The Footballer Who Could Fly

Duncan Hamilton is the author of *Provided You Don't Kiss Me: 20 Years with Brian Clough*, which won the William Hill Sports Book of the Year for 2007. In 2009 he was awarded the William Hill again for *Harold Larwood*, as well as winning the prestigious Wisden Book of the Year for 2009 and Biography of the Year at the 2010 British Sports Book Awards. He lives in the Yorkshire Dales.

Praise for The Footballer Who Could Fly

'As a memoir, it is heart-crackingly nostalgic. As a record of historic moments in British football, it is eye-wateringly evocative.'

The Times

'Duncan Hamilton traces an idiosyncratic path through the post-war history of English football, exploring his relationship with his father . . . All Hamilton's books have an elegiac quality, this more than the rest.'

Independent, Books of the Year

'Hamilton takes us on a hugely enjoyable nostalgia trip . . . a moving depiction of how football can bind together a family.'

Sunday Express

'Although a fine tribute to former greats including Welsh striker Wyn Davies, it's the relationship between the author and his dad that makes his post-war pilgrimage through the game such a rich read.'

FourFourTwo Magazine

'A beautiful, heart-cracking memoir by a sublime writer.'

aga Magazine

The Footballer Who Could Fly

Living in my Father's Black and White World

DUNCAN HAMILTON

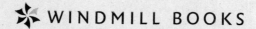
WINDMILL BOOKS

Published by Windmill Books 2013

10 9

This book is a work of non-fiction based on the life, experiences and
recollections of the author. In some limited cases names of people, places,
dates, sequences or the detail of events have been changed solely to protect
the privacy of others. The author has stated to the publishers that, except
in such minor respects not affecting the substantial accuracy of the work,
the contents of this book are true.

First published in Great Britain in 2012 by Century

Windmill Books
The Random House Group Limited
20 Vauxhall Bridge Road, London SW1V 2SA

Addresses for companies within The Random House Group Limited can be
found at: www.randomhouse.co.uk/offices.htm

The Random House Group Limited Reg. No. 954009

www.randomhouse.co.uk

A CIP catalogue record for this book
is available from the British Library

ISBN 9780099558576

Typeset in Minion by Palimpsest Book Production Limited,
Falkirk, Stirlingshire

Printed and bound by Clays Ltd, Elcograf S.p.A.

To my father. And to those fathers who understand
that football is always better shared with their
sons and daughters than watched alone.

Contents

The Number Nine Shirt

Whenever I think of my father, I always see him first beside the Tyne Bridge. His face comes back to me with photographic clarity, as if the camera's shutter had opened and closed on him just a moment ago. He is caught in the cathedral light of a late September morning, the lattice-work architecture of the bridge rising behind him. The sky is the colour of an unpolished pearl, the sun so watery that it casts almost no shadow as it nears its noonday peak.

I remember everything about this long-ago hour.

I remember that summer had long since left Newcastle, scythed away by north-easterly winds and the rapid advance of a russet autumn, already noticeable in the dampish air. I remember my father was wearing his brown herringbone coat, buttoned to the neck, and that his hands were tucked into its slanting pockets for warmth. I remember his shoes had a high-shine lacquer. They were new, and squeaked like mice whenever he walked. I remember his hair shone too. It was Brylcreemed and combed back, revealing his widow's peak, the dome of his forehead and the soft mesh and hatching on the flesh. I remember the short bristles of his pencil moustache and the crinkly spread of crow's feet around his eyes, the effort of thinking narrowing them into slits. I remember the small boats which cut long furrows through the treacle-black water of the Tyne. The engines of these boats panted and chugged, as though the drag of the current was too much of a strain for them. But I remember that each made it beyond us, and moved gradually down a straight stretch of the river before banking and holding the gentle right-hand curve which carried them out towards the chop of the North Sea. I remember watching one boat vanish into the middle distance before another rolled by, bringing with it a strong smell of oil and acrid petrol and the much fainter scent of sea salt, seaweed and lichen, which clung to its grubby red hull. I remember hearing the wing-flap of a bird close by and spotting a grey gull dive across the boat and its wavelet before pursuing it in widely extravagant swoops. The forlorn caw-caw-caw noise it made was like a cry for pity.

Revisiting the past is often like walking through mantles of drifting fog. One hazy memory dissolves into another – and then another still. The shape and firm detail of what you're trying to recall is obscured or distorted. You only half glimpse again what once was exact and distinct, or see it in a series of fragmentary vignettes that refuse to become a coherent whole. But this day returns to me so vividly, as though in High Definition, because it is among the most pivotal of my early life.

It is 1973 and I am almost 15 years old. I am shy and I stammer badly; so badly that the pronunciation of the simplest words is an appalling trial. Conversation is frequently impossible for me. What comes out is indecipherable – a low guttural moan, as if I might be choking. Sometimes, in trying to speak, I resemble one of those tormented figures in a Goya painting. For even extreme facial contortions – teeth clenching and the solid tensing of each muscle – cannot pull entire words free. My mouth spasms and gurns into all sorts of ugly shapes to produce a single syllable. I am obsessed with books and newspapers; I have an insatiable appetite for them because I am only fluent on the silent page. The mind deals perfectly with sentences I have no voice to say aloud. My first Careers Adviser, appalled that I want to become a newspaperman, has recently told me to focus instead on manual labour – 'like the mines', he said – or a factory shop-floor job. 'Be grateful for it,' he added. The winter to come will be memorably chaotic and lit by candlelight. It will be scarred by strikes and social unrest, inflation at 8.4 per cent, recession and shortages, rising oil prices, a three-day week, dark nights spent searching for a box of matches and waiting for the electricity to be turned back on. At the end of it Newcastle United – the team I and my father support

– will reach the final of the FA Cup for the first time in almost 20 years, and we will sit together, sing the opening verse of the 'Blaydon Races' as if it was the 'Battle Hymn of the Republic', and watch our players walk out at Wembley, trailing history behind them. But, for me, nothing will dominate these convulsing months more than standing on the quayside.

We have come 'hyem', my father dissolving into Geordie to describe the city of my birth and the place he gladly adopted as his own. And we are here because my maternal grandfather is dead. My father is dealing with the mundane bureaucracy of death: the registration and paperwork, the funeral arrangements and also the sorting out and distribution of possessions left behind. I am dealing with the realisation that death devours all things lovely, and also the marks it leaves: injustice, anger, confusion and a visceral, howling grief. I know where death's sting is. I can feel it; I am conscious of its physical weight. I had never conceived of life without my grandfather. He was my idol and I was his blue-eyed boy – the grandson who loved what he loved: cricket, football, boxing, walking and reading; and who loved him above any and all of them.

My grandfather had callused, bucket-like hands and didn't so much breathe as wheeze. He was also deaf and always wore a hearing aid in his left ear. The pack accompanying it, clipped to his belt, was connected by a pink, twisty cord. He and I made the oddest couple. I was the boy who couldn't speak. He was the old man who couldn't hear. We found friendship and profound understanding in our companionable silences, which were disturbed only by the slow turn of a page and the chime of the clock on the sideboard. With each book, our bond became stronger.

My grandfather was peculiarly different from the rest of the family: he supported Sunderland. His allegiance to the Wear rather than the Tyne began as a schoolboy crush. He was smitten by a side he never saw – Sunderland's 19th-century Team of All the Talents, the first to score 100 goals in a season and also winners of three Championships in four years from 1892 to 1895. Eventually he became a fixture on the Clock End at Roker Park. His devotion ran contrary to fashion. When it hardened, in 1908–09, Newcastle were indisputably the League's dominant force – overtaking Aston Villa in the Edwardian era – and about to claim their third title of the decade. But that season's crushing embarrassment for them was a 9–1 defeat to Sunderland, which my grandfather saw through a fine drizzle at St James' Park, a ground he playfully considered to be 'enemy country'. 'There were eight goals in less than half an hour and the last five came in under ten minutes,' he'd said to me, adopting a tone that suggested it was one of the unranked Wonders of the World. Counted among his Red Letter Days was the 1937 Cup Final. He went to Wembley by train, his ticket pinned to the inside of his jacket pocket. 'Your grandmother did it for me in case I drank too much ale on the way,' he explained.

In the heave and sway of the crowd, he yelled so much he lost his voice as Sunderland, a goal behind at half time, won 3–1 in front of George VI. 'A day in London and I saw two Kings,' he'd say. The other, albeit honorary, sovereign head was Raich Carter, Sunderland's sleekly immaculate captain, who my grandfather maintained had 'drops of blue blood in his veins'. He recalled the beery homecoming afterwards. 'There were Sunderland fans who were drunk for a week after winning that Cup,' he said, preparing me for the punchline. 'And there were Newcastle fans who were drunk for *two* weeks just because Sunderland had won it.' The word 'two' was delivered with such emphasis that I saw a battalion of exclamation marks chasing after it.

In my naivety I supposed the bliss of my grandfather's company would never end. He had survived the trenches and the bloodiness of the First World War, returning from it devastated to the core and mute out of respect for the dead. What he saw, felt and experienced there remained buried inside him because his brother was buried in Belgium and his 'pals' were buried in France. He had survived the death of his first wife in childbirth to remarry the woman who became my grandmother. He had survived the Great Depression, another war and the constant hardships it brought. He had survived half a century underground – tunnelling, burrowing and hacking coal with a wooden-handled pick, aware at any moment, in this Russian Roulette-like way of living, that a pit prop might snap, a seam could collapse, a full tub could jump from its rails and mow him down. He risked losing a limb or his life. He hewed enough coal to have created a mountain range along the Scotswood Road, and every breath he took doing this dismally repetitive work drew dust and disease into his lungs. But he survived that too. I thought he was indestructible.

Only four months earlier, on an afternoon when soft rain smudged the front window of his council house, he'd risen time and again from his square leather chair beside the fireside. Hands aloft or flaying the air with a clenched fist, he could not believe what he was seeing on his ancient television. He felt his eyes were betraying him; that somehow he was locked into the dazed improbability of a sweet dream in which whatever he asked for was promptly given to him. *His* Sunderland were winning the FA Cup again. This was the mid-table, 50–1 against Sunderland of the Second Division; the Sunderland of lanky Bob Stokoe with his pork pie hat and flapping fawn mackintosh; the Sunderland of Ian Porterfield's hooked in, first-half goal; the Sunderland of Jim Montgomery's point-blank, push-away save from Peter Lorimer. Even after I watched and re-watched the replays – each time expecting the ball to beat Montgomery's reflex lunge and bulge the net – I was unable to work out how this implausible act had been achieved. But then the result itself was illogical, and went far beyond rational sporting belief. At the whistle, after Sunderland had beaten Don Revie's skilled and professionally ruthless Leeds United, my grandfather sagged back into his chair, as though he'd run every yard with Watson and Tueart, Horswill and Pitt and had also shared Stokoe's wide-armed, goggle-eyed sprint from the bench and across the wet turf to embrace Montgomery. He raked his fingers across his forehead, as if wiping away sweat, and exhaled – a prolonged breath that signalled relief. On the bottom of the screen the score and scorer were printed in white letters.

Leeds 0, Sunderland 1   Porterfield, 31 minutes

My grandfather shook his head. 'The football shock of the century,' he said quietly, as if to acknowledge it too loudly would render the result null and void. The following morning he read the newspapers to make certain that he hadn't been tricked. He stared at the photographs: Porterfield's close-range winner, the pale ball rushing off the player's boot; Montgomery's upturned palms, which made him look like Superman deflecting a bullet, to deny Lorimer; a tearful Stokoe with his gappy smile; and Sunderland lips on the Cup, the fond kisses like a meeting between long-lost lovers. 'It's true,' my grandfather said, as if the rest of us doubted it, 'we won the Cup.' His favourite headline was spread across the back page of the *Sunday Express*:

IT'S SUNDERLAND IN WUNDERLAND

It expressed exactly how he felt. The metre and musicality within that simple phrase also made it sound like a terrace chant. He continually recited it to me. I put together a scrapbook for him of every cutting I could find and slid a copy of the match programme, bought by post, inside it. On the cover of the scrapbook I stuck a colour photograph of the captain, Bobby Kerr, holding the trophy, the handles adorned with Sunderland's ribbons. My grandfather went through the cuttings from front to back and then from back to front. He treated the scrapbook as though it was as precious as the Cup itself. Returning to Newcastle for his funeral, I knew the gift was about to be returned to me as part of his inheritance, along with his war medals and the compass he took to France to navigate the battlefields and point him towards home. On the journey from Nottingham, where we lived, I thought about my grandfather and his child-like joy at Sunderland's Cup win. I took solace from the fact he'd seen it; that this little piece of history hadn't been denied to him.

My father didn't learn how to drive until he reached his mid-40s. Having a licence, however, didn't mean we could always afford a car. They came and went as our finances allowed. Normally we travelled to Newcastle on a single-decker bus that rattled like old bones and was swathed in the dark vapour of its own exhaust. It was uncomfortably cramped and the driver had to follow a ponderously winding route north-eastward. We endured it because the five-hour trek was cheap. But, after news of my grandfather's death, my father bought rail tickets. The carriage had a sliding teak door and the seats, covered in scratchy fabric, faced one another. Our luggage lay in the loose netting of the overhead rack, which was stretched across the compartment like a sailor's hammock. My father smoked. My mother fussed. I stared out of the window, which I misted with my own breath. Squat houses and shorn fields rushed by. Stations and other travellers came and went again. I was oblivious to them. I wondered about the man my grandfather must have been at Wembley in 1937. No photograph of his younger self existed, and so on the journey I strived to create something of him in my own imagination, as though he was sitting in front of me posing for a painted portrait. I rubbed away the crevices and gauntness of age. I gave him lively eyes and removed the bagginess beneath them. I washed the grey out of his hair. I put him in a three-piece navy suit, a watch-chain draped like braid across his waistcoat, and a high white collar and sober tie. As long as I kept him alive in my mind, I felt that he couldn't really die, a consoling thought which I held close to me until the girders of the Tyne Bridge came into view. It broke apart as we unloaded our cases on to the platform.

I was sharply aware of the clip and scrape of my own heels on the bare concrete. The echo was unnaturally loud and seemed to ricochet off the high canopy roof and come back to me amplified. I heard the shrill melancholic pipe of a guard's whistle and a sudden whip of wind emphasised the bitter emptiness of the afternoon. Looking around I recognised nothing and no one. There was only the press of strangers hurrying through dingy arches and up a wide flight of steps, the sound of competing, raised voices, the stark black-on-white station sign and the huge arrivals and departures board. Another train was about to pull out for Nottingham, and I wanted to climb on to it and be gone. For if I left I wouldn't have to accept that my grandfather was dead. It was like choosing not to slit open a letter that you know contains bad news. I could continue the fantasy that he remained alive, either much younger or exactly as I last saw him, because I wouldn't have to confront the truth. I understood then that to travel hopefully really can be a better thing than to arrive; for in arriving I couldn't refute the overbearing and undeniable reality. There could be no more displacement, no more pretending. I was in Newcastle for a purpose which could not be avoided. I felt as though my heart had left my chest and lodged in my throat. I sat down on my case and wept. But there was no relief in my tears; for more followed them. My father kept his distance from me, as if not wanting to trespass. He registered the tangled knot of grief turning slowly inside me and agonised over it; but, as if unsure about how to demonstrate his understanding, he was unable to speak to me about it. He was not immune to emotion; he merely chose not to show it. Like so many men of his era, he found it difficult to express his feelings and avoided situations where it might be necessary. Even the natural, innocent physical intimacy of parenthood – a hand folded around my hand, a palm resting gently on my back – was territory into which he never strayed. It wasn't in his instinct. He'd been raised in a household where the relationship between father and son (my father had four brothers) was taken for granted and preserved in respectful silence; he wanted the two of us to abide by the same etiquette. We acknowledged our caring and support for one another through gesture rather than words or touch. The prime example of it came as a consequence of my grandfather's death, which is why it stays with me.

People are like rivers. To understand them properly you have to find their source, a realisation which in my father's case came too late to be useful to me. This is what I know about the man who everyone called Jim or Jimmy.

He worked, aged 12 to 14, in a bakery. From 14 onwards he took the only road open to him. Like almost everyone around him, he went into the pit and stayed there. Wherever he went there was always the lingering smell of coal in the air and the crunch of coal underfoot and the coal dust of the mine beneath his and his friends' fingernails. Escape was impossible. If he didn't like one mine he could at least move on to another. In the beginning, during the mid-1930s, there were 121 coalfields in Northumberland employing more than 25,000 miners.

At the end, there was nothing – no turning wheels or sheds; scarcely a sign that a mine had once been sunk through the soil and no imprint of the boots which had clomped daily towards and away from it.

In the 1960s he dragged his miner's kit from Newcastle to Nottingham because the seam of the pit in which he worked was exhausted. The terraced house in which we lived – net curtains at the windows, paved slabs for a front garden and an outside toilet – was made rubble by a wrecking ball. When the preliminary phase of its destruction was over, we stood in the carcass of what had once been our home and stared at the remains of a staircase now resembling one of Escher's; it led nowhere. Our flowered blue wallpaper, which my mother loved, hung in long, torn strips from what was now only half of a living-room wall. Shattered glass from the front windows cracked beneath our feet. The street itself had always been scarred by a heap of slack coal, which blocked off one end of it. Acres of scrubby wasteland stretched beyond. My father still didn't want to leave the house, the village or the North East. He felt the simultaneous loss of home and job was a conspiracy against him, and it exacerbated the hurt. He said goodbye to Newcastle with the reluctance and resentment of a refugee, displaced by force of circumstance and through no fault of his own. The fact of it gnawed painfully away at him and his yearning to return existed well before he'd even left.

Every summer we went back there. For one thing, we

could only afford to holiday at my grandfather's home, which was three miles from the coast. For another, my father didn't want to go anywhere else. He wanted the Geordie air in his lungs. He wanted the *Newcastle Evening Chronicle* in his hands. He wanted to drink Newcastle Brown Ale in the working-men's club of which he was still a member and where the regulars sat bowed over round tables wearing flat tweed caps, smoking pipes and shuffling dominoes, like a Newcastle version of Cézanne's *The Card Players*. He missed Newcastle so much that the chorus of Lindisfarne's 'Fog on the Tyne' made it a heartbreak song for him.

> *The fog on the Tyne is all mine, all mine*
> *The fog on the Tyne is all mine,*

He believed it was true. The oddity is that he wasn't a Geordie. He was born in the central band of Scotland in the early 1920s. In the plague years of the Great Depression, first his grandfather and then his own father had to head south because their local pit had closed. My father saw a grim symmetry in his own migration further south still.

He loved Newcastle. For one thing, he loved the Tyne the way Twain loved the Mississippi. For another, he admired its landmark bridge and those who built it. The scale and strength of it never failed to inspire anything but overwhelming pride in him, as if he'd soldered the rivets himself. As he saw it the bridge was more than a functional construction. It was an emblem of the city, an instantly recognisable and stupendous piece of art – long before *The Angel of the North* was thought of, let alone iron-forged – and proof of what the ordinary working man could make. I could not comprehend how its pieces were cast and transported, hoisted and locked together in such geometrical perfection. But my father once told me about a strip of film he'd seen of the bridge's creation in the late 1920s. The bridge was only half-finished. Cranes taller than a galleon's mast were swinging girders into slots, where men in steel-capped boots, wearing ordinary woollen jackets and Newsboy caps, waited to manoeuvre them with ungloved hands for welding. Other men casually strolled along the girders already in place, some with a rolled cigarette lolling from the corner of their mouth, and never glanced at the 100-foot drop below them. They were as nonchalant as tightrope walkers. I've since seen the film myself. The camera pulls back, snapping a panoramic view of the ribbed skeleton of the bridge, and suddenly each of the men shrinks to the size of a full stop in relation to it. The ingenuity of the engineering and the bravery necessary to take it from pencil drawing to metal life contributed to my father's certainty that Newcastle was a blessed spot on the map.

Of course, there was more to it than that; the ordinary men and women mattered most of all. He saw Newcastle as an earthy, honest, hail-fellow-well-met city without the need for spit, polish and snooty airs. Geographical remoteness gave it an identity. It had its own way of doing things. With detachment came customs and habits which made it seem to my father as though Newcastle was an independent state within the Nation of the North East. It deliberately chose to be only tangentially connected to anywhere else. Another clinching factor for him was the dialect. One of the best lines in Lee Hall's *The Pitmen Painters*, a compassionate and insightful play about the Ashington miners' art group formed in the mid-1930s, comes in its first act. The pitmen, setting up their easels, meet their posh-speaking tutor, and a brief misunderstanding occurs about whether he is or is not a Professor and whether he does or does not teach painting. Finally, and to settle the matter, an exasperated miner asks him.

'Ye de de art, divvint ye?'

The sentence captures the cadences and rhythm of the Geordie language as well as its incomprehensibility to anyone who does not know it or speak it tribally. My father didn't have a Geordie accent – until he went back to Geordieland and slipped into it, as though dressing linguistically for an occasion. Everything was *bonny* or *canny* or *alreet, lads*. He had *marras* instead of friends. He saw *bairns* rather than children. He'd ask whether we were *gannin te the match*. And he'd say *whey, man* and *howay* and *goodneet*. On the terraces of St James' Park, he could have passed for pure Geordie. My father sang hymns for Newcastle with the gusto of the newly converted. For him it truly was the land of singing waters and winds from off the sea. Improbable though it seems, he regarded Newcastle in the same romantic way that Housman thought of those Blue Remembered Hills. In hindsight, I see this level of zeal was only achievable in someone desperate to establish his attachment to it, his loyalty towards it and his profound regret that both weren't automatically his through birthright; though, curiously, it coexisted with his pride as a Scot.

He demonstrated faithfulness towards everything Geordie. The first of these was to Newcastle United. Everyone who has ever worn a scarf in team colours likes to think *their* club represents something of the heart of football; and that the football itself is inherent to the place. But there are particular spots on the map steeped in and shaped by football to the extent it is defining. The people's perception of themselves, as well as the way outsiders see them, is gained principally through football. To imagine them without it is impossible. It sounds trite to say that the football in these cities is far more than a game. But, if nothing else, cliché can convey an unambiguous truth. In Newcastle, long before my father arrived and began supporting them, there was an emotional and compulsive need for football and it indisputably influenced mood and self-worth. Saturday afternoon governed how much beer was swilled in the Bigg Market on Saturday night. What football provided was much more than an escape from the trap of the shop, the office, the factory floor, the colliery head and the din of shipyard hammers. It bound

Newcastle together as one people. Even those who knew little or nothing about football looked for the results and shared, however vicariously, in the fortunes of the team. It touched and affected everyone.

Football was at the centre of everything to my father and, like the rest of us, he had his heroes. I was given luminous descriptions of each of them.

Hughie Gallagher, whom he worshipped. 'He wasn't as big as your thumb,' he'd say, 'but he could dribble the ball all afternoon and no one could take it from him – unless he became bored with it.'

Len Shackleton, who he regarded as football's equivalent of a circus troupe. 'More tricks than a stage magician,' he claimed. 'Better balance than an acrobat too.'

Bobby Charlton, who he said could thump a left-footed shot into the top corner and 'make it rip clean through the net'.

The super-hero of these heroes was Jackie Milburn, whom he spoke about with reverential awe. He was 'The Greatest of the Very Great', the capitals evident in the sentence as my father spoke it. And he was always 'Wor Jackie' too, as if he lived just down the road from us. My father made Milburn sound like an amalgam of alchemist, Norse God and Knight, who wore his Newcastle shirt like silken armour. 'You were unlucky,' he'd say to me, 'not to see him play.' My father said this of Milburn: 'He could run with the ball without his studs touching the ground. When he really took off, it was like a roar of flame across the pitch. As for the ball after it left his boot . . . well, you barely saw it – just the vapour trail as it sped through the air. I'm surprised the thing didn't burst.'

These were my father's fairytales, and I first heard all of them at bedtime and at an age when I was unable to distinguish between hard fact and playful exaggeration. 'You know,' he'd tell me, 'they used to run a clothes line from one crossbar to another at St James' Park, hang 11 black and white shirts on it and 60,000 people turned up to see them blowing in the wind – and there'd be another 20,000 outside waiting to get in.' He never read to me. Instead, he described footballers and the matches he'd seen them play on grounds of which I was then only vaguely aware: Hampden Park, Villa Park, Wembley, Old Trafford, Hillsborough. He described them clearly and with dramatic effect, sometimes kicking an invisible ball or smartly darting out his right hand, fast as a lizard's tongue, to signify a goalkeeper's leap across the line. As my father told it, shots thrashed against the net from impossible distances and at improbable angles. Saves were made with elastic arms and fingers or sacrificial plunges on to a flaying boot, as if the green-jerseyed goalkeeper was smothering an explosion from a grenade. He talked about pitches – some groomed like the lawns at Hampton Court and others resembling a sodden, ploughed field, where the ball needed to be towed from one box to another. I always knew Milburn would figure somewhere. He'd either claim a goal or make one after a mazy slalom beyond more players than the Football Association's rules allowed any team to field.

In the early 1950s Newcastle won three FA Cups, beating Blackpool 2–0 in '51, Arsenal 1–0 the following year and Manchester City 3–1 in '55. Of those fevered and much fêted successes, the win over Blackpool had the greatest effect on my father. He never forgot it. 'The first time is always the best,' he'd explain. 'The beer tasted better than it had ever done before.' Milburn scored twice in that game. To prolong the pleasure of them my father spent one late summer weekend in the dark of a fleapit cinema, sitting through multiple screenings of *The Lavender Hill Mob*, simply to see the newsreel of Milburn's goals, which were still being shown in Newcastle months after the event. He committed each to memory. Milburn's second was spectacular, a long-range shot struck with his left foot. The force of it left him on his rump. The ball went into the top corner while he was on his backside. 'You could say he scored sitting down,' my father used to claim. But Milburn's first – a runaway effort covering nearly 40 yards – was regarded as 'special' in our household. No matter how many times he saw this goal, my father felt excruciating tension in the few seconds between Milburn collecting a pass in the centre circle and scoring inside the box. When describing it to me, I always saw what my father saw. The baggy-shorted Milburn glancing around him, half expecting to be flagged offside and astonished at the space he's found himself in. There is no one between him and the goalkeeper. He is on his own, alone except for his shadow, and in pursuit of the ball – just as a Blackpool defender is in pursuit of him. The frantic defender chasing him looks like someone caught out in a game of musical chairs, and the goalkeeper shuffles uncertainly off his line before retreating in surrender, the low drive beating his right hand. Watching it replayed in the cinema, my father said the men and boys around him would jump up as soon as Milburn got the ball and repeatedly shout '*Gann on, Wor Jackie*' until the ball was safely in the net again.

This is how I grew up – living in my father's black and white world. But the man who created it was a mystery to me; a code I couldn't crack.

I perplexed my father because I was so unlike him. Although he never complained about it, or questioned the reasons why, he couldn't comprehend my need for books. I was not what he expected. He believed I'd become his mirror image: stout and brawny, adept at physical lifting and with a head for mental arithmetic. He could divide, multiply, add up and subtract numbers as long as buses without the need for pencil and paper. But I only ever saw him read three books from first page to last: *The Story of Newcastle United FC*, Jackie Milburn's autobiography, *Golden Goals*, and a two inch-thick account of the development of the northern coalfields, which was bound in stiff blue leather and contained copious diagrams, concertina maps and plates. He saw no point in 'made up novels' or poetry. The towers of books in my bedroom – borrowed, bought for pennies secondhand or taken out of the library – flummoxed him. Which is why I know one thing unequivocally. Without football we'd have had nothing to say to each other. The game alone pushed us into one another's orbit.

I still regret, as if part of my childhood was denied to me, that our talks about it never led to back garden kickabouts. Only in retrospect do I realise that he frequently came home fatigued to the point of collapse. He worked relentlessly because the extra hours made the difference between enduring life and living it to some small degree. It meant, however, that for weeks at a time he was a vague presence in the house – either absent altogether or seen briefly as he ate and then slipped his aching body into bed to recuperate for the next shift. By the time I was born – an only child – my father was almost 40. When I began to thump a football against the outside wall, he was already prematurely middle-aged through fatigue, disappointment and over-work. Repeated pleadings for him to join me were ignored. He sat in his chair smoking and reading the newspaper. Back then I resented him for it. But I know at last what I failed to recognise in my boyhood or – I am ashamed to confess – in my early adult years either. The mine and a miner's life of back-to-back shifts was no place in which to age gracefully. He was a backyard non-combatant purely because he lacked the vigour and physical strength to become one. He strived to make up for it in other ways. He bought me copies of *Goal* magazine and *Charles Buchan's Football Monthly*. He returned home with a once-a-week packet of football stickers, which he propped up on the mantelpiece. And the day after my grandfather's funeral he offered something material to help me forget, however fleetingly, the ache of his loss. I was sitting on the sofa, staring dejectedly into the flames of the coal fire, when my father appeared carrying my limp coat, draped across his right arm. 'We're going into the Toon,' he said. 'The two of us. I'll buy you a Newcastle shirt. We'll get a badge for it and a number nine to stitch on the back.'

In my boyhood, replica kit was neither ubiquitous nor cheap. There were no long rows of shirts in brightly lit club shops, no gleaming footballs on hooped metal display stands and no vast racks of boots vivid with the maker's name or mark. I played in whatever I could find.

The sports shop, a goal kick from St James' Park, belonged to Frank Brennan, a veteran of two of Newcastle's three FA Cup wins in the 1950s. In the window was the head and torso of a hollow-eyed mannequin modelling the shirt my father was about to buy me – rough nylon, round-necked and long-sleeved. I looked at it for a while through the glass before pushing open the oak door, the clang so shattering that the bell above it must once have rung in a church tower. The inside of the shop was as dark as a cave. The displays were formal and unreachable, the socks, shorts and shirts tucked into buff-coloured boxes, the footballs on shelves and the boots laid in pairs with the long white laces tied together. The middle-aged man serving us – Brennan, much to my father's disappointment, wasn't in the store – wore a poorly fitting grey suit and had fingers as thin as splinters. His nails were bitten down. He did not welcome us warmly from behind the counter. Instead he measured us sullenly with his eyes, as if our entrance was a disturbance to him. There was no attempt at small-talk either from my father, who disliked it, or the assistant, who immediately struck me as someone who did not relish the fetching and carrying of his work. He found a shirt, held it against my chest and announced it was the right size. The badge, as grand as a council crest, and the poppy red number nine on a rectangle of white cloth came separately. My father reached inside his wallet and produced a £10 note so stiffly crisp that it could have been printed that day. Saying nothing as he did so, the assistant wrapped everything in brown paper, which crackled as he wrestled with it, and then weaved a line of coarse string around the parcel he had made. He passed it to my father, who passed it on to me. I looped my fingers under the hard central knot of the string and carried the package out of the shop. With my bundle, I looked like a child evacuee during the Second World War. 'You'll be champion in that,' my father said as we walked out of the store, the bell thundering again.

I asked whether we could watch the boats on the

Tyne. My father thought about it for a second or two, as though calculating the distance to the quay, before telling me: 'We'll take the long way.' Newcastle was a different city then; drabber, grubbier and less vibrant than today. Especially in winter, as smoke and smuts spread across the rooftops, it seemed as though a permanent black haze trimmed the skyline. On the streets we saw women in paisley silk or plain chiffon headscarves, mouths dark with lipstick, and men that my father identified instantly as miners. The unhealthy complexion of someone who had spent too long out of the sun gave them away; their skin was the colour of china clay. We walked to the Monument, and saw the robed Portland stone figure of Charles Grey staring down at us from the magnificence of his 133-foot Doric column. A huddled flock of pigeons flew around it like a low rain cloud. We headed off along Grey Street, its ochre Georgian buildings streaked in soot, and veered towards the Tyne. It was like descending into a labyrinth. There were narrow streets and passageways, and steep, uneven steps made greasy by earlier rain. Gradually the city seemed to be sliding into the river. The landscape abruptly flattened out when we reached the quayside. The bridge stood majestically in the middle distance.

We'd walked less than 100 yards before my father stopped near a short rail and let his gaze meander down the river.

'You like the shirt?' he asked, almost tentatively and without looking at me.

I nodded and gave a wan smile in return as he finally turned his head.

His hands momentarily gripped the short rail in front of him and he said, as if addressing an audience. 'In the 20s and 30s they used to sail the football ship from here. It was a biggish ship with a funnel and two masts. I saw a photograph of it once. They went from Tyne to Thames – all along the North Sea coast – in time for the FA Cup finals at Wembley. There were thousands of people – standing where we're standing now – just to see the ship and to hear the hooter and wave it off as it pulled away, leaving the bridge behind.' He made it sound like a carnival parade. There were coloured flags, he said, and caps being spun in celebration like rattles, and a roar, as though a goal had been scored, as soon as the ship broke properly into the water. A ship sailing to Wembley? I wasn't sure I believed him. But I visualised it all the same – the ship's bulk rocking along a watery Wembley Way and anchoring below the Twin Towers.

'I remember the 1932 Cup Final on the wireless,' my father continued. 'The signal was so faint we pressed our ears against the set to hear it.' He said it as if remembering his own father beside him. 'That was the Over the Line Final against Arsenal. Afterwards, all the photographs showed the ball *was* over the goal-line *before* it was crossed for our equalising goal. Arsenal complained about it. And they're still complaining about it. Mind you, I think we'd have beaten them in the end anyway.' His certainty about it was unshakeable. 'Newcastle were made to win Cups. We were *the* Cup team. The FA may as well have given it us for keeps. We thought we'd never have to hand it back. But then you know what I'm going to say next, don't you . . .?'

My father glanced across at me and I nodded at him again. He was talking about Jackie Milburn. 'Well, you've heard all the tales,' he said, half-sighing as though reluctant to retell them, but waiting for me to signal my permission for a repeat performance.

For the third time I nodded.

'Wembley, 1951, Newcastle v Blackpool and Stanley Matthews,' he began, eyes far brighter and his hands conducting his words. 'Milburn has the ball. He's suddenly in the clear . . . the Blackpool back line is chasing after him . . . the black and white half of the stadium is shouting him on . . . the tangerine end is absolutely silent.'

The retelling of my father's favourite story led to another. Through the 50s he went, diverted occasionally into the 30s and 40s to provide some important context, before dashing into the 1960s. He ticked off the Cup Finals, relegation and promotion, new managers, the arrivals and departures at Newcastle. With recollection came precise detail – all of it accompanied by numbers: crowd figures, times of goals scored, appearances and League position. The next hour had everything in it. Milburn scored his Cup goals, Len Shackleton duped defenders because of his virtuosity and Bobby Charlton consistently whacked the ball with vehemence. Tottenham took the Double. England won the World Cup. Manchester United claimed at Wembley what had been denied them on a snowy airfield in Munich a decade earlier. And Newcastle – *our* Newcastle, post-Milburn – were buffeted by the vicissitudes of Fate, never quite fulfilling the hope we had for them. 'If only we had Milburn now,' he said. My father only stopped talking when a tug of chill wind sent skeins of cloud across the diluted sun, blotting it out entirely, as if Nature were reminding us to mourn. 'We should be heading back,' he said, aware of the deepening chill of the day and half-turning to make sure I was following him. I held the Newcastle shirt more tightly than ever as we set off into the heart of the work-grime city again, eventually turning a sharp corner and losing sight of the bridge.

Most moments pass through us, like light through glass, before vanishing. They leave nothing traceable behind. This was different. Not because of what was said – the stories were as familiar to me as my reflection – but because of the effort my father put into each one; and what the sum of them explicitly meant. I was aware that his evocation of a life now past was done to avoid talking about the present; and aware, too, that his stopping at the end of the 60s was done deliberately to avoid encroaching at all into the then and now. But there was something more to it. My father knew I was not just closer to my grandfather than to him. He was aware I loved him more too. And so, on that strip of Tyneside quay, he was beginning to address that fact, as if making up for Time lost and preparing for Time to come. For him football was the safe and neutral territory, and he made me feel better because we were occupying it together, intimately. Even in the confusion of growing up, I understood this much.

I knew him as an intensely private and taciturn man, who revealed almost nothing of his deeper self – at least not to me. Early on, he accepted that he could neither refashion his life nor reinvent himself. He wasn't satisfied with what he had, but he never attempted to grab for something more in case he wound up owning even less. He was typical of the pre-war working-class generation to which he belonged. It adhered to a creed of stoicism, self-reliance and self-effacement. It played the cards Fate dealt – however bad or inauspicious – and seldom complained. He prepared for rainy days because he'd been taught to expect them.

There'd be occasions in the future – and a lot of them too – when my father would frustrate or infuriate me because of his reticence, his detachment and what I perceived as his apparent lack of tenderness towards me. But, whenever I was in danger of mistaking it as ambivalence, I'd remember that football shirt and the efforts he made on the quayside. And I think of it whenever I hear anyone say, dismissively, that 'football doesn't matter'; or that 'football is just a game'; or ev 'well, it's only football'. No, it isn't. Not for me. It bound us together when nothing else could. Without football, we were strangers under a shared roof.

With it, we were father and son.

PART ONE

The Time Before You Were Born

1

The Man Made of Metal

He lingered in the half-open doorway, partly hidden in shadow, as though wary of escaping into the pale afternoon light. He was wearing a grey suit, the colour of hot ash, and a dark thin tie, its tight knot the size of a penny piece. In one hand he held a small spiral notebook and a rolled copy of the *Newcastle Journal*. In the other was the stub of a burning cigarette. A row of pens was hooked into the top pocket of his jacket.

I saw him glance both ways before stepping on to the uneven pavement and then walking away at a brisk clip, as if fleeing from something or someone. His head was bowed, the chin resting on the chest. After a yard or two, he broke into a steady half-trot and began to thread his body in between and around straggly rings of arriving and departing travellers, who were too busy with their luggage to take much notice of who was passing them. But my father was instantly aware of him, recognising his features as soon as he appeared, framed in the rectangle of lintel and posts. He nudged me gently with his elbow. 'Over there,' he said, whispering, as though passing on a secret no one else should hear. I had no idea why I was tracking this slim figure, whose inky-black hair fell in loose lanks across his forehead as he stooped and swerved away. I had no idea, either, why my father was still staring into the far distance – his eyes chasing him through the traffic and the thick choke of people – long after his departure.

'Who was that?' I asked, innocently.

'Jackie Milburn,' my father announced, as if together we had witnessed something godly.

Milburn, then in his mid-40s, worked as a journalist for the *News of the World*. The newspaper's district offices were in Newcastle's Marlborough Crescent – an open-to-the-elements and bleakly inhospitable slab of concrete where long-distance coaches tipped out passengers. The stench of oil and gasoline filled the air. The bus station was such a desolate and unwelcoming place that the Brutalist architecture of Gateshead's Trinity Square car park, where Michael Caine's character avenges his brother's murder in *Get Carter*, counted as a sculptured wonder by comparison. But, with sublime timing, our coach from Nottingham had juddered to a halt, throwing us forward in our seats, almost directly opposite the *News of the World*'s front door. We were waiting for our suitcases when my father picked out Milburn. Years later, I understood this: I didn't see what my father saw on that unseasonably mild October day in 1970. I knew Milburn only in Newcastle's black and white – the sleeves of his shirt bunched up, the hem of his shorts almost touching his knees, the heavy boots laced near the ankle. So I saw a middle-aged gent, smartly attired and smoking (as everyone constantly did back then) who was surprisingly adroit and darting in his movements. My father saw a centre forward – sleek, fast, sure of himself: the starry youth Milburn had once been. For him fume-filled Marlborough Crescent became the upturned bowl of St James' Park. The growl of bus engines became the roar of the crowd. The pavement became a strip of grass down which the predatory Milburn danced, the ball at his feet, and around him were defenders in pedalling retreat, unsure of whether to lunge or block.

My father could have chosen the life of John Edward Thompson Milburn as a specialist subject on *Mastermind* and trounced all-comers. He knew everything – including the trivia. He could tell you the date and place of Milburn's birth: 11 May 1924 at 14 Sixth Row in Ashington. The terraced house overlooked the pit heads, which dominated the landscape and controlled the daily rhythm of a community built on coal. He could tell you Milburn's height and weight – 5ft 11¾in, 12st 12lb – and even the fact he took a size 8 shoe. He could tell you that the boyish Milburn, unable to afford a leather ball, had kicked a stone from home to school and back again to sharpen his close control. And he could tell you, in an incredulous tone, the haphazard way in which

Milburn prepared for his trial at St James' Park. 'You wouldn't believe it,' he said. 'He turned up *four hours* early. He sat on the steps that led up to the main entrance and ate two meat pies and drank a bottle of fizzy pop. And he played in a pair of borrowed boots.'

What came next was a wage of 30 shillings per match and travelling expenses amounting to a glittering half crown. Milburn's signing on fee was £10, paid in two notes that Newcastle's godfather-cum-monarch, Stan Seymour, spread mesmerisingly between finger and thumb, like a card sharp fanning out a deck in front of him. This was Seymour's showy way of giving the occasion legal solemnity. Seymour *was* Newcastle – an FA Cup and League Championship winner in the 1920s who became a director, honorary manager and chairman. He was balder than a Bigg Market pigeon and had a pot-belly, constrained in his over-tight black waistcoat. To the impoverished Milburn family – wholly reliant on the pit for a home, food, clothing and heat – the money was like a pools win. 'It was a fortune. I'd never seen, let alone owned, quite so much,' said Milburn, still astonished half a century later by the windfall and Seymour's implacable faith in him. He handed £5 to his mother to buy a new dress. He gave £1 to his father for a pint and a tin of tobacco. What remained was spent on a plain suit for himself. My father knew all this, as if recounting his own life.

A goal scored in today's game is filmed by more than a dozen High Definition or 3-D cameras. It is replayed from multiple angles even before the whooping yells of celebration for it are over. In Milburn's day a goal was fixed in the eye of the beholder alone. The perspective from which it was both judged and stored in the memory depended entirely on where you happened to be standing in the ground. From behind the posts, my father believed he was staring down the wide barrel of every goal Milburn scored and he described them to me, believing his anecdotes would preserve what no cameraman had been there to capture. I heard about the tap-ins, the shots that left his boot in a great whoosh, the noise of them rattling around the sky, and the rare headers. There was one goal in particular that stood out. It was *the* goal. 'Against Tottenham,' my father said. Those two words were his deliberately bland prequel to an amazed account of it. They were always followed by a pause to crank up the anticipation. Milburn fastens on to a short pass, which is pushed to him on the half way line. He has sufficient space and time to take two touches. The first controls the ball. The second nudges it barely half a yard in front of him. 'Everyone expects him to look right or left and knock a pass away,' my father said. Instead Milburn stares straight ahead. He sees the Spurs goalkeeper beyond his six-yard box. Instinctively he shoots. To listen to my father, the ball was in the top corner of the net – tearing against the thick cord – barely a nanosecond after Milburn's boot connected with it. But he stretched out the story, as if he was seeing everything in super-slow motion – the arrow-like trajectory of the shot, the revolutions on the thickly laced ball as it blasted through the air, Tottenham's defenders twisting their necks to watch it in flight and the goalkeeper impotent as it cleared his upward dive. 'A goal from nearly 50 yards,' my father said, as though the statistic alone made further elaboration unnecessary.

My father could recite Milburn's League, FA Cup and wartime scoring record: 238 in 492 appearances. And, perched in one of the middle tiers of Gallowgate End, he had seen the very first, which came in Milburn's home debut against Bradford City in the wartime, lamp-light flicker of 1943. It was scored with his first kick too – a swinging left foot from ten yards. I was always told: 'He barely raised his boot to make contact with the ball and the shot hardly got off the floor. The goalkeeper didn't move at all. It went past him too quickly – and he turned his head too late – to even catch sight of it.' Statistics prove Milburn's worth. But aesthetics were more important than data to my father. Figures could never convey the way he moved with the ball or articulate the lyrical body-swerve and smooth back-lift which preceded a shot.

Where football is concerned, style is usually a matter of deportment; the way possession is carried, received and distributed. The question of whether the game qualified as an art was categorically answered for my father whenever he saw Milburn. For him St James' Park was the working-man's Sadler's Wells, and Milburn remained unchallenged in my father's affections – venerated, whereas others would be merely admired. The realisation of this struck my father when, in October 1946, he witnessed Len Shackleton's six-goal arrival on Tyneside in a 13–0 humiliation of Newport County. Shackleton was mischief; he had more colour about him than Matisse. His penchant was for excess; he was purposely as idiosyncratic and playful as possible – the Clown Prince. Why, an England selector was once asked, is Shackleton not in the team? 'Because we play at Wembley Stadium and not the London Palladium,' he replied tartly, unimpressed by his whimsicality. My father saw Shackleton, easily bored, sit on the ball near the touchline and wait for a defender to come to him. He also remembered how he'd lightly rest his studs on the top of the ball, as if posing stiffly for a photographer's camera, and glance impatiently at an imaginary watch strapped to his left wrist before beckoning the opposition towards him with his right hand. Sometimes he would mime puffing on a pipe like a puckish gentleman character in a Rattigan play. He even acted out the process of striking a match to light it. The routine ended as Shackleton, cupping the pretend pipe in one hand and crooking his other arm – as though propping himself up against the wide mantel of a fireplace – blew sham smoke rings towards the opposition. Another party-piece was to fake losing his balance. There'd be a practised stalling during his run to goal, a deliberate series of long, maladroit mis-steps, which sent him into a low crouch, and then his upper body would sway and list. Shackleton made it look as though the touchline was a high ledge and he was stumbling awkwardly along it. The nearest defenders would be conned into expecting an ignominious fall. But, at the very moment any move was made to rob him of the ball, Shackleton snapped himself gracefully upright again, jumped clear of the tackle and whipped his limbs into a gallop. He swept into the space the defenders' gullibility made available for him. 'They'd wait for him to end up on his backside,' my father said, 'but he never did.' He saw Shackleton use his leg like an axe-blade too, chopping his boot through the base of the ball, which made a five-to ten-yard pass come directly back to him, as if he was controlling it on a long strip of elastic. 'It was like watching a yo-yo drop and then spin back into the palm of your hand,' my father remembered. 'The poor bloke sliding in to make a tackle found that Shackleton had gone – and the ball was nowhere to be seen either.' Another trick was to play the ball deliberately off a corner flag or the foot of a post to bamboozle a full back or goalkeeper.

Shackleton eschewed anything simple, as if it counted as a serious dereliction of his duty to be a showman. On a churned pitch my father saw him sprint so far ahead of a defence that it surrendered early and left the goalkeeper to confront him alone. The keeper slid towards Shackleton and made a wild grasp for the ball; Shackleton simply nudged it around him. The goal was unguarded. The closest defender was marooned in the centre circle. The keeper was face-down in the mud, as if he'd been run over. Nothing more elaborate than a toe-poke was necessary to score. But Shackleton couldn't resist the final flourish. He walked the ball directly to the line before flicking it languidly from his left foot on to his right knee. As the airborne ball drew level with his forehead he nodded it smartly into the net. He retrieved the ball himself and juggled with it from the six-yard box to the half way line. With an outstretched hand, he presented it to the referee, like a postman delivering a letter on the doorstep. 'It was slapstick,' my father said. 'He would nutmeg one chap, take the ball forward half a dozen paces and then backtrack to nutmeg him again.' The smart-alecky Shackleton made twisty runs on slim feet – he often wore rugby boots because nothing else fitted so comfortably – and frequently hair-pinned back on himself to dizzy the defenders lunging after him. He flowed across the pitch in huge bright swathes and made even the best defences look disorderly. My father thought Shackleton buttered up the crowd because he wanted what any entertainer wants, to be loved and so went to extremes to achieve it. Still my father's footballing heart belonged to Milburn. 'Even though Shackleton got half a dozen against Newport,' he said, 'I was a Milburn man. He played inside left. He played right wing. But I knew he was a goal-scorer – a proper centre forward.'

My father thought Bobby Mitchell, also of Newcastle,

dribbled the much more cumbersome 1950s ball better than George Best would have done. He spoke almost breathlessly of George Robledo, Chilean-born and partly Yorkshire-bred, whose hair rose like a surfer's wave and whose shots, my father insisted, sizzled through the air and landed like shell-fire. There were others he purpose-fully went to see, among them Tommy Lawton and Stanley Matthews, Tom Finney and Billy Liddell, and thought each capable of dominating any era: Lawton for his heading – 'his neck muscles were like springs,' he said; Matthews and Finney for the devilish cut inside or the dash to the goal-line before the inevitable cross, which arched into the box dangerously; and Liddell because he was as tough as a middleweight champion. 'Couldn't be roughed up. He was bare-knuckled,' he maintained. But no one compared to Milburn. He described him in tabloid language, as if he were a force of Nature. He would wash over defences in 'a flash flood', he explained. Or hit them in a 'lightning strike'. Or deracinate what-ever stood in front of him like the sweep of a 'huge tornado'.

My St James' Park hero was Malcolm Macdonald, who always came on to the pitch with a bow-legged swagger, like a gunslinger in a High Noon western. There was an air of edgy confrontation about him. In midfield Newcastle had Terry Hibbitt who was short and wiry with eyes as big as Eddie Cantor's. He would curl his boot around a pass and float it forward for Macdonald to chase. The ball went from Hibbitt's left foot and on to Macdonald's and then into the net. Super Mac's left foot was like a fairground hammer. But if I dared suggest he was better than Milburn, my father would have none of it. 'You don't know what you're talking about,' he'd say. The way he talked it was as though the sun always repositioned itself in the sky if a mucky cloud obscured its view of Milburn on the run. I found it extraordinary. My father was no doe-eyed, impressionable youth when he first watched him. He was already 24 – two years older than Milburn. But, like others around him on those crammed terraces, my father recognised a quality in Milburn that went far beyond goal-scoring.

I am sure his esteem for him was loosely rooted in the belief that he and his hero were very much alike: diffident and inhibited, placid and undemonstrative. Milburn's temperament and demeanour, as much as his talent, impressed him. He did not strut. There was nothing arrogant or brazen about his bearing – even after a hat-trick. He was neither self-indulgent nor self-aggrandising. Shackleton was a self-confessed non-conformist and show-off, pleasing himself as much as those who watched him, and he gave off a seemly dazzle. Milburn had a different mind-cast. He was an altruistic Everyman, ostensibly ordinary except for his footballing skills, and what he did was for Newcastle first and foremost – even if obligation and duty meant the graft of some heavy lifting rather than the glamour work up front. He was also aware of the responsibility of the number nine on his back, explaining it in a homespun way: 'The people who watched wanted to be in your position . . . I never forgot that . . . I knew how much football meant to them . . . You have to be born here to realise it . . .'

Milburn didn't consider himself great in any sense; he was humble because he thought he ought to be. He was constantly bewildered that anyone – especially long after his retirement – should make a fuss about him or what he'd once done with laced pieces of leather. He regarded himself as 'just an ordinary chap' who had 'been lucky' and knew 'nowt else' except football. In saying it, he was neither indulging in false modesty nor fishing for flattery in return. He simply believed it to be true.

The 1950s began in austerity – no jam today or the next – and ended in affluence and coffee houses and rock 'n' roll, albeit only for some. Harold Macmillan exaggerated his view that: 'You've never had it so good.' For in the far corners of the country, especially within the boundaries which my father occupied, the claim was patently nonsense. Affluence was a chimera. At one end of the scale there were drab pre-fab houses and progressive high rises, every day a kitchen-sink drama. At the other there was the swish of debutante balls and London society. A footballer such as Milburn was a working man only marginally better off than the others. The players who appeared on cigarette cards still lived in the same cramped houses and travelled on the same corporation buses as the fans who followed them. There were no wide metal gates, high walls or vast acreages of land to separate the performer from his public. On Saturday the double-deckers bound for St James' Park pulled up to snaking queues, two or three deep, at uncovered stops in Milburn's Ashington. 'They would yell at me to get to the front of the queue,' said Milburn. 'I waited my turn like the rest.' Once on board, it was standing-room only, and he refused the offer of a seat. In these dotted villages, where coal shards clogged the gutters and pit seams criss-crossed underground, blood relations grew up beside one another. Each cobbled road, street or cul-de-sac was a line of an extended family tree. In Ashington, there were 73 'Milburns' looking out for one another in the embodiment of community spirit.

Milburn was no different from my father – or from tens of thousands exactly like him. He went down the mine. As a fitter, he began a shift at midnight on Friday, clocked off with his black minstrel's face between 7 a.m. and 8 a.m. on Saturday, went home to scrub off the grime and less than six hours later replaced pit boots with football boots, one pair scarcely lighter than the other. The night before one match, against West Bromwich Albion, Milburn crawled on his back along an 18-inch-high seam to repair the pawl on a diamond coal cutter. The job took nearly four hours and he spent most of them on his knees. 'You know what it's like when you're down there by yourself?' he said, the bite of remembering traceable in the tight vocabulary.

'The props are popping and creaking. The stone's falling. The roof's laying on.' Only a doctor who ignored the Hippocratic Oath, bending it on the back of a white lie, allowed him to break free of the Friday night– Saturday morning shift. The doctor diagnosed external otitis – an infection of the ear canal causing pain, inflammation and a gluey discharge – and gave Milburn a hospital chit to prove it. 'But my ears never ran at all,' admitted his patient.

It wasn't as though football paid Milburn handsomely for his genius. My father saw him as representative of the unrewarded – a group of players never given their financial dues. 'He got bugger all,' he said. In 1947–48, despite being capped for England, Milburn had a measly £17 in the bank. His salary was £12 a week and every piece of furniture in his four-roomed semi-detached house had been bought on hire purchase. He was paying off the debts slowly, and said he 'needed every penny I could lay my hands on'. As Milburn collected his third Cup winners' medal in 1955, he was earning £16 during the season and £14 in the summer. Newcastle made enough pounds and pennies to have shared the profits more equitably among the team. The club's average home gate exceeded 56,000. But football was not an egalitarian business; and footballers were not elite earners. They were ranked as artisans rather than artists.

Newcastle's directors regarded themselves as lordly, and were not alone in the delusion. The attitude was prevalent throughout the Football League. In the boardrooms sat men who were parsimonious, self-important and as self-protective as the Medicis. At worst, most players were viewed as chattels. At best, they were considered hired help – just as disposable as a handyman or a gardener. Players were given bonus money – £3 for a win and 10 shillings for a draw, which was set aside, as Milburn remembered it, 'to get the groceries in'. To the board, believing itself virtuous, generous and also socially and morally superior, the brown packet payments were akin to flipping a token tip to a waiter or a shoe-shine boy. Even the Milburns of this unequal world were supposed to be grateful and say please and thank you, grovel if necessary and doff the flat cap in gratitude at the charitable benevolence of the board.

He had been taught a lesson in 1948, and felt the lash of it. Asking for a transfer, he was told to stand in front of Newcastle's directors to defend his case, as though occupying a court dock. The club's boardroom, with its long polished table and its sepia photographs hanging in dark wooden frames, resembled the headmaster's study in a slightly run-down public school. It was gloomy, swirling with the smoke of cigars and pipes and forbiddingly austere for someone as unconfident as Milburn, who disliked dealing with authority because he confessed to an inferiority complex. Milburn pretended his wife was suffering from bronchitis and needed the cleaner, fresher air of the south to recover. He was still standing when the directors refused his request, dismissively waving him out of the room. Milburn lacked the belief to argue. His tepid response, delivered after a decade's hindsight, was to blame himself. 'On reflection, I realise what a foolish young chap I'd been to think there was easy money to be made out of football . . . I know now that easy money isn't the kind of money I would like to handle,' he said. Hard though it is to believe, he defended the directors, stressing what he felt were the 'tremendous overheads of the club'. Newcastle's total wage bill was then £700 a week. The 'easy money' went to the club.

My father thought Milburn never appreciated his self-worth – or just thought himself unworthy. He told me this after quoting the final lines of Milburn's autobiography to me. It was published in 1957. This was three and a half seasons before the abolition of the maximum wage, which tethered salaries to £20 a week, and six years before the official end of restraint of trade, which allowed a club to cling on to a player's registration after it expired – sometimes for reasons of expediency and occasionally out of pettiness – until he became superfluous. Milburn put a question – and then answered it – with the humbling charm of someone lacking a greedy gene in his DNA. He wrote: 'We professionals can't really grumble, can we?' He insisted that players should neither be classed as 'underpaid slaves who do not get a fair return for our services' nor think of themselves as 'little tin gods'. Then, as now, these statements sound ludicrously naïve, anachronistic and fawning. But his passiveness towards peppercorn wages revealed again the acquiescent nature of his character rather than his deference towards – or excuse-making for – avaricious directors. And the warning about bloated egos stemmed from Milburn's dislike of the tint of celebrity, from which he sought to detach himself.

Milburn never envisaged the revolution to come, the blasting away of convention. George Eastham, given the clichéd title of 'lone rebel with a cause', broke Newcastle's hold on him in 1960 to sign for Arsenal and then went to the High Court in 1963 to get the Retain and Transfer system proclaimed illegal. Eastham's QC likened it to 'treating men like cattle' and added that a footballer's contract was so damagingly restrictive that 'any intelligent apprentice in the Middle Ages would have rejected it with scorn'. As a consequence of a planned strike in 1961 – what the Football League called insolent insurrection and the players described as a freedom fight – Johnny Haynes, the Maestro of Fulham, became the first £100 a week footballer. In both instances, the League acted like the Director of Public Prosecutions responding censoriously to *Lady Chatterley's Lover*. The cold horror and panic and high-handed effrontery the League displayed made it look pathetically tyrannical. Worse, it seemed trapped in an upstairs–downstairs world where servants had to honour and obey without a peep of protest. Anyone breaking ranks was branded as an uppity troublemaker.

Born much too early, Milburn's generation missed the benefits of financial emancipation, which were necessary because the oppression preceding it was often loathsome. In setting up his sports shop, where my father took me to buy that Newcastle shirt, Frank Brennan inflamed a member of Newcastle's hierarchy. When he opened the store in 1953, Brennan was only 28, the pivotal figure in the previous year's FA Cup Final win over Arsenal and a performer at his peak. But from 1954 until his transfer into the non-Leagues in 1956, he played just 16 First Division matches, saw his salary halved to £8 and was denied the chance of a third Cup winners' medal in 1955. All this disproportionate spite was poured on Brennan because he wanted to better himself through business. The instigator was the dictatorial Seymour, who made a series of condescending claims, which arrogantly presumed anyone who heard or read them was a block-head unable to differentiate between truth and lies. He claimed Brennan's branching out into the sports goods business was a 'distraction'; that he was 'on his way out as a player' anyway; and that he didn't fit in 'with our scheme for the development of younger players'. His words were soaked in self-interest and carried the stench of the sewer about them. There was already an established sports shop in Newcastle; and Seymour was the owner of it. The rival stores were less than half a mile apart. Seymour's response to Brennan's challenge to his monopoly was corrupt, damnable and transparent. His subsequent maliciousness was more

transparent still. Brennan was forced to play his testimonial match at Roker Park because Newcastle's board
blocked the use of St James' Park. Brennan was anointed
'The Rock of Tyneside'. He wore size 12 boots and told
team mates who got in his way in defence to 'piss off
– let me deal with this'. In his way, he told Seymour to
piss off – though it was only a pyrrhic victory.

After the Premiership was established, like a gold rush,
there were a lot of things my father found unacceptable.
Cheating: a dive in the box or an injury feigned to con
a referee; the vituperative disputing and colossal whinging
indulged in if a decision, no matter how trivial, went
against a player; the false declarations of club loyalty,
such as kissing the badge of the shirt, before mutinous
flirtation with another club led to a lucrative departure;
the arm-waving attempts to have an opponent yellow- or
red-carded; and the general child-like antics of adults.
But he never complained about the salaries being paid.
He refused to think of them as insanely exorbitant even
when I told him about one Premiership player who would
buy a newspaper with a £20 note and then refuse the
change because a handful of coins spoilt the smooth line
of his suit. He only regretted that Milburn hadn't earned
enough to do the same; and that Brennan had been
treated so contemptuously. 'Look what happened to those
two,' he said, ashamed and angry on their behalf. 'It was
exploitation. That bloody Seymour should have been
locked up for it.'

* * *

My father was concerned about my choice of journalism as a career. Not because he thought it an unsuitable profession – he read newspapers assiduously – but because he worried about whether I could cope with the limitations my stammer imposed. His way of dealing with that stammer was never to mention it. He taught me to box without saying why; though, I suspect, it was to counter the bullying he wrongly believed would be commonplace. He was aghast when, aged 13, I wrote to David Coleman at the BBC to ask how to become a commentator. Coleman was then the Corporation's sporting voice. His typewritten reply was routinely straightforward. 'There's no traditional way of becoming a sports commentator,' he wrote, 'but most people I think come through sports itself or journalism.' The letter, arriving in its smart BBC envelope, knocked my father sideways; he assumed I thought my stammer would one day just clear up, the way measles and chicken pox had done. He spoke to my mother. Almost immediately, I was dispatched for speech therapy, which proved all but hopeless.

Four years later he was similarly troubled when I began in newspapers. As usual, he said nothing to me about it. He confided his fears to my mother again. Was I capable of interviewing anyone? Would I be teased or tormented and find the struggle to speak too 'painful' – his euphemism for embarrassing? Since I was so inarticulate in speech – each word broken as soon as it left my lips – how would I ever achieve fluency on the page?

He made almost no comment on any of the stories I wrote – even though he read them in the broadsheet *Nottingham Evening Post*, which he yanked with a clatter from the letterbox each tea time. He made no mention, either, of my nascent, but slowly developing, working relationship with Brian Clough. Everyone else wanted to know how long Clough had kept me hanging around in the grubby corridor, like a footman waiting for a finger-clicking summons from the master of the house. After our daily audience in his cluttered office, my friends expected me to reveal to them what I'd found unprintable – the real story, cloaking the one which had actually appeared, and also to detail the small foibles and blatant eccentricities of his behaviour. In my early days on the *Post*, the business of gathering copy for it was a severe chore. Often, it was a pantomime minus the music: the two or three fingers of morning Scotch in stocky tumblers; Clough's occasional tempest rages; the frequent acts of generosity which stemmed from a core of principled kindness; and the tests he set like traps – being purposefully late or deliberately obstreperous – merely to see if I was sufficiently tough enough to pass them and come back for more. You survived or were crushed; I promised myself I would survive. To be in Clough's presence was to witness a stage performance, a peculiar kind of whirling vaudeville act. The consequences were often troublesomely chaotic or gloriously memorable. My father was the only person close to me who never asked about any of it. He feigned disinterest. I once mentioned him in a column I wrote about Newcastle and the club's attachment to the FA Cup. I waited for him to reach the piece, tucked on the inside back page, and I saw him read each line of it too. And then I prepared myself for a sparky reaction. The article may as well have been written in invisible ink. He made no reference to it.

I can nevertheless pin-point the precise moment my father finally accepted that I'd chosen the right career. At the beginning of the 1980s, I went to St James' Park to cover a mid-week match in Division Two: Newcastle v Notts County. It was early April, a warm spring night. Newcastle's press box was built into a curved wooden pediment in the main stand. It looked like a half-closed, sleepy eye. The only way in and out of it was via a corkscrew staircase forged from thick metal. The box slightly overhung the pitch and provided a panoramic view of the city beyond it – the slant of blue and red tiled roofs and the high windows of Georgian buildings in the middle distance. It felt like sitting in the lamp room of a lighthouse. If a blaze had ever broken out in the stand, there would have been no escape. I climbed the tight spiral towards my seat, clutching the rail hard and aware with every step of where I was placing my feet on the rungs. I refused to glance down in case the sight of the drop induced vertigo. When I reached the box, I took a vacant place near the end of the back row and bent to unpack the paraphernalia from my case – notebook, pen, team sheet and programme – and then began arranging them on a wide bench. I was aware someone else had already occupied the end of the row beside me. I turned to offer the usual handshake and make my introductions, half swivelling in the seat to face my new neighbour. It was Jackie Milburn.

His face was gaunt, making the grooves from nose to mouth distinct. The eyes were slightly sunken, as if set in a shallow well, and the hair was flecked with peppery touches of grey. He was dressed in a collar and tie, and wore a light brown mackintosh over his suit. His hand-shake was solid, and the expression accompanying it struck me as genuinely warm, as if I were being re-acquainted with an old uncle instead of meeting a stranger. In one way, it was true. I had heard so much about Milburn from my father – his background and his goals, his FA Cup Final medals and his idolatry status – that I felt I *did* know him, if only by proxy. I'd seen him only through my father's eyes, and from grainy scraps of old film, which were occasionally shown to coincide with Cup landmarks or for the purpose of wallowing nostalgically in all our yesterdays. Whenever he saw the film, my father's stock response to me was 'the time before you were born', which was said in a way that implied that a Golden Age had come and gone without me in it. Milburn was nonetheless part of my growing up, and I came to respect him because my father did.

It's said that the cure for admiring someone famous is to meet them. Not in Milburn's case. I discovered he was every bit as humble and unprepossessing as my father had suggested. At first we spoke in innocuous generalities about the game we were about to watch, and the season so far. But, at one stage, in a yawning lull early in the opening half, I owned up to being a Geordie, born so close to St James' Park that Milburn, in his heyday, could have kicked a ball into the maternity ward from the half way line. 'My father's a great fan of yours. He watched you play all the time. He says you were the best,' I said, knowing how flat the line must have sounded as I spoke it; and how often Milburn must have heard it. I mentioned Len Shackleton and Tommy Lawton, Billy Liddell and Stanley Matthews. 'No one else came close to you for him, though,' I added, cautiously. With another friendly, but perplexed smile, Milburn acknowledged what he sensed from experience was shaping into a grandiose compliment – a full soliloquy about his skills. In the pause which followed, he pressed his lips together in a minor grimace; a look which reminded me of someone bracing themselves for the short jab of a doctor's needle. He ran his hand across an unopened Silvine notebook which lay in front of him. 'That was a long time ago,' he said, kindly brushing the praise away. 'You won't have seen them, but there were a lot better players than me.' Milburn uncapped the Biro, found a clean page in his notebook and scribbled a slanted note across it. I took the hint and shut up. There was so much I wanted to ask: about the physical demands of swapping the pit for the pitch. About that opening goal against Blackpool in 1951. About the homecomings after each Cup win. About the fervour of the crowds who came specifically to see him score. About the differences between his era and the better paid one immediately following it. About his loyalty to Newcastle and why he regarded Tyneside as unique. I longed to go home and regale my father with Milburn's replies. I wanted to succeed with verbal anecdotes where I had failed with the printed word. After their telling, he would surely look at me differently – his son, the established journalist at last. But I didn't want to press Milburn because, without being curt or awkward, he didn't want to talk about himself. To do so would have been a form of boasting; and Milburn didn't boast. The hope and expectation he generated in Newcastle brought him oppressive fame. The city thought it owned him. He could go nowhere without being stared at, pestered or pointed out. He'd wait until a cinema darkened before entering and slip into the nearest aisle seat. The depth of his discomfort is explicit in one paragraph he wrote.

I have found that fame has deprived me of some other pleasures. For one thing, it is many years since there has been any privacy for me and my family while we have been out and about in the area. If we go to the seaside for the day someone is sure to recognise me. I daren't even play football with my children on the beach for fear that someone will think I am showing off. So I just sit and watch the children playing and hope that no one will come up and want to talk to me about football.

I understood why he'd looked so furtive, as if on a mission of subterfuge, as he escaped the bus station crowds all those years before. He didn't want to be recognised. In the final ten minutes of the game I summoned up the courage to ask him about his goal against Blackpool. I told him my father would want to know, and that I daren't go home with the question unasked. 'Well,' he said, making light of it. 'The longest run of my life. I seemed to be running for ever. No matter how fast my legs went, I didn't feel as if I was getting anywhere. I had so much time to think. I just hoped I wouldn't make a mess of it. When I scored, I felt relief before I felt any joy.' At the end of the game he shook me by the hand again and said generously, as if he meant it: 'If your dad is ever here, bring him over.' An hour or so later I watched Milburn leave St James' Park. It was impossible for him to slide away inconspicuously. He couldn't walk more than five feet without being slapped on the back, taking a hand which had been offered to him or signing an autograph. I saw in the gaze of old men and young boys alike that Milburn was far more than a mere footballer to them. He symbolised the club, as if it had been built around him.

With the picture of Milburn solid in my mind, I rehearsed what I'd say to my father. He was a two-pack-a-day smoker who sat in a blizzard of ash from his fags. His brass ashtray, containing a stack of dead butts, curled and crushed, was always precarious on the arm of his chair. He was either reading a newspaper or just putting one away. This is how I found him – cigarette smouldering and a newspaper open. I put my bag next to the sofa, walked over to him and said: 'Here. Take the hand that shook Jackie Milburn's hand.' He took it edgily, as if I was playing a practical joke on him. And then he stared, smiling, at his own palm, as if expecting to see the whorls and swirls of Milburn's prints on his own fingers.

'You spoke to him?' he asked.

'He sent you a message,' I replied. 'If you're ever at another Newcastle game, he'd be pleased to say hello.'

My father rebutted the notion, his desire to meet Milburn instinctively smothered by shyness. 'I wouldn't like to bother him,' he said. 'He must have all sorts of people bothering him.' In that moment he both looked and sounded a little like his hero.

My father did meet Jackie Milburn. In November 1991, he caught a bus into Newcastle with one intention. He walked along Northumberland Street until he found the nine-foot bronze of Milburn, unveiled only 48 hours earlier and incongruously sited beside a branch of McDonald's. The man, now immortalised in metal, had died in 1988. Milburn is frozen in the act of shooting. The boots are high and long-studded. The left foot is planted solidly beside the ball, the right poised to strike it. The face is stern in concentration and the body is powerful-looking. Magnificent in its visual strength, the statue captures both the sense of motion and power within Milburn, the folk hero.

Someone had tied an old black and white scarf around Milburn's neck. A withered red rose and a fresh carnation lay beside his feet. My father walked around the statue, remembering goals and matches and all those times when his eyes followed Milburn around the pitch – even when the ball was elsewhere. 'I'd just be waiting for him to get it,' he said. He stood behind the plinth and imagined the ball Milburn was about to kick disappearing in a long, high arc down Northumberland Street. When he told me about it, his mumbled afterthought of regret was: 'He should be outside St James' Park. He'd be sure to score from there.'

2

When Christmas Day
Came Every Spring

Depending on his mood Brian Clough could be the very best or the worst possible company. To work with him was like living under the volcano. I was always expecting, and braced for, an eruption. He took delight in argument and provocation.

Almost every January I found myself writing the same story about Clough. Either explicitly or tacitly I put the question: is this the season he will win the FA Cup? Clough had won everything else, including two League Championships and two European Cups. But the FA Cup refused to yield to him. He tried to pretend it didn't matter, always insisting: 'I'd prefer to win another Championship. In fact, I'd prefer to win another Championship rather than another European Cup. The Championship is the thing that matters to me. Nowt else.' He'd say it with grand conviction, blocking any counter argument I could offer. Accompanying the words was either a provocative, stabbed finger – aimed between the eyes – or one of his low, contemptuous glares, colder than a gust of arctic air. At such uncomfortable moments the benefits of invisibility became sweetly attractive to me.

There was an expectation that Clough would one day win the FA Cup for Nottingham Forest. In a city which celebrated its last win in 1959 – ten-man Forest beating Luton Town 2–1 – there was a need and a longing for the trophy to return. By the late 1970s and early 80s, the young lads who had gone to Wembley with their fathers were middle-aged men with sons of their own. They wanted to recapture their own youth by retracing the path of it. Most of all, they wanted their children to experience the same thrill of an FA Cup Final Saturday at Wembley, and the dizzy feeling of winning there. At every notable '59 anniversary, at each old players' reunion or whenever one of that team died, the Cup and what it had meant to Nottingham surfaced again. Stories about it never lost their allure – either to those who had been there and had originally told them, or to others hearing about that long, memorable weekend secondhand and for the first time. There was the unexpected sight of Forest's players, holdalls in hand, pushing through the tide of the crowd after the club's coach got caught in traffic. Arriving less than an hour before kick off, the driver hurriedly parked a quarter of a mile from the dressing-room entrance. There was the human drama of Roy Dwight, who lifted a close-range shot into the net for the opening goal and was later stretchered off after cracking his shinbone, forcing outnumbered Forest to hold on for 40 minutes of the second half because no substitutes were then permitted. And there were the ordinary tales from the Wembley terraces: of decorated buses and special trains that left Nottingham and the supporters with treasured tickets, who went to London wearing pinned-on rosettes the size of dinner plates, carrying home-made placards that urged 'Up the Reds' and wore long knitted scarves. Finally, there was the homecoming – the impromptu street parties, the spilling into and out of the Market Square pubs, the unsynchronised jigs that passed for dancing and the drunken, loud sing-songs. Nottingham then was exactly as Alan Sillitoe described it in his novel *Saturday Night and Sunday Morning*, published only six months after that Cup was won. After a week of monotonous graft in the mines or on the type of factory floor where Sillitoe's protagonist, Arthur Seaton, worked – lanes of capstan lathes, drills and hand-presses and the thump and slap of motorised belts and well-oiled wheels – Saturday nights were rowdy relief. It was, as Sillitoe said, the 'best and bingiest glad-time', supping pints and small gin chasers in a fug of smoke. Most men did follow the maxim that Sillitoe gave Seaton – 'be drunk and be happy' – and thought as he did: 'Well, it's a good life and a good world . . . if you don't weaken.' The Sunday mornings were for sobering up, hoping the hours would pass slowly before the piecework began again, which Sillitoe said was 'cramp-inducing, back-breaking, knuckle-knocking'. The Saturday Night and Sunday Morning after Forest's Cup win were unforgettable, worthy of capital letters like the title of the book, and those who drank through them wanted to live another exactly like it. Clough was supposed to fix this for them. He'd won back-to-back European Cups in 1979 and 1980. He'd taken Forest to Wembley for three successive League Cups too, and won twice in 1978 and 1979. But he was either prickly about the FA Cup – 'I've told you before, the bloody thing doesn't bother me much' – or treated conversations about it with detachment, like someone weary of repeating himself. 'You're raking old coals again,' he'd say to me.

I always thought Clough was protesting too much, as though afraid a frank confession about his desire to win the 'bloody thing' would make him appear needy or illuminate too brightly his failure to do so. I believed, too, that his public indifference towards the Cup masked a private ambition. He conceded the fact to me in his office only a week before the 1991 final against Tottenham. 'I want to win the FA Cup very badly,' he said. By then his reasons went beyond filling in the only remaining blank on his CV. He wanted to make another barbed point about his abilities to manage alone; and specifically to win another trophy without his former partner, Peter Taylor. At its successful height, the relationship with Taylor was more than friendship. It was marriage without a licence. Their compatibility, a meeting of minds and football philosophies, suggested an unbreakable, happy-ever-after bliss. But failure, the maladroit dismantling of the European Cup-winning squad in 1980, led to insecurities, trivial jealousies and suspicions before the two of them separated and then slipped into a cold silence that lasted seven years. Taylor died suddenly, and in bereavement Clough felt guilty, as well as remorseful, about the futility and waste of their rancorous falling out. But the Cup Final provided his chance, which I'm sure he sensed would not come again, to achieve something substantial alone. He was resentful of anyone who thought he was only half a manager without Taylor. The League Cup, which Clough won again in 1989 and 1990, had neither enough tradition behind it nor sufficient kudos attached to it. You had to do your Wembley lap of honour in May to make it indelible on other people's memories. Clough knew it, too.

There was no lap of honour for him in '91 – only a 2–1 defeat to Spurs and proof that the saddest words of mouth or pen truly are what might have been. That Cup Final comes back to me in a slideshow of single images. The rabid tackles from Paul Gascoigne, threatening to decapitate Garry Parker and dismember Gary Charles; and Gascoigne being carried off – rather than sent off – after shredding his knee ligaments in the second of those challenges. The lashed-in dead ball from Stuart Pearce which put Forest in front from the resulting free kick. The headed own goal from Des Walker that gave Tottenham the Cup in extra time. And the poker-face Clough wore afterwards as he came out of Forest's dressing room and boarded the coach, which was waiting for him in the tunnel. What I recall above all is his inexpressive marble gaze, as if his eyes were suddenly sightless. After his retirement I sat with Clough in his living room reminiscing about his career. There were only a few regrets. Not managing England was one. 'That bunch of bastards,' he said of the Football Association committee who decided, well before his sham interview at the end of 1977, that Clough's combustible nature made him unsuitable for high office. Another was the Cup Final. 'Should have been sent off,' he said emphatically of Gascoigne, shaking his head as if still unable to believe it hadn't happened. Clough stared out of the window, the left side of his face in profile. 'Should have been sent off,' he said again before adding: 'If he had been, we'd have walked that final. We'd have beaten them, good and proper, in any replay too. I'm certain of it. We'd have kept a clean sheet and probably scored four or five.'

The closest Clough came to an FA Cup winners' medal was to hold one in a photograph, which I arranged to be taken before a semi-final against Liverpool at Hillsborough in 1988. Billy Gray, the Forest groundsman, had played in the '59 final. With a shimmy, a step inside and a far-post cross he'd created Forest's second goal. He was a genial man, devoid of hubris and apparently content with his lot. He bore no grudge about the fact he'd played in the era of the maximum wage and frugal perks. I never heard him complain about the fiscal unfairness and injustices of the past. And I never saw him glance enviously around the City Ground's car park at the rows of smart sports cars that symbolised a level of success beyond both him and his fellow Cup winners. Nor was he resentful about the position he found himself in – replacing muddy divots and rolling the grass for a different generation. There was no jealousy; just an appreciation of the skills he saw on 'his' fine pitch.

The newspaper where I worked, the *Nottingham Evening Post*, wanted something more than a stock picture to accompany the semi-final preview I wrote for Friday's back page. I thought of Billy and his medal; I also thought of myself. Watching film of Newcastle's 3–1 win over Manchester City in the 1955 final, I'd seen Bobby Mitchell stop near the foot of the steps shortly after the presentation of the trophy. The box containing his medal sat in the well of his hand. He looked down at it and flipped open the lid. For a second or two he looked at the medal intently. It was as if only the sight of it, rather than the silver Cup, persuaded him that Newcastle's achievement was real. He lingered over the medal until Jackie Milburn yanked the baggy sleeve of his shirt, pulling his friend towards the photographers waiting with bulky cameras. From that moment on, I wanted to hold an FA Cup winners' medal too.

Some sportsmen buy glass-fronted cabinets to show off what they've won. Others value the achievement of winning itself far above any token given to them as reward for the effort; the knowledge that they were the best is more important than actual proof of it. Billy fell into this category. I asked him whether he would bring his medal to the ground. He pushed his left thumb into the strap of his navy dungarees and dropped his head in a pose of studious thought. 'If I can find it,' he said amiably, as though he was talking about a sixpenny prize he'd won at a fairground. 'To be honest I can't remember the last time I saw it. I think it's in a drawer at home. I'll dig around for you.' Billy arrived the following morning with his medal and handed it to me. 'Just give it back when you've done with it,' he said. 'There's no rush.' The gold medal lay in its blue leather presentation box, faded and lightly scuffed at the corners. Like Mitchell, I lifted the lid. The gold was dull and in need of polish. But I imagined what it had looked like, fresh and shiny, on the afternoon Billy had won it. On the front were two footballers, hands resting loosely on hips, standing beside three lions. On the back was an inscription which declared him to be an FA Cup winner. When I caught up with Clough – I was still holding the medal as though it was a breakable antiquity from the Victoria and Albert Museum – he decided he wanted to be photographed beside Billy. 'Let's go and find him,' he said. 'You're not getting my ugly mug on its own.' I trailed beside him along the bank of the Trent

– Clough speed-walking and waving at whoever waved at him – until we saw Billy, who had changed into his blue overalls. He was wading calf-deep through weeds on the apron of Forest's training ground. The term 'training ground' is an over-elaboration. The facilities comprised a couple of bare pitches, and frequently the goal posts lacked nets. The pitches were fringed with long grass and stinging nettles. Overlooking it was the hulking and disused British Waterways building, an austere block blandly designed. The setting was primitive-looking and bleakly windswept; no one would ever have thought European Cup-winning teams had been raised on it.

Clough sat on Billy's tractor, a flat cap on his head and a fleeced coat buttoned almost to the neck. He wore a pair of dark green Wellington boots. The medal sat delicately in his left hand. Clough understood the mechanics of newspapers. He knew what constituted a good intro, a good headline, a good photograph. He posed like an old pro. Billy, though smiling, seemed mystified by the attention. It was as though he couldn't conceive why Clough and I thought the picture was remotely newsworthy. When the photographer finished his work, Clough gave the medal back to Billy. 'Hope this doesn't bring me bad luck,' he said. Billy casually tucked the medal into his top pocket and went back to hack at the weeds.

Forest lost that semi-final to Liverpool (and also the one which followed it 12 months later – the second result inconsequential in the aftermath of the Hillsborough tragedy). The *Evening Post* sold the photograph of Clough and Billy on to the *Daily Mail*, who used it on the morning of the match. After the game, I was sitting on the team coach, a row back from Clough. He climbed into his own seat, saying nothing at first except to tell the driver to head for home. The coach, as the dressing room must have been, was forlornly quiet. No one else spoke. But, as we headed out of the Hillsborough gates, Clough turned to me and said sternly: 'I agreed to that picture because it was for you and my local newspaper. And then I pick up the *Daily Mail* and find it on the back page. Tell your bosses on Monday morning to shove it up their arse.' I said sorry and also lapsed into the obvious excuse – which happened to be genuine – that I knew nothing of the decision. But I found the exchange revealing. For here was Clough in the aftermath of a semi-final defeat – so close to Wembley he could have touched it – sliding into a mini-rage about a newspaper photograph. I put it down to the basic psychology of displacement; someone suffering such hurt and disappointment that he looked for a way of avoiding, however fleetingly, what he felt.

Less than six months later, as a quotidian conversation on a dull autumn afternoon meandered harmlessly into another discussion on the FA Cup, Clough leant back in his office chair and rested his feet on the desk. 'You want me to win it more than I want to win it myself,' he said to me, irritably, as if the act of willing him on to Wembley was an offence. 'You're all about the grandeur of the occasion, the community singing before the kick off, the coach journey and the walk down Wembley Way. You have a bloody romantic notion of all this that I don't possess. Never have. Never will.' Clough sounded as though the final was too ostentatious for his plain tastes. He got up from his desk, snapped himself straight and began walking out of the room. 'Ah well,' Clough said distractedly, loitering in the doorway. He was an eloquent evoker of silences, and waited a second or two before breaking the one he now held: 'You live in the fairytale version of the Cup. I live in the real world.'

I knew he was right. I also knew my father was responsible for it.

Today the FA Cup is incorporated into the fixture list almost as an irritant, a chore to be fulfilled out of duty and sentiment. Its currency has been steadily devalued as other competitions have made themselves worth so much more. To anyone weaned as a fan on the Premiership alone, the Cup seems antiquated. To the rest of us, the competition – and the way it once ignited the season – is longed for. It was integral in making football indispensable in our lives. It began properly with that Monday lunchtime draw for the third round, always held in the dead-yellow gloom of the Football Association's headquarters, which were then in Lancaster

Gate. As a boy I had a distinct idea of what the inside of Lancaster Gate must look like: high white ceilings and marble Ionic columns, gilt mouldings and plush crimson carpets, delicately cut glass chandeliers and polished teak tables. I imagined the walls covered in ornately framed sepia photographs and oil paintings of the FA's former dignitaries, Victorian gentlemen with fat faces, waxed handlebar moustaches and wing collars, or old Corinthians such as W. N. Cobbold, The Prince of the Dribblers, and the centre forward G. O. Smith, dressed in long breeches and high stockings, his granddad shirt tied at the neck.

This image grew from the respectful way the draw was relayed on radio. The commentary was as solemn as a Royal investiture or the State Opening of Parliament, and the broadcaster spoke quietly, as if anything but a whisper would be an affront to the dignity of the FA and the decorum of such sacred surroundings. The draw was one of those shared experiences common before the arrival of multiple choice in broadcasting. In offices and factories and pubs, as well as in the football clubs themselves, the radio was switched on. We all listened for the soft click-click of minute wooden balls shaken in a velvet bag. We all waited for our team's number to come out. The draw was announced in plummy and ever-so-slightly pompous 'telephone' voices by anonymous men, who I supposed wore immaculately brushed blazers, the FA's crest stitched to the breast pocket. As though it was a recognised medical condition, there also existed every year what newspapers diagnosed as 'Cup fever'; the high voltage of hope and anticipation and a crackly, edgy atmosphere around each tie that was quite separate and distinctly different from a League game. It *was* true. It swirled around grounds mostly jammed to overflowing. Because of the gladiatorial, live-or-die element of it – and because then the status of the competition was unchallenged – the Cup's gravitational field proved irresistibly powerful. Even anyone only casually interested in football was pulled towards it. The Fates produced genuine giant-killers – postage stamp 'towns' such as Yeovil, Hereford and Colchester – that whipped big city clubs who never fielded weaker sides with the excuse of conserving energy for more important matches to come. In the pendulum-swing of fortune, your team could actually win the Cup too. From the end of the war to the beginning of the Premiership in 1992, 47 finals produced 23 different winners. From 1992 onwards the Cup has been mostly passed around between Arsenal, Chelsea, Manchester United and Liverpool, as if it contractually belongs to them. There is a depressing sameness about these finals, the event dulled and diminished by repetition. The fascination of the Cup was its unpredictability. But, if the early rounds produce upsets now, the final has latterly failed to bring one consistently. The engraver's steady chisel too often spells out in silver the name of one of the big four.

When the Cup truly mattered, the spectacle of the final and its commemorative sense of occasion always captivated my father as much as – and probably more than – the match. 'It's football's Christmas day,' he said. He transmitted his enthusiasm for it to me. There was a showbizzy glamour attached to the final and, para-doxically, a rigid formality too – as though its staging was an act of High Church. Conventions were formed; small practices, each of which became a ritual in an established ceremony. There was the first glimpse of the cream-washed Twin Towers climbing out of the grey flat-land around the stadium. There was (as Clough had said to me) the deliberately slow walk down Wembley Way – beyond the vendors peddling souvenir scarves and silk flags, the programme booths, as square as tele-phone boxes, and the peanut stalls. And there was (as Clough had said again) the uniformed, brass-buttoned band and the sorrowful verses of 'Abide With Me'. There was the shoulder-to-shoulder emergence of the teams from the gaping black mouth of the tunnel, the unrolling of the red carpet and 'God Save the Queen', the white-paper song-sheets waved as the last note of the anthem died on the air. All this mattered – and seemed so important – not only because the game's focus was narrower, but also because of what the Cup Final repre-sented. Nowadays, whenever the Champions League swallows up the mid-week scheduling, it is possible to watch more domestic and European club matches in eight days live on television than my father and I saw in our first two and a half decades of watching football together at home. What now we routinely take for granted was once a rarity, almost comet-like in its appearance, which made it special. Beginning in the 1950s, as newly bought televisions replaced the mantle and the hearth as the focal point of the living room, the Cup Final found its armchair audience. Everyone who had a set switched it on. The Cup Final captains appeared on the cover of *Radio Times*. Cup Final trivia dominated newspapers for a week. And the Cup Final was tantamount to the season's full stop, the precursor to the start of the cricket season, because so few games were played after it.

To appear at Wembley was also the sunlit peak of a player's career; and few were given the privilege. Apart from internationals, the Cup Final used to be the solitary professional game staged there. Wembley is now open all hours – for the Cup semi-finals; for the League Cup final; for play-off finals in three divisions; for the Johnstone's Paint Trophy final; for the Community Shield. Familiarity long ago stripped Wembley of its veneer. The first person to express it cogently to me was Tommy Lawton.

I occasionally ghosted his twice-weekly column for the *Nottingham Evening Post*. Lawton had been a Championship winner with Everton, aged 19 in 1939, before Hitler interrupted the upward momentum of his career. He scored a record 44 goals in 43 internationals, and another 635 in 731 games for Burnley, Everton, Chelsea, Notts County, Brentford and Arsenal. In his life Lawton came to intimately know Kipling's two impostors, triumph and disaster, and found it impossible to treat them both the same. At the end of the 1940s, the weekly magazine *Picture Post* ran a feature on the 28-year-old Lawton, photographing him at home in one of the smartest addresses in Nottingham after his record £20,000 transfer from First Division Chelsea to Third Division Notts County. His annual income – from football, endorsements and business – was nearly £3,000 a year. The average worker took home less than £300. But, only a decade later, the end of his playing career and failure as a manager led to ruinous decline. Not only did the cheering stop, the money stopped too. What followed was drink, unemployment, bankruptcy and the contemplation of suicide. He thought about throwing himself into the River Trent, which divides Nottingham's two grounds. It seemed to him to be an appropriate place to end his life. In 1973, ashamed of being on the dole, he lied to his family both to protect his dignity and to give them hope that softer times were ahead. He told them he was working regularly, and every morning dressed as neatly as his shabby wardrobe allowed and went out punctually, as if adhering scrupulously to the discipline of nine-to-five. He'd wander the streets of Nottingham, sit on the hard benches in Market Square and buy cups of tea in Parliament Street's cheaper, cheerless cafés with their misted-up windows, garishly coloured Formica-topped tables and unscrubbed, black and white chequered floors. Everything he owned from football – medals, caps, shirts – was gradually sold, often in pubs or saloon bars, to buy food and pay utility bills. At his nadir, in 1975, he was sentenced to three months in prison for unpaid rates; he was locked in the court's holding cell when the kindness of a friend expunged the debt and released him.

When I came to know and speak to him properly, Lawton was already in his mid-60s. Because of the cumulative stresses of the previous two decades, he appeared far older – a vague outline of the poised, physically handsome athlete he had once been. His face was cleaved with the grooves of worry. His swept-back hair was dark, and yet noticeably thin, and the hairline was extravagantly high on the forehead. His shoulders had dropped, giving him a half-stoop. And his neck, which had been the spring for formidably powerful, trademark headers, seemed shrunken and slightly scrawny in the collar of his shirt. Every Monday and Thursday morning, he'd arrive at the newspaper's Victorian stone office, wearing a short beige mackintosh over a dark jacket, and piece together a column, which proved redemptive. The *Post*'s broadsheet page brought renewal for him, and the respect of those who read his words; not even Clough challenged Lawton's opinions. He'd smoke as he talked; indeed, thin veins of blue smoke encircled him like Saturn's rings, and long fingers of ash fell and scattered on to his trousers. He'd brush them away, using the back of his left hand, without ever glancing down. Lawton never sought to consistently argue the superiority of his own era except in the context of behaviour on the field and the camaraderie off it. The column he signed was almost always about the present. But, once each was written, he'd reminisce, exactly like my father, as if he was also educating me. Lawton dropped easily into the past. The footballers of my father's generation had either been his friends or his team mates. There was Lawton and Stanley Matthews climbing through a toilet window the size of a cat flap to smuggle themselves back into the England hotel in Lisbon at an ungodly hour after breaking curfew to visit a casino. 'Didn't affect our performance,' he'd say. 'We beat Portugal 10–0 – and I got four of them.' There was his whist and poker partner, the goalkeeper Frank Swift, who would clap, as though wedged among the crowd, if he admired the shot which had just beaten him. There was Joe Mercer, who would wait until the referee and linesmen were looking elsewhere and then playfully hook his huge boot around Lawton's ankle, nudge him in the back with his forearm and wink before watching him stumble on all fours.

Despite all the trouble he'd seen, Lawton gave the impression that the final destination of his life had been worth the full journey. There was one professional regret: 'No Cup winners' medal,' he said, shaking his head as though the absence of it had always baffled him. 'All my best pals won the Cup – Stan and Swifty and Joe. I was envious of them. Never had a stroke of luck in it and so never came close – apart from a quarter-final on a mud heap at Wolves in '39. Odd, really, because there'd been no rain for a week there. But when I stepped on the pitch I sank into it up to my knobbly knees. Someone had "accidentally" left the hose pipe on.' Lawton, I remember, took a long drag on his cigarette, as though a dose of nicotine temporarily assuaged the disappointment. He stubbed out the cigarette in a white saucer and leant forward in his chair, right hand overlapping the left. 'In my day there was just the Championship and the Cup, you see. If you won the title you felt as though you were the best. You'd got the bragging rights, hadn't you? But it was an endurance race. A bloody long one too. And you went to some rough places and you were relieved to get over the line – and exhausted at the same time. The Cup Final was a different kind of glory – much more glamorous. Like a treasure hunt, I suppose, from round to round. I wanted to wake up one Saturday morning and know I was playing in a Cup Final that afternoon. I wanted to know how that felt. To experience everything about it – all the trappings – and to know that every pro in England who wasn't there that day would murder you to be in your place. Sad I never made it. You see, a player had to be good to get to Wembley then. Like Stan Matthews. Now nearly every bugger goes there – whether they can play or not.'

Lawton drifted into a recollection of 1953 in which Matthews, 38 years old and playing his third Cup Final in six seasons, at last shed the habit of losing. 'The very greatest of Cup Finals,' Lawton said before adding flatly and factually: 'I wanted to win a medal more than ever after watching it. But my career was nearly over then . . .' Blackpool, 3–1 behind to Bolton, won 4–3 in injury time because Matthews' composure and control, and the prospect of defeat again, galvanized him into creating both the second goal and the winner. Matthews' shadow rapidly elongates as the sun descends on that May final. Lawton recalled the white number seven on the back of Matthews' tangerine shirt, and a side-step on the fringe of the Bolton box – 'the sort of side-step Stan could do semi-conscious', he said – and the perfection of the cross that unravelled the defence again in the last seconds of injury time. 'You knew *someone* would score from it as soon as it sailed off his boot,' said Lawton. Matthews expected to find Stan Mortensen, already scorer of a hat-trick. The ball found Bill Perry instead. Mortensen, tightly policed, dragged two defenders to the far post to create room for that goal. 'I was better than no one and no one was better than me,' was Matthews opinion of himself. Lawton disagreed. He regarded Matthews as infallible. 'Stan,' he'd say, 'was so accurate that he could cross a ball with the lace pointing away from your fore-head. That right foot was stardust.'

Tommy Lawton died in 1996. I went to the funeral wearing a tie – maroon stripes on a black background – that he'd given me. After the service, the mourners quietly spilled out of the crematorium and gathered on a narrow strip of concrete; there was nowhere else to go. In this confined space we were jammed alongside one another, each struggling to turn or move sideways. I took a step back and felt the hard heel of my shoe come down on someone else's foot. I heard a sudden anguished yelp and then a long, pained groan. I turned around and saw Stanley Matthews visibly wincing, as if he'd been felled by one of those grotesque tackles from Gascoigne in the '91 Cup Final. His hair was white, the wrinkled features lightly tanned. A black, three-quarter length leather coat with wide stiff lapels hung on his wiry frame. He lifted his hands chest-high to balance himself, and eventually looked down at his polished shoes, where the dusty imprint of my heel remained. I had trodden on the toes of that revered right foot – the foot that had scored mesmerising goals that lit up four decades of football; the foot that Lawton had described as 'stardust'; the foot that had struck the cross for Blackpool's decisive goal in '53. I stammered an unsatisfactory apology to Matthews, who graciously told me the mishap didn't matter – even though, from his still-grimacing expression, I knew he was in extreme pain. He limped away, using a friend's arm as a crutch. When I told my father about it, he was seriously atten-tive at the sound of Matthews' name and seriously appalled at what I'd inflicted on him.

From a drinking friend, a former England inside forward called Jackie Robinson, my father had listened, star-struck, to a description of one of Matthews' training routines, which he could repeat as long as the fancy took him. The ball would be swopped from left to right foot, from right to left knee, from left to right shoulder and on to his head, where Matthews held it still on his forehead. The ball wouldn't touch the floor until he became weary of juggling it. He'd casually drop his shoulders, flick his head and let the ball run down his spine. Finally, he'd back-heel it high into the air before trapping it as it fell. With his right foot, of course. My father's response to my clumsiness in walking over it was a prolonged and reproachful tut-tut, as though I'd set out to maim deliberately. 'Count yourself lucky,' he said. 'In the 1950s Matthews would have kicked you back for that. Or given the nod to one of his defenders to do it for him.'

My father grew up listening to Cup finals on what he called 'the wireless'. The *Radio Times* published a diagram of the pitch in numbered squares, which were marked from one to eight. As the commentator described the flow of the game, another voice – more sonorous – read out the number appropriate to the location of the ball as it travelled across the pitch; Sky Sports, it certainly wasn't. 'You let your imagination do the rest,' he said. 'The crowd . . . the flags around the ground . . . the teams coming out . . . whichever Royal turned up to present the Cup.' When the final was over, my father added, it would be replayed time and again throughout the summer on dirt roads and down back alleys with chalk marks for goals.

The final came to him through the eye of childhood; but childhood shows the man. 'I knew I'd go to the first

Cup Final I could,' he said. It turned out to be 1950: Arsenal v Liverpool. Jackie Robinson gave him the complimentary ticket. As a 17-year-old Robinson was part of Sheffield Wednesday's squad for the 1935 Cup Final against West Bromwich Albion. Only five days earlier Wednesday had played West Brom in a dress rehearsal, which the fixture compilers – and serendipity – had arranged. Robinson, taken along for experience, was told just an hour before kick off: 'Get a shirt on.' Wednesday cannily rested their captain, Ronnie Starling, whose butterfly nimbleness earned him the sobriquet 'The Man with the Fluttering Feet', and replaced him with the unknown Robinson. With no boots of his own in the team's wicker kit hamper, Robinson played in Starling's and scored in a 1–1 draw. 'The boots pinched a bit,' he said, unfazed.

There's a photograph of Robinson inspecting the Wembley pitch during the afternoon before the final. He is slim and inconspicuous. His hands are tucked inside the pockets of a pair of pale pleated slacks. His tie is askew over a dark V-necked sweater. Robinson stands slightly apart from the others and has a faraway look, as if what he is seeing for the first time – the steep bare banks of the empty stadium and the smooth clipped turf beneath his feet – hasn't fully registered with him. The veterans around Robinson are jaunty, confident-looking. One of them, dressed like Douglas Fairbanks Junior promenading along Hollywood Boulevard, is blatantly brash, as if tomorrow's result isn't in doubt. In a natty plaid suit, the billowing plus twos tucked into white socks and the peak of a flat cap angled across his brow, he gives a cocksure smile directly at the camera. It's as though he thinks the photographer is there just to follow him. From the bench Robinson watched Wednesday win 4–2. He wouldn't be a spectator again. By 1937 – only 19 years and nine months old – he was an England international. The defining moment of his career came in May 1938 – a match that lives on in infamy because of politics and propaganda, the craven nature of the Foreign Office and the jellied spine of the Football Association.

It happened like this. With the non-stop talk of war, and with Neville Chamberlain's government placating Hitler to avoid it, Germany invites England to play in Berlin. The city Robinson sees is smothered in swastikas and posters of Hitler, which cover buildings in red and black. The army strides around the streets directly below his hotel window. The military occupy the Olympic Stadium, too, strategically positioned at all points to demonstrate its uniformed muscle. Each pliant German in the 110,000 crowd holds aloft, between thumb and first finger, swastikas printed on squares of thin card. A huge rectangular portrait of Hitler hangs above the VIP box, where Goebbels and Goering, ribboned medals pinned ostentatiously across that barrel chest, expect to see *the* classic demonstration of the Nazi philosophy of Strength Through Joy – a demonstration of Aryan supremacy so complete that the message it conveys across the Channel will be unequivocal. If you can't win a football match against us, how can you win a war? In the dressing room Robinson gets changed beside Stanley Matthews. He is already in his kit when an FA official arrives. He tells the players that each of them will have to give the Nazi salute at the end of the anthems. 'There was silence for a second or two,' Robinson told my father. 'And then the old pros went mad. The air turned blue. Someone told him to bugger off. Matthews, I think.'

This was the FA's meek, unresisting response to the direct order of Sir Neville Henderson, the British ambassador in Berlin and the archetypical suave Foreign Office time-server, who moved effortlessly through its titled ranks. He had slicked back hair and a cut-glass accent. His thick moustache was impeccably trimmed. A silk handkerchief puffed out from the pocket of his Savile Row suit. Here was a man who Nazi-saluted Hitler whenever he met him; and his judgement of him was the egregious: 'If we handle him right . . . he will become more pacific.' In the summer of 1939 he would urge Chamberlain to accept the Munich Agreement – certain that war would not come as a consequence.

Henderson knew the footballers of England could be conveniently used without risk of rebellion or public dissent. They were powerless; players such as Robinson earned less than £1 a week. The demeaning coercion was arranged to appease, giving Hitler the tacit, diplomatic message that his annexation of Austria two months earlier was acceptable to Chamberlain. The FA were willing collaborators and the salute was non-negotiable: anyone who rebelled would never be picked again. The team had no voice and so had no choice. 'What could we do?' Robinson asked my father, who could give no adequate reply. With a pair of binoculars strung around his neck, Henderson sat in the VIP box in a feathered hunting hat, as though he was shooting on Scotland's grouse moors.

The Germans, also absorbing the most talented Austrians into their team, had been preparing for ten days in the seclusion of a Black Forest training camp. England were bone-tired after 48 hours travelling, sailing first from Harwich to The Hook of Holland and then boarding a train to Berlin. Drilled into the Germans-Austrians was the importance of establishing the image of the Fatherland as an iron fist. So fervently obsessed were the Nazis with the need to enfeeble England that the German goalkeeper, Hans Jacob, was refused permission to return home to care for his dying four-year-old daughter.

Angry beyond belief at the Foreign Office, pathetically abandoned by the FA, Robinson was humiliated along with his colleagues for the sake of cordiality towards fascism. Retribution for it was delivered in the only way Robinson knew how. He claimed two goals in a 6–3 win. Those goals, scored on a blazingly hot day, seldom illustrate reports of the match. The lingering image is 11 honourable men giving the Nazi salute against their judgement and their will. Their heads are turned slightly to the left, so avoiding direct eye contact with the Germans. What came next – the emphaticness of the result, a Len Goulden shot so fierce that it tore the net off its hooks beneath the bar and the fact Matthews regarded the England performance as 'perhaps the finest . . . I was ever involved in' – became irrelevant. The story went around the world. Even obscure newspapers printed in remote places published the photograph of the Nazi salute and juxtaposed English football's capitulation alongside the dignified defiance of Jesse Owens in running and leaping to four Olympic gold medals on the same field two years earlier. The players shrivelled in shame, and the FA's guilty conscience peeked through. Each player was given a canteen of cutlery for the achievement of licking Hitler, as if fish knives and forks could atone for the collapse of administrative courage. 'It was the only bloody thing we ever got from them,' complained Robinson to my father. 'I looked at it and thought: We did all that – for this.'

Robinson was born and brought up in Shiremoor, another pit village less than three miles from where my father made his home. The two of them originally met in a pub; and Robinson would eventually own one after his playing days came to an end prematurely. From Sheffield Wednesday, he was transferred to Sunderland and, finally, became player-coach at Lincoln. When Robinson gave my father the Cup Final ticket, he was recovering from a broken leg, sustained on Christmas Eve 1949, and waiting for the birth of his second child. 'I bought the drinks that night,' my father said. 'He wouldn't take payment for the ticket any other way.'

As in every city targeted repeatedly during the war, the reconstructive surgery to repair London was on-going, the healing scars still evident. To visit the capital, however gutted and monochromatic, was a shining adventure, which had the feel of a holiday. It was an enormous journey from Newcastle – a bumpy and tedious ride, which began at dawn. Arriving in London, the rain already falling, he bought a pink carnation to signify his neutrality and slotted it into the buttonhole of his suit. It was eventually squashed under his raincoat.

It was the Cup Final in which The Brylcreem Boy, Denis Compton, three weeks away from his 32nd birthday, was given a swig of whisky at half time and received his own private instructions from Tom Whitaker, Arsenal's manager. Whitaker wore a pair of spectacles with circular frames, which gave him the eyes of a startled owl. In a softish voice he told Compton: 'You've probably got only 45 minutes left in first-class football. Give all you've got – even if it means falling flat on your face at the end.' It was the Cup Final after which Billy Liddell wept on the way home to Liverpool, distressed at the inadequacy of his own performance. And it was the Cup Final in which Arsenal's second goal of a 2–0 win was described by the *Sunday Times* as coming from 'the old fashioned Soccer copy-book'. It reported the 'smooth accuracy and quick passing' between Goring, Compton and Cox – the ball flicked between them – before Reg Lewis finished the move with a single touch.

My father saw it from a place near the half way line. Decades later, he could still recall a Liverpool player buckle and fall in the final minutes because of the constant strain of chasing. It was as if his legs had turned to sawdust. He remembered the crowd singing 'The Lambeth Walk' and watching Whitaker repeatedly dart from his seat, as though attached to it by a volatile, jack-in-the-box spring. And he saw Compton slap his brother Leslie on the back and lock him into a brief, coiled embrace at the foot of the steps to the Royal Box. 'The small boy had his dream fulfilled,' said Compton of his winners' medal. The small boy my father had once been had his dream fulfilled too. What came back most easily to him was the majestic sweep of the stadium. Wembley was a paradise; even on an afternoon when pitiless drizzle – from clouds like grey belches of smoke – rinsed the air and made it cold. A Liverpudlian allowed him partial shelter beneath a black umbrella because he'd left his flat cap on its hook at home. The steady rain saturated the crowd, settled on the pitch and soaked the flags, leaving each to hang abjectly from its pole. But the scale and spaciousness of Wembley, compared to the cramped League grounds, was magnificent nonetheless. My father talked of chessboard squares of Cumberland turf so vividly emerald that it hurt the eyes to look at them. The grass seemed to him as if it had been varnished. To be there, he implied, seemed to heighten every perception, as if each aspect of the game had been magnified. At the end he was reluctant to pull himself away from it, waiting until the stadium emptied. He stood among the discarded programmes and song-sheets for one last look at the place.

'I wanted to go to *every* Cup Final after that,' he said to me. 'Most of all, I wanted to see Newcastle win there.'

My father never saw Newcastle win at Wembley. He saw all the semi-finals (each of which went to replays) but couldn't get a ticket for either the 1951 or 1952 final, and reluctantly sold the one he was given in 1955. He and my mother had arranged their wedding for that summer. My mother had set her heart on a console TV in a walnut case. The case was the size of a modern fridge freezer. The screen was hardly bigger than the cover of a Penguin paperback. My father used his ticket to partly fund the initial payment for the set. But, 24 years later, I bought him tickets for another Wembley FA Cup Final.

Since 1967, when the first ever all-London final pitted Tottenham against Chelsea, we'd watched the showpiece together on TV: Manchester City edging out Leicester by a single, Neil Young goal . . . Leeds claiming the Cup on its Centenary after Allan Clarke's diving header beat Arsenal . . . Second Division Southampton replicating Sunderland's feat by beating First Division Manchester United . . . and United then denying Liverpool a treble 12 months later. Always, our morning and afternoon viewing was militarily mapped out to accommodate every trivial aspect of the final. We bought extra news-papers, reading the predictions of each star writer. We were then glued to the box. We missed nothing: the finalists relaxing in their hotel; the round-by-round Journey to Wembley; the early arrival of supporters; the profile of the managers and the camera-on-the-team-coach. We'd watch the game again on *Match of the Day* that evening; and again on Sunday afternoon. We'd buy all the Sunday and Monday newspapers too, rating the quality of analysis against what we knew to be true. I saw no end to this simple routine. I thought we'd see every Cup Final from the sofa.

But, in the autumn of 1978, my father suffered a bad heart attack in his mid-50s. It marked the beginning of the end of his working life. In its immediate aftermath he became morose and introspective – aware for the first time, I think, that all of us live on the minute hand of the clock. Overnight he became sickly, far older and greyer to me. He lost weight, stopped reading the news-paper and didn't talk much. He slipped into his chair and stayed there, staring at the television even when the screen was blank. After a listless day came a sleepless night. It was as if he was afraid to close his eyes in case he never opened them again. The heart attack made him reluctant to leave the house. He moped around it, unsure what to do with himself.

Football was the cure. I got him tickets for the City Ground. These were prized seats – he no longer wanted the strain of standing on the terraces – because Nottingham Forest, already defending League Champions, were about to win the European Cup in Munich, striking another blow for provincialism. This was a giddy season in a small city, and I pushed my father to share in it. With each game, his self-confidence slowly returned. He became something of his former self.

He'd spoken so much about 1950, and Reg Lewis' two Wembley goals, that another Arsenal final – against Manchester United – seemed the logical and poignant next step in his rehabilitation. A day trip to the capital to remind him of better times; Liam Brady and Graham Rix to admire rather than Lewis and the Compton brothers. I insisted he took the friend who always accompanied him to the City Ground; it seemed fairer that way. I told him I didn't mind watching the final without him for once, which was a lie. 'I'll video it for you,' I said. 'We can watch it again tomorrow morning.' He dressed as he'd done in the 1950s: suit and tie and shiny laced shoes. I waved him off and I remember the jaunty roll of his walk as he vanished down the path and turned the corner. A few hours later, studying the screen, I hoped to find him interviewed on Wembley Way or catch sight of him in the crowd, one face among the throng.

This was the Three Minute Final – much of its drama, and a hat-trick of goals, compressed into an unbelievably frenetic 180 seconds. Blink and you almost missed it. United, 2–0 down, scored twice to equalise in the 87th and 89th minutes before Alan Sunderland filched Arsenal's winner with an outstretched leg at the far post when extra time seemed certain. Shaking his head and his poodle-mopped hair, Sunderland went on a celebratory dash, glancing up at the sky as he did so, as though sure Heaven and some Other Hand, as much as Brady's ingenious run and Rix's cross, had fashioned the fantastic finale.

I was worried that my father – choosing to avoid the crush – might have left five minutes early and so hadn't actually seen one of the greatest ever climaxes to a Wembley final. I waited up for him like an anxious parent. Near midnight, I heard the knock on the door. I found him on the doorstep, still digging into his pockets for his key. His tie was slightly askew. He was unsteady on his feet and trying to disguise it. One beer and a whisky chaser too many, rather than ill-health, was the cause. He sat in the armchair and I went to boil the kettle, ignoring his offer to pour us both a nightcap. He was tired and in no state to give me a proper précis about what he'd seen. He kept repeating one phrase: 'Well, that's the magic of the Cup.'

His tea went untouched and cooled in the mug. He fell asleep, still wearing his suit and shoes, and I had to nudge him towards bed. I followed my father up the stairs, watching him grip the handrail like a mountaineer gripping a guide-rope. 'That's the magic of the Cup,' he said again, instead of wishing me goodnight. But I thought then, as I do now, that the Cup's real magic was the way in which it reinvigorated him. The man I had known before his heart attack had come back to me.

3

A Goal of an
Unconquerable Heart

Nearly half a century old, the album shows the wearing signs of age. The cardboard cover has creases and spidery cracks, and the bottom right-hand corner is ripped off after some forgotten, minor calamity. The narrow spine is torn too, and the rusted staples have come away from some of the ragged, partly foxed A3 pages which crackle whenever I turn them. Afraid it might become powdery dust, I handle the album gently now. For to lose it would mean losing an important part of my past.

It is grandly titled *The Wonderful World of Soccer Stars* – 24 pages, 22 First Division teams in alphabetical order and 330 players. It cost 3 shillings and 6 pence. On page one George Graham, his hair immaculately side-parted, looks suave and urbane, as though he ought to be dressed in clothes from the King's Road rather than

Arsenal's plain, round-collared red and white. In Chelsea blue, Peter Osgood seems as if he's about to wink conspiratorially at the camera. The head and shoulders portraits of Billy Bremner and Johnny Giles are over-colourised, as though both belong to a football annual of the 1950s instead of the 1967–68 season, which the album represents. England's World Cup winners are scattered throughout: Alan Ball, his hair redder than maple; Roger Hunt with Liverpool's Liver Bird badge huge on his chest; George Cohen, already looking middle-aged – even though he's only 28 – with a high forehead and waxy features. There's the West Ham triumvirate: Geoff Hurst, Bobby Moore and Martin Peters. Hurst doesn't smile; Moore seems caught off guard, as if he hasn't groomed himself satisfactorily for the photographer; Peters' face is trapped in semi-shadow, which hangs over him like a pale mask, and beside him is an absurdly young-looking Harry Redknapp, aquiline nose and prominent cheekbones, a crafty jack-the-lad expression in his dark eyes.

This relic of an album marks a rite of passage for me – the point at which football became fully part of my life rather than peripheral to it. The game took off in my imagination and dominated it. To watch football then was thrillingly visceral because everything about it was new and unexplored. The album and its packets of sealed stickers pulled me into it. It represents what was – and remains – the season of all seasons to me, like the first love you can't forget. The photos are as fondly remembered as family shots – even if, like a lot of family pictures, I can't place or recognise some of the more distant and obscure relatives. Who was Smith of Burnley, Sharkey of Leicester City or Shaw of Sheffield United? Whatever happened to Henry Burrows of Stoke City? Or George Kinnell of Southampton? And where and when did the final player in the album – Leslie Wilson of Wolverhampton Wanderers – end his career? I look at it now with the wondrous hindsight Time brings – the simple fact of knowing what came next for most of the faces who stare back at me from my boyhood. There is the bristly sideburned Terry Venables, who will go on to manage England and Barcelona. There is Martin Chivers, with his long jaw and hooded eyes, wearing the wide stripes of Southampton. Before the season is over Spurs will buy him – for a club record fee of £125,000 – and he will lead the line in successful League Cup and Uefa Cup teams during the early 1970s. There is Peter Shilton, then scarcely old enough to be shaving – or even to have left school – who will play for 11 different clubs over 30 years and win 125 caps, more than anyone before or since. He will become a friend of mine too, a fact that my younger self would have regarded as preposterous. And there is Shilton's England rival Ray Clemence, his nose prominently bent, and Pat Jennings posing almost sideways on and narrowing his eyes against the sun's glare. These three will establish themselves as the finest goalkeepers of the decade to come.

Like the plot of a tragic novel, sorrow also permeates these pages. There is Emlyn Hughes, who will die of a brain tumour, aged 57; Gordon Banks, who will lose his right eye and his career in an horrendous car crash in 1972; Jeff Astle spectacularly scores the only extra time goal in the FA Cup Final for West Bromwich Albion just a few months after I glue him into the album – a rising 18-yard shot. He will die at 59 of degenerative brain disease in 2002. The coroner found Astle suffered repeated minor trauma because of his prodigious heading of the ball. The recorded verdict was 'death by industrial injury'.

There is only one black face. It belongs to Albert Johanneson, whose story is the saddest of all owing to the self-destructive nature of it. Johanneson was called 'Our Albert', because Leeds adopted him, and also 'The Black Flash' because of his winger's speed. In 1965, the first black player to appear in an FA Cup Final, Johanneson's salary was £200 per week – the equivalent of almost £3,000 today. But then drug-taking and excessive drinking became the dark part of his life. Johanneson fell precipitously, uncontrollably. He signed for York City, then in the Fourth Division. He began to take part in kick-arounds with a Sunday League side, self-mockingly called Gluepot United, on the wide, trim parkland of The Stray in Harrogate. 'I couldn't handle the fame,' he said in an unpitying attempt to provide some mitigation for his decline. He tried to anaesthetise himself against it by drinking rough cider from litre bottles.

He lost his money, his family, his self-respect, his mind. Near the end of his life Johanneson's cheeks were jowly and bloated, his voice thick with constant drink and his memory patchy. Alcohol rubbed away whole parts of it. The eyes, once so alive, were streaked yellow. Johanneson died, aged 53, five months after the 30th anniversary of that Wembley Cup Final, which Liverpool won 2–1. He was found in his broken-down, tower-block flat near Leeds city centre. His body had lain undiscovered for a week. The album preserves the Johanneson I saw once in the flesh – clean and brave and handsome.

These stickers became my obsession. I bought, begged and traded; I regarded them as preciously as stock-market gold. Three in particular were highly prized: Moore, Bobby Charlton and George Best. Indeed, Best was sought after by those who weren't interested in football but wanted him purely as a pin-up. It made the competition to acquire him much more difficult. In the free market of the playground and the classroom, Charlton and Moore were valued at 15 stickers apiece. The exchange rate for Best was 25 to 30 and upwards – not so much a sum as a ransom demand. I paid it eventually, giving in return blue chip figures such as Dave Mackay, with sticky-out ears and missing incisor-tooth, Mike Summerbee and Charlie Cooke; and also the local hero, Ian Storey-Moore, of Nottingham Forest. Most reluctantly of all, I handed over Jimmy Greaves, his brown hair brushed into a quiff. I believed Best was worth the sacrifice. He was glamour. He summoned up marvels. He filled the eye. And he transmitted vitality and vigorous energy – even sitting down.

Watching him on *Match of the Day* was to appreciate instantly the trickery of his feet on a wiry, narrow-hipped physique. He shimmered on the screen, a completely rhythmic mover, who glided across pitches which during the sharpest edge of winter were rutted and muddy with rain or heaped with shovelfuls of sand to disguise the lack of grass on them. With Best in possession defenders were nervously active, twitching and fidgeting in a futile effort to second guess where and how he might smooth his way past them. Their rapid calculations – you could almost hear the tumblers of their brain click and spin in panic – were almost always trumped by his quick thinking as much as his pace from a standing start and the beguiling, gifted touches that he produced regularly and miraculously. Best's football intelligence – his clear awareness of angles, positioning and pitch geography – meant he was nearly always two brilliant thoughts ahead of those who tracked him; he was there one moment and gone the next. How he did it was an unyielding mystery. An entire back four could fold itself around Best, and he would still escape them. Legs lunged at him, the studded soles of boots rapped him on flimsy shin-pads (when he chose to wear them) and there were crudely violent efforts to charge and bundle him off the ball with arms and elbows. The vast proportion of these challenges escaped censure, let alone a booking, because then the bloodiest, most brutal tackling was permissible and blithely accepted. Referees took a lenient attitude towards actual bodily harm; even grievous bodily harm was tolerated, as though it was innocent rough and tumble. By the end of a match Best's hacked at flesh was Prussian-blue and welted. Without protection he still prospered. With it, however, he'd have been uncatchable; for an incredible tensile strength existed within that stem-like frame. He got chopped down and beaten up and rolled over. On each occasion he rose again, as if his disregard for physical punishment bordered on the masochistic.

In his album photograph Best is 21 years old. He has a beatific smile and his coiffured fringe touches the ledge of his right eyebrow. His sideburns are long and trimmed, and his mouth is open slightly, as if he's about to speak. Apart from Graham, he looks different from everyone else in the album – an example of chiselled beauty: porcelain skin, sculptured facial bones and prominent Hollywood cleft in his chin. The camera lens loves Best and he responds naturally to the demands it makes of him. He is self-aware and more male-model than footballer – as though he's just stepped, cocksure and nattily attired, from the dressing room of a bespoke tailor's. Those, like me, whose idolisation of Best was manifest in our relentless pursuit of his face on this prized sticker saw him only in the arc light of athletic perfection. He was the jinky presence on the pitch. His high-jinks off it were unknown to us. We were unaware that Best was Matt Busby's problem child and ignorant of the hedonistic extravagances and daily gadding about that were to end prematurely both his career and his life because of the irreconcilable impulse to drink as well as to play. We saw only the glittering talent and none of the turmoil beneath it. To us Best was the sort of man we hoped to become; the name evoked most often during park matches where each goal post was an untidy heap of coats and sweaters. He had skill to burn and so he burnt it. But to say those skills were wantonly wasted is to ignore the impact Best made and the impression of unmatched genius which his 11 years at United – beginning in 1963 and ending in 1974 – created.

It naturally helped that Best was at his zenith in 1967–68, which made him more glamorous still to me. He moved unstoppably from match to match, the First Division's irresistible force giving performances which were masterpieces of one-man theatre. Whoever tried to mark Best couldn't get close to him; nor even to his shadow. He was too quick, too mercurial, for them. Best was top scorer – 28 goals – and the Footballer of the Year, the European Footballer of the Year and a European Cup winner. It can take a lot of persuasion to convince a new generation – raised on Ryan Giggs, Cristiano Ronaldo and Wayne Rooney – about the claims of a world of which it bore no witness; especially without supporting evidence comprising several miles of cine film. Every goal, near miss or pass of a Premiership player's season is recorded and can be watched again. Not so in Best's case. Enough of it exists nonetheless – admittedly, a good deal is in black and white – to capture his brand of fantasy football: slanting runs, bicycle-kick crosses, elegant leaps over slide tackles, top-corner headers and bottom-corner shots. Watching them is proof of Best's pre-eminence. The clinching clip is a fragment of beauty against Spurs in which, confronted by four defenders, a goalkeeper and a margin of error calculated in millimetres, Best cushions a punched clearance on his chest. As the ball drops, he is 15 yards from the impossibly cluttered net, and almost no one anticipates what will follow except the architect of it. Best's mind has already weighed up the complicated variables – the weight of the ball, the height of the bar, the direction and knot-speed of the wind. He leans back and with a feathery, caressing touch sends an angled lob over the head of everyone in front of him. The white ball spins slowly, looping off his right boot before dipping under the bar. The Spurs defenders follow its gentle curved flight, fully aware in that instant of two things: exactly where the ball is travelling and their powerlessness to stop it. When the goal is scored, each gazes silently at the other, as if the embarrassment Best has just inflicted on them cannot be articulated.

I remember sticking Best into my album at last, as if he was a trophy. He completed my United set, which included each of the players who, six weeks earlier, had won the European Cup at Wembley. A month later, a new season almost underway, the entire album was full. The final gap was filled by Burnley's Ralph Coates with a generous shock of strangely blonde-gold hair. Within a few seasons, it would be all gone except for a Max Wall-like mane, which dropped to his collar. It swayed and it spread as he ran, most famously after his winning goal in the League Cup Final for Tottenham against Norwich.

I carried the completed album in triumph to my father, who held it at arm's length until he found his brown-framed spectacles and jammed them on to the bridge of his nose. Reaching the Manchester United page, he studied it as though looking at something only he could see. 'There's someone missing here,' he said finally, pointing to a slender separation of the boxes on the second row between Tony Dunne and Bill Foulkes. His ran his stubby finger down the page 'That,' he added firmly, 'is where Duncan Edwards ought to be.' My father began to talk about Edwards the way I now talk about Best. I looked at him uncomprehendingly, as though he'd given me a riddle to solve.

'Who,' I asked 'is Duncan Edwards?'

I knew nothing of Duncan Edwards. I'd caught no sight of him in a team group. I'd heard no mention of his name. I could dredge up no memory of him on *Match of the Day* or from any of the dozens of newspapers which came into our house every week. 'Who,' I asked again, 'is Duncan Edwards?' My father initially hesitated, as if Edwards could not be summed up easily. But I retain a vivid recollection of what came next. It seemed significant that I should know as much as he could tell me about Edwards. Who he'd been and what he could have become. I recall, too, what my father didn't say; though I appreciated the gaps and silences only in retrospect. At the end Edwards, of whom there was no trace in my album, seemed realer to me than some of the others whose photographs I had already collected.

My father put down the sticker album, still folded open on the Manchester United page, and reached for a fresh packet of Embassy, using his thumb to flick open its hinge lid. With the practised sweep of the habitual smoker, he was able to flick open the box, remove and light the cigarette, dispose of the spent match, lean back in his armchair and take his opening drag in almost a single, seamless movement.

I presumed Edwards pre-dated Jackie Milburn and had long-since retired; that he existed only in the memory of men of my father's or my grandfather's vintage and was now an old man comforted by the past and combing his grey hair. His story – new then and so familiar now – came to me chronologically, built up block by impressive block so that the Edwards who appeared from its telling was formidably tough and even more formidably talented: a 16-year-old who had the physical attributes of a man of 30 and possessing the maturity of someone older still; capable of playing at inside left, centre half or centre forward; the youngest capped player for England, aged 18 years and 183 days; the 'complete all round player' who could tackle, head and pass 50 yards with unerring accuracy, defend and attack, and shoot so hard that, according to my father, 'goalkeepers would get out of the way of the ball'. My father even gave him the sort of bulging muscles I saw only on the marble statues of ancient warriors or in cartoons where Popeye swallowed five cans of spinach. 'I saw him play once,' he said, summoning up a personal memory of England's 1–1 draw against Scotland at Hampden Park in April 1956. 'He was so strong he could shoulder-charge whoever he liked off the ball. If anyone tried to do the same to him, it was like running into a stone pillar. He stayed on his feet. They were on the floor.' There was nothing, he added, that Edwards could not do; nothing, in fact, he could not have achieved if circumstances had been different. 'He was a very great player – the sort you see once in a generation if you're lucky,' my father said before fastening on to the still-perplexed expression on my face. He realised he hadn't adequately conveyed either the scale of Edwards' power and ingeniousness or placed him into the sort of context which I could understand conceptually. 'Imagine George Best,' he said, 'but bigger . . . and rougher . . . and better.'

I voiced the thought which immediately occurred to me: 'How many stickers was he worth?'

'The whole album,' he said, unhesitatingly.

I asked: 'So who does he play for now?'

My father looked at me sadly, shaking his head, and replied abstractedly with a single word which seemed senseless to me until he explained it.

'Awful,' he said.

'And so they are ever returning to us, the dead,' wrote W. G. Sebald. It is true of Duncan Edwards, for ever 21. He returns to us on the February anniversary of the air disaster which killed him and seven other members of his team, plus three backroom staff, eight football writers, the aeroplane's co-pilot, a steward and two passengers. He returns to us on the October date of his birth. And he returns to us – first, foremost and with striking clarity – whenever someone who knows the grim details of Matt Busby's Babes and Manchester United's Wonder Team stares at the white, twin-faced clock at Old Trafford and reads the date and place written above and below its slender black hands.

FEB 6th, 1958
MUNICH

The minimalism of this clock is the perfect memorial, beautifully wrought. The simplicity of it belies the symbolism attached to it: the fact it records the tragedies of another Time and the requirement to remember them. At first my father spoke to me about Edwards as a player and gave me the barest account of the crash. But, as I grew older, he made larger points. I learnt everything about Munich from him: the slush on the runway, the snow in the air, the ice on the wings of the chartered Elizabethan aircraft. One aborted take-off and then another on this necessary refuelling stop. The third attempt and the calm, routine words swapped between pilot and control tower:

TOWER: Wind two nine zero – eight knots – cleared, to runway two five.
PILOT: Thank you . . . ready for take-off.

When the disaster happened – the plane failing at 3.04 p.m. – my father had already been in the belly of his pit for nearly two hours. He was on afternoon shift, two miles below ground and insulated from every sound and movement above him. Only when the shifts began to change did the basic facts, sparse and confusing, reach him. The plane had clattered along – bumping and buckling through the runway, beyond the grass stopway and into a house, a wooden hut and towards a copse and a fuel compound. The news was shouted so it rose above the grind of machinery and the thud of boots on the hard floor of the mine. Those who heard, or half-heard, what was said to them asked for it to be repeated. 'No one believed it. A whole team couldn't die,' my father said. A team, moreover, which had won back-to-back Championships in 1955–56 and 1956–57 and were FA Cup runners-up in 1957. A team which only the previous Saturday had gone to Highbury and beaten Arsenal epically 5–4. A team – including Bobby Charlton – which had just drawn 3–3 with Red Star Belgrade to reach the European Cup semi-finals and done so on a surface, according to Geoffrey Green of *The Times*, 'where the last remnants of melting snow produced the effect of an English lawn flecked with daisies'. The still and moving images of Munich and its aftermath remain with whoever sees them: the bent, churned metal of the aeroplane – everything ravaged, everything burnt – and the tail section wrenched away from the main body. Smoke plumes rising in slanted columns, drawn eastwards by the wind. Snow smothering the runway; more snow fluttering in the damp, dark air. What remains in the mind, too, is the final photograph of Manchester United in full kit – the smart row of red shirts standing on that pitch in Belgrade, a *carpe diem* moment if ever one existed. Edwards is nearest to the camera, as if Fate wanted us to take a good last look at him. The fingertips of his left hand are tucked into the elasticised band of his white shorts. He is pictured in stern right profile, glancing along the line and looking at the friends who will soon die with him: Eddie Colman and Mark Jones (closest to Edwards) and Roger Byrne, his captain. Others in the squad, out of the picture, came home in flower-decked coffins too: Geoff Bent, David Pegg, Tommy Taylor, Billy Whelan. The average age of United's eight dead was 23.

My father's history lessons about Munich were frequent. Eventually he talked of Manchester, a city where there was suddenly darkness at noon, the emotional damage done to it then irreparable. Elsewhere the wider world in which Edwards lived intersected the smaller worlds which men like my father occupied. The experience proved communal and profound. All the miners on my father's shift were football fans. The game sustained them. 'Some couldn't bring themselves to drink a pint that day or the one after. It felt disrespectful to enjoy yourself,' he said. 'These were people we'd never met, but it felt as if we'd known them, like pals, because you were so used to reading about them.'

My father said that an entire country had its heart broken because of these deaths. It didn't matter which colours you wore – the numbing effect, the ineffable sense of loss was the same. So was the bitter, unfathomable injustice of it. In Manchester, the people went to Old Trafford because nothing else was appropriate and because being at the empty stadium brought them some comfort. The disaster made football at once both trivial and, paradoxically, significant. Among those who mourned, there was relief that the game went on because it allowed them to grieve and find solace together. This grief united strangers in pubs and bars, at the newspaper kiosk, in the tobacconist's shop and corner store, on the bus and in the train and, especially, on the terraces. But there was also an acceptance that football wasn't – and could never be – more important than life. Edwards broke his ribs and his pelvis and fractured his right thigh in myriad places. One of his lungs collapsed. The most grievous injury lanced his kidneys. He clung on improbably for 15 days on the fourth floor of Munich's Rechts de Isar hospital before those kidneys wore out. For Manchester – the city as well as the club – his dying was the final crushing. 'We thought he was going to live,' said my father. The 'we' he used encompassed everyone he knew, whether football was their sport or not. 'That's the effect he had,' he explained.

The future has a habit of never turning out the way we expect, but there is no quarrel about what Edwards would have achieved. He'd have been among England's World Cup winners in 1966; probably, the captain. And he'd have held the European Cup long before that sweltering May evening in 1968 when, at last, the winning of it constituted Manchester United's emotional memorial to the dead. It was an occasion when football's greatest need – a United win – coincided exactly with the grittiest of performances. Each player knew he was a bridge between a tragic era and a triumphant one. The final was played for ghosts.

There is far less film of Edwards than of George Best, and most of it was shown only on cinema newsreels. But one small strip of it – less than nine seconds long – reveals the essence of him. It is 1956 and England are in Berlin facing West Germany, then World Champions, in a match which Arthur Walmsley, of the *Manchester Evening Chronicle*, remembered as 'assuming a significance in the German mind far beyond the game of soccer'. England had not played there since before the war. In its aftermath, the resentment still raw and conspicuous, Walmsley wrote that the team and those accompanying it 'met with dumb insolence in our own hotel and open hostility in public places outside it'. In the stadium, he added that 'the near-hysteria of the Germans was almost tangible and unnervingly unhealthy. Here were all the frightening, ugly undertones of those pre-war Nuremberg rallies; a people reduced to robots in the insane pursuit of superiority.' Walmsley, who deplored nationalism – calling it 'a rapidly increasing evil in sport' – found himself infected with it. Early on England were battered and out-passed. 'Then it happened,' wrote Walmsley, 'the most spellbinding, dramatic experience of my sporting career.'

This is what he saw.

Mid-way in the opposition half Edwards gathers a loose ball from a white-shirted German midfielder, who has lost it and his footing in the tackle on greasy turf. Edwards tracks back on himself, unselfconsciously manoeuvring around the German, who is on his back and flailing, like a turned turtle. He takes no notice of him. With a long-legged run he cuts a straight path. His body is bent forward, as if pressing into a head-wind. A pace and a half later two more white shirts converge on him simultaneously. Neither is able to touch Edwards, who powers beyond them, like a tank travelling over flat land. The ball is under his total command, and he side-steps a tackle from the German centre half. From 20 yards he draws back his boot and buries the shot inside the base of the left-hand post. Because of Edwards – born in 1936, the year the Nazi Olympics were staged in the same stadium – England win 3–1. 'Emotion was naked,' said Walmsley. 'Tears sprang spontaneously to my eyes. I wanted to break out of the press box and scream at every shocked and silent German: 'Have you got a boy of 19 who could do that?' He said it was the 'goal of a Titan; the goal of an uncon-querable heart'. When I read Walmsley, I remembered my father's friend, Jackie Robinson, being co-coerced into giving the Nazi salute in Berlin while Edwards was still learning to walk and talk.

Today a player like Edwards would be a carefully coiffured brand wearing designer-chic labels. He'd be allowed to go nowhere in public without the dragonfly buzz of camera shutters accompanying him. He'd have an agent-cum-consultant, an image rights company to enable him to wriggle through legitimate loopholes in the tax system, a Twitter feed written for him by a flunky, a portfolio of high-profile and lucrative sponsorship deals and something shiny on four wheels made by Lamborghini or Porsche. Edwards wore an ill-fitting tweed jacket and rode a Raleigh bicycle from his land-lady's boarding house in Birch Avenue, less than two miles from Old Trafford. He would cycle down the road that is now Sir Matt Busby Way and tie his bike to a drain pipe with a piece of twine, which he kept in his pocket. He didn't smoke. He drank sparingly. He briefly promoted the use of glucose tablets – his only commercial endorsement. Like Jackie Milburn, he hid himself in the cinema and endlessly watched films. And he taught himself to type slowly with two fingers on a portable grey Remington which belonged to his fiancée. He tapped out the draft of an instructional book for boys on that clankerty machine. The book, *Tackle Soccer This Way*, was published posthumously. The copy I found in the library was slim – only 112 pages. Edwards appears on its cover in a roll-neck training shirt and is flanked by Stanley Matthews and Billy Wright. At 41, Matthews is old enough to be Edwards' father and Wright, though just 34, looks as though he's already nudging 50. Together the two of them accentuate Edwards' youth; he could be an autograph hunter chasing them for a signature. *Tackle Soccer This Way* is his credo in ink, a manifesto that left behind something of his spirit bound between hard covers. Pressed within them is Edwards' ripping passion for his trade. Most impressive – re-reading the book nearly half a century after originally finding it – is the gee-up enthusiasm he transmits and the explicit message he weaves into the text: there are life-lessons to be learnt from football. About character and courage. About team solidarity. About stiff-upper-lip decency. About generosity and fair play. Edwards lived and died well before the word 'professionalism' was defined in the *Shorter Oxford English Dictionary* as 'engagement in an occupation, especially a sport, for money rather than as a pastime' and wouldn't have recognised its use as a vulgar euphemism for anything sly and underhand or as an excuse for dirty tricks. Edwards sounds like a Corinthian, playing purely for the untrammelled joy of it. Which, given the pitiful amount of his salary, he effectively did. Every professional player ought to read this book.

'Never seek revenge,' Edwards warns anyone in pursuit of the man rather than the ball.

A losing team should leave the field 'with dignity', he adds.

And he abhors dissent: 'Never argue with the referee . . . and never, never mob a referee.'

The Publishers' Note accompanying his six chapters claims the typescript was not 'altered . . . in any way; it remains entirely as he passed it on to us'. However unlikely that scenario – surely a kindness to the dead – Edwards' ideals are preserved in the finished copy. 'Football is a game that rewards those who show courage' and 'No person can play football unless he is a complete master of the ball,' he says. To become one himself, Edwards revealed, the Black Country streets on which he was bred 'were transformed into palatial Wembley'. He turned park matches into training exercises designed to improve his weaker left foot. 'I would try to go through the whole of these games (and remember they would go on from after tea until it was too dark to see the ball) using only my left foot,' he wrote. Edwards' advice alternates between the philosophy of shooting – 'I favour the hit 'em hard method. I slam the ball at the iron stanchion . . . and congratulations to the goalkeeper who saves it' – to quaint instructions about taking care of your boots: 'Never put them in front of the fire to dry . . . the leather stiffens and cracks. And it will play havoc with the skin of your feet.'

For hours I practised what Edwards preached, kicking the ball repeatedly against the pale brick wall at the rear of our council house, once cracking the lower half of the frosted backdoor window after a skewed pass flew off the outside of my foot. I tried to control the ball instantly before sending it thudding into the wall. If my father was right – if Edwards was as good as he claimed – I couldn't fail to improve by following his other drills on heading and tackling, chesting the ball or cushioning it on the upper thigh. Absent-mindedly, though, I forgot Edwards' advice about never putting sodden boots on the hearth of a coal fire. The leather of mine shrank and the boots became so tight and uncomfortable that I could barely walk, let alone run, in them.

I did all this unaware of the posthumous role Edwards played in my life, a minor but personal sequel to the story of Munich which my father left out of his account that day; I assume because it embarrassed him. And it embarrassed me to ask him about it later on, which left something else unsaid between us. I was born ten months after Edwards died, and I owe him my name. My father was christened James after his own father – despite being the family's fourth-born son. He wanted me to be called James to perpetuate what he hoped, and confidently expected, would become a traditional naming ceremony among the Hamiltons. My mother, however, had always set her heart on calling any son she had Duncan. I knew nothing of what followed until, in my mid-teens, I asked her how my name had been chosen. She was in the kitchen, arranging patterned cooking pans on various rings, a white apron tied around her waist. 'Your father was adamant you'd be called James – until the air crash at Munich,' she said, turning on the gas. 'That changed his mind. He said he'd been thinking about it. If we ever had a boy, he wouldn't mind calling him Duncan after all. A week or so later I found out I was pregnant.'

Everything fell into place. At last I knew the reason why my father had given me the impromptu biography of Edwards, and also the reason for the intensity of it. He thought so highly of Edwards, and had been so affected by the catastrophe of Munich, that it dictated the name on my birth certificate. My sticker album had served a purpose. It had allowed him to talk about Edwards and explain him to me. But he'd found it impossible to come clean about why I was christened Duncan. It was withheld, another emotional step too far for him to take. The words which would have told me stayed wound up inside him.

A stranger never knows whether he is leaving Dudley or entering it. It sits in the messy sprawl of the Black Country, where one crowded boundary is indistinguishable from another. The town isn't easy on the eye. Mostly rebuilt in the 1950s and 60s, the era in which form meant functional for architects and planners, the charm was bulldozed out of it, leaving behind slabs of blackened concrete, wide-windowed high-rises and harsh-looking buildings, which are now unsightly or drably forlorn. There are few architectural flourishes. The centre of Dudley is dismally run-down. Stores are empty, boarded up or closing. The pavements are litter-strewn and dirty.

This is where I found Duncan Edwards in February 2011. The weekend marked the 53rd anniversary of Munich, which fell on a Sunday. But, coincidentally, Manchester United had played at Wolverhampton Wanderers, the club geographically closest to Edwards' home, the previous evening. If Edwards' United had returned safely from Munich, Wolves would also have been their next opponents instead of becoming a cancelled fixture.

I arrived in Dudley with United supporters, who had made a detour to pay their respects. Scarves were quietly laid on the plinth of his statue in Market Place, where Edwards stands beside street-stalls and vendors huddled beneath worn, striped awnings. I followed the fans to the next stop on the pilgrimage, which constitutes aesthetic beauty in Dudley: the rust-coloured, elaborately carved and columned stone of its Victorian museum. Inside is a 12x12 room devoted to Edwards. It contains the things he won, wore or owned, and all afternoon a procession climbed the wooden, balustraded staircase to find them. The walls of the room are washed in beige paint. The carpet is Wembley green. Behind glass cases are cream-coloured England shirts and a neat arrangement of 17 velvet international caps, the pale-gold tassels of each hanging like a curtain cord. His medals are in leather boxes. There are silver polished plaques, grey pewter tankards and miniature Cups. Numerous photographs, faded programmes and press cuttings hang in dark frames.

In one of these, taken just a week or so before his death and published on the cover of *Charles Buchan's Football Monthly* as he lay dying, Edwards is in kit and tying the lace of his left boot. His foot rests on the bench inside the Old Trafford dressing room. His Brylcreemed dark hair is swept back and his black-button eyes are raised towards the ceiling, no doubt at the photographer's request. The sadness of this picture comes from the way in which it succeeds in capturing the boundless energy within Edwards. He has a fresh, pink complexion and looks so vibrantly alive that I imagine those who studied it contemporaneously refused to believe that he was then on the edge of death. The idea must have seemed an impossible fiction to them. As I looked at it, I listened to the Pathé News account of the Munich crash, the film of which is played on a loop on a pull-down cinema screen. The narrator's intonation is slow and mournful as he reads the names of those who have been killed or injured. The glare of the strip lighting in the room dilutes the projected images, and the outlines of the plane and the people appear so faintly as to be barely visible. But the voice – strong, richly resonant – negates the need to see what is being broadcast. Indeed, I didn't want to look at it again. I thought about the orphans, widows and parents numbed in a grief common to all but also individual to them. I remembered my father telling me to think about the survivors as well as the dead: that those who came out of Munich alive carried so much with them. They carried the dreadful memory of it. They carried the sorrow it brought. They carried a degree of survivor guilt and incomprehension. They carried within them a need to remember – to commemorate the dead – and also the need to forget; though the circumstances made forgetting impossible.

In Dudley's St Francis Church I met one of its regular congregation. Growing up, he lived less than a mile from Edwards and played in the same school team and also alongside him in casual kick-abouts on the nearby recreation ground. He's 75 now, grey-haired and portly. He wore a pair of gold-rimmed aviator spectacles. His coat was as scarlet as a United shirt. He was standing with the vicar, who admitted she knew 'nothing' about football, and the church wardens, who were polite and kindly and also ever-so-slightly incredulous that groups of us had trekked to an unprepossessing corner of the West Midlands that otherwise you'd pass by. But Edwards' old friend comprehended it. He understood the pull of the story: the sad romance of promise unfulfilled in a what-might-have-been life – the goals which were never scored, the medals and honours never won and the fact, too, that Edwards has become almost a mythical figure. I asked him the obvious questions; the questions I suspect he's always asked. The word he chose instantly to sum up Edwards was 'awesome' and he said it emphatically, as if anything else was inadequate to describe an unclassifiable talent. He remembered Edwards cracking and bending the bar from the half way line in an Under-23 international against Holland. The bar vibrated like a tuning fork. 'If Duncan hit the ball, you made sure you didn't get in the way because you'd get hurt. That was more difficult for me because I was the goalkeeper,' he said, raising his hands as if trying to block one of those shots. Other reminiscences tumbled out of him like psalms and, as he recalled them, I knew he saw Edwards as easily as he could see me in the half-light of the Assisi Chapel. To him, he remained perfect in the imagination – the same unlined face which boarded that plane, a hulking physique that will never turn to fat. 'You never saw him without a ball of some sort at his feet . . . after school he'd always be ready for a game on the park . . . there was never any side to him . . . he was just one of the lads . . . even now I can't believe I knew him and lived so close to him or that he died so young.' He turned to look at a pair of tall, perpendicular stained-glass windows commemorating his friend. In the first window Edwards wears United red. In the second he is dressed in England white. The gorgeously crafted glass in the panels above and around him glows rose, emerald, Kingfisher blue and a warming, soft yellow. He said, finally and truthfully after a pause during which he's weighed up what Edwards was and has since become: 'I don't think he'll ever be forgotten.' There was the faintest catch in his throat as he added without any high-flown nonsense: 'They'll keep on coming here, you know. I'm sure of it.'

The prophecy seemed precise the following morning at Edwards' grave. The cemetery is beside a main road and surrounded by black metal railings and rows of houses. The grave is only a few minutes' walk from his pebble-dashed family home. The graveyard slopes upwards, the carefully tended acreage scattered with trees and divided by ochre-coloured, gritty pathways. In 1958 more than 50,000 people stood in absolute silence, still convulsed by shock, along the route of his funeral procession. An incalculable number have been drawn to him since. Edwards' headstone of black marble with distinctive gold lettering rises above the others around it – just as he rose above those alongside him on the pitch. It stands next to a gnarled, listing trunk of a tree, its branches almost leafless. To the far west, the mauve roll of the Malvern Hills, where Elgar walked, beautifies the horizon. To the east – in the middle distance – loom tower blocks with ugly balconies and dark windows. The grey-bellied sky, as gloomy as a Turner storm, looked full of rain.

However loose and tangential it may be, I feel connected to Edwards. I always wonder how many other boys were named Duncan in tribute to him. As I read the rhyming couplet inscribed on the headstone – *A Day of Memory Sad to Recall/Without Farewell He Left Us All* – and studied the image of him chiselled into its gently curved top, my peripheral vision registered the arrival of more fans. A group of men came up the pathway. A further two groups were parking nearby. Every visitor was looking for Duncan Edwards.

There was a sallow-faced man with crinkly hair, who had come from the south coast. He'd seen Edwards play at Molineux for Manchester United. 'It makes me tearful,' he said, looking at a blaze of red carnations arranged in various vases and a collection of scarves tangled beside the flowers. A young woman in a dark brown coat, carrying her infant child, did cry; long, low sobs that made her eyes sore. She yanked out a large white handkerchief and her husband rested a consoling arm on her shoulder as she repeated the same two words: 'So sad.' There was an elderly couple, arm-in-arm and heads bowed, who stood in front of the headstone before whatever memory of Edwards it conjured forced them to turn away and regain their composure. The husband took off his square tortoiseshell glasses and began massaging the bridge of his nose to disguise the drip of his own tears.

Earlier I'd gone to the wrong graveyard and had wandered around it searching for someone who wasn't there. But there was a serendipitous twist attached to getting lost, as if it was pre-ordained. I was thinking of Edwards' father, Gladstone, who began his working life as a metal polisher and finished it as a gardener at the cemetery. Often he directed visitors towards his son's grave and talked to them alongside it without ever disclosing his identity. At that moment, a tall, thinnish middle-aged man appeared in a pale grey windcheater. He had a brush and a wash-bucket with him. In a Black Country accent, he pointed me towards the graves of Edwards' parents, which are close by, and then ran a hand through his short mousey-coloured hair. He began to wash down the grave, the gold lettering suddenly becoming much brighter. 'I'm a relation on my mother's side,' he explained. Shortly before her death, aged 93 in 2003, Edwards' mother, Sarah Ann, asked him to tend the graves. He's been doing so, once a fortnight, ever since, an obligation he regards as a privilege.

'I throw away the dead flowers and take some of the scarves home and wash them after the weather's made them grubby,' he said, scraping away a heap of soggy, russet-coloured leaves. He was four years old when Edwards died and could vaguely recall him. 'My mother used to tell me how Duncan grew up so quickly,' he added. 'He'd only been at United for a few months. When he came back she realised how much he'd changed. He'd gone from boy to man almost overnight.' His side of the family own some of the mementoes in Dudley's museum. 'A chap came a year or two back and asked us to sell them to him. The sum he was talking about would probably have been enough to buy a house around here. I couldn't do it. Didn't seem right.' As he spoke he worked briskly and diligently, the water and the rip of the wind already reddening his hands. 'Most people come on Duncan's birthday in October,' he said. 'It's remarkable, isn't it? To think he's still remembered? To think people still care?'

'Remarkable,' I said in inadequate reply.

I felt a spit of rain and so I thanked him and moved away. In parting we briefly shook hands, his fleshy palm and fingers cold to the touch. After only a pace or two, I glanced back and saw him on his knees again, still scrubbing the grave and fulfilling the promise he made to an old woman for the sake of her son. Someone who never saw the moment of his greatness flicker. Someone whose whole life will always be defined by the manner of his death.

I left thinking of imponderable 'what ifs'. What if the plane hadn't tried to take off in the snow? What if it hadn't snowed at all? What if Edwards and the others had lived? Today he'd be a dignified and fêted septuagenarian sitting in the Old Trafford directors' box beside Bobby Charlton. Instead, he profoundly touched so many other lives. Men he never knew, such as my father. And children, waiting to be born, such as me.

PART TWO

Flesh And Blood And Super-Powers

4

A Drink for Mr Baxter, Please

My father noticed the shoes first: the sheen of expensive leather and the slenderness of the toes, which were cut into the sharpest points, each glinting like the tip of a chef's knife. He'd always describe them as winkle-pickers, long after the term, like the style itself, ceased to be in fashion. 'I'll never know how he walked in them,' he'd say, shaking his head at the absurdity of it. He could nonetheless recall the walk – the lightness and kingly step of this lone, suited figure and the deliberate turn of the shoulders.

He came into the pub and sat on a high wooden stool, as if he owned the room. My father watched him lay the flat of his hands on to the bar. He ordered a bottle of Bacardi and a jug of Coke, and asked for a small bucket of ice. My father was drying a glass and he tucked the cloth into the deep pocket of his white barman's coat to fetch each of these things for him. He set down the bottle, unscrewed the cap, found a tall fresh glass and yanked the top off the Coke and then prepared to pour both it and the Bacardi for his new customer. 'No bother,' he was told. 'I like to pour my own measures – you get more that way.'

This is how my father met 'Slim' Jim Baxter.

Throughout my boyhood my father tried to escape the drudgery of the mines. For a while he sold an assortment of things door-to-door: insurance policies, plastic household utensils, square boxes of tea, which were stored at home. Nothing worked for him. On each occasion he was driven dejectedly back underground to crawl again through low labyrinthine coal seams. Finally, he decided to try the brewery industry. He moonlighted with part-time jobs – fulfilled in between tiring pit-shifts at weekends or on days off – in the hope of training himself and acquiring the tenancy of a pub. He learnt to change barrels and clean the pumps. One of the pubs he worked in lay on the rural fringes of Nottinghamshire. It was out of the way and slightly upmarket, a place where the customer could arrive and leave without being overly conspicuous, and drink discreetly – frequently after last orders were called and the doors were bolted. And, as everyone knew, Baxter liked to drink whatever the hour and as though it was a competitive sport.

Baxter had been dropped off by a friend who, he claimed to my father, would be collecting him later for a tour of the town. He was dressed spiffily. Along with the impressive shoes, he wore a dark suit, the trouser legs as narrow as drain pipes, a white shirt and a pencil blue tie. He was no stranger to my father, for whom Glasgow Rangers were the Scottish club of his heart; the club, in fact, that his own father – and his father's father, too – had owed allegiance to. To my father, Baxter – the 'blue Brazilian' – represented the precocious best of Rangers. They and he were bound together in a dovetail fit. To see Baxter in any other colour on the field was to catch him inappropriately dressed. But he left them nonetheless and the lustre he possessed soon left him as a consequence.

Most people have to chase fame and achieve it only at the end of something. At the beginning, there is the toil to get through. Baxter was different. Fame came to him almost as soon as he beckoned it, and he grew accustomed to the adulation the public gave him, which was there from the start. This made his rapid climb straightforward – three Championships, three Scottish Cups and four League Cups at Rangers between 1960 and 1965. But the descent from that high of The Baxter Years was dire: an ill-judged, money motivated transfer to unglamorous Sunderland in 1965, which ended in struggle and misery, and then another – more woeful still – to Nottingham Forest at the end of 1967. Forest paid £100,000 for an image of Baxter as he used to be. They got stuck with the player as he really was then: alcohol-dependent, truculent, impossibly lazy and irre-deemable. What used to come effortlessly became a labour, and Baxter went through the motions out of self-preservation because to do anything else – to actually *try* – would have made his deficiencies more obvious than ever. Baxter was a spent force and an idler, his best years as a footballer already behind him. There were a few jolly tricks – a side-step or two, the foot rolled over the top of the ball, a playful back-heel – but no sustained performance; no match that anyone could say Baxter had entirely bossed for Forest. He'd still tell the City Ground apprentices to fetch his boots, which he called 'my magic wands'; but there were few spells left in them. He did score one spectacular goal, against Southampton, after controlling a headed clearance with his right foot and then volleying it back into the net with the left from 20 yards. As a legacy, it was meagre.

That his full-time command on the Scottish game was also brief – a span of half a decade – didn't negate the splendid things that had happened during it for my father. He always defended Baxter. It was 'unfortunate', he explained, as if Baxter didn't aid and abet his own downfall, that he played when specific players – he meant George Best as well – were treated like 'pop stars', a social status denied to the generations before them. The temptations that came Baxter's way because of it embraced each of his fatal weaknesses: drink, betting, women, and the inability to say no to any of them. The corrosive effects of this celebrity were clearly visible. When my father served him Bacardi, Baxter was only 29, but looked 40 years old. Within months he'd leave Forest, later calling his period there 'a disaster', and return to Rangers, where another awaited him. Sometimes you just can't go home again – because, so long after parting, either you or that home are unrecognisable and therefore incompatible. Baxter is proof of it. He wasn't the sprightly Baxter on the T-shirts sold outside Ibrox, which proclaimed *The King is Back*. The merit of the statement was factual truth. But the tacit promise contained within the message went unfulfilled; Baxter's bags were packed for him after 22 games.

The decline in Baxter – and the reason for it – was evident in his appearance in the pub. The 'Slim Jim' sobriquet cultivated by, and particularly useful for newspaper headline-writers, no longer applied to him. In early photographs Baxter is so thin he seems to be made out of wire. There is virtually no muscle on his bones. But this once-lean youth was an overweight and unfit man when my father saw him. The belly was big to the extent that his paunch hung like a ledge over his belt. The face was rounder than it ever had been – the sort of moon face you find in a child's drawing – and crowned by heavy dark hair, the fringe cut flat against the forehead. The eyes were heavily lined, as though he had missed several nights of decent sleep. My father said he could have passed for a travelling salesman, over-fed and over-lubricated in his nicely cut clothes, with an undeniable charm which instinctively elicited empathy; and sympathy too. He registered both the physical change in him and his insatiable taste for alcohol. He saw Baxter gulp his first drink, as if taking thirsty relief in it, before constantly sipping the rest, barely diluting the Bacardi with splashes of Coke. Well over a quarter of the bottle vanished in under half an hour. Neither the level of his intake nor the pace of it had any significant effect on Baxter. Frequent use had made him immune to it. But he drank – or at least it seemed so to my father – through the need to do so rather than because of the pleasure it brought him. 'I don't think he tasted it,' he said. 'He just had to have a glass in his hand.'

My father recognised the hunched body language of men who came into pubs to find solitude and the signals of other drinkers hunting out, and hurting for, companionship. From the beginning Baxter had an inclination to talk. My father gave me the edited highlights. 'There's a hint of a Scots accent in your voice,' Baxter said to him. My father said he came from Stirling. He knew Baxter had once been a miner and admitted to being a colliery-man too. 'I was a miner,' said Baxter, pointing at his chest. 'Bloody awful – couldn't wait to get out.' My father said his name was Jim. 'Two Jims – sitting here with just ourselves for company then,' said Baxter. 'Let me buy you a drink.' My father took a half of bitter – 'for later', he said – and Baxter poured himself another stiffish Bacardi with a finger of Coke. He said that he might take a pub himself one day. He didn't want spit and sawdust on the floor. 'I want something a bit classy,' he said. Already envisaging a well-upholstered and leisurely retirement, Baxter wanted to arrange the glasses, lean against the bar and talk his middle and old age away.

The footballer didn't mention football. He hadn't even alluded to the fact he was *the* Jim Baxter. 'He was waiting for me to mention it first,' my father reckoned. The discussion between them meandered on inconclusively until my father said: 'I remember you at Wembley in '63 – and how you scored there.' Baxter became coy, perhaps remembering the player he used to be. My father saw him stare, almost shyly, into his glass, as if the image of the game – and the two goals which he'd scored – might settle there. England had beaten Scotland 9–3 at Wembley in 1961, a shaming result for the tartan. The 1962–63 team grew out of that lacerating and shambolic defeat. My father thought it represented what he said to me was the true bloom of Scotland. There was talent to spare besides Baxter: John White and Denis Law, Dave Mackay and Billy McNeill, Ian St John and Paddy Crerand, Willie Henderson and Davie Wilson. In '63 Baxter saw Wembley's groomed acres and said: 'If I can't play well on this turf, I'll sell brushes round the doors.' The brushes went unsold. The score was England 1, Baxter 2. 'I was a brilliant player then,' he said to my father, nodding his head, the use of the past tense accepting his present chaotic state. 'I could beat a man as easily as falling off this stool. At Wembley that day, everything worked for me. If I'd shot from my own goal-line, it would have gone into the net.' He added that the obvious 'trick' was to have the ball. If he didn't, he said he felt like a spectator and the game became boring for him. He chased it, wanting to own it for himself. 'Some days,' my father remembered Baxter saying, 'you had to tear the bloody thing away from me.' My father knew Baxter wasn't exaggerating about any of this.

Football is a collaborative art, and yet he'd seen Baxter nail the opposition down and be ruthless without the need of support. He did it in a cavalier way, as if style mattered to him as much as substance. My father asked about his ideals and the reply distilled Baxter's ideology into a single word. 'Enjoyment,' he said with a mildly startled look, as though anyone who'd watched him ought to have worked it out for themselves. My father understood Baxter's 'enjoyment' meant giving as much as receiving, which sharply distinguished his contribution. 'You knew he was there to entertain you,' he said. 'He wanted you to go home smiling.'

The evening wore on. It began to rain, the drops hard against the windows. More Bacardi was ordered and drunk. More minor confidences were traded. Baxter was still alone, hardly caring that no one had turned up to claim him. Occasionally he'd glance up from his glass and look at the clock on the wall and sigh before taking another mouthful of his drink. My father – and he told Baxter this too – grew up in a village where Protestants and Catholics were separated by the main street, which ran like a dividing river through the middle of it. It gave him a hatred of any type of segregation or bigotry – especially religious. I think his outlook on football

mirrored the view of the sagely stoic referee, Mr
Armistead, in Jack Rosenthal's drama, *Another Sunday
and Sweet FA*, which is based around a park game played
on a pitch surrounded by sooty factory chimneys, electricity pylons and dark church towers. The sprawl of
an unidentified, northern city sits below the plateau of
the lime-marked field. Mr Armistead's approach is all
about common sense. He keeps a photograph of Dixie
Dean in his wallet, withdrawing it wistfully to remind
him of his youth, but retains his sense of proportion.
For him football isn't – and can never become – the be
and end all of everything; and the spirit of the match
is always more important than the result. Drawing the
feuding, antagonistic captains together before kick off,
Mr Armistead tells them:

> What we are about to witness is called a football match. Not
> the beginning of World War Three. Not the destruction of
> the human race . . . it is a football match.

My father felt the same way. He could never grasp
the divisiveness and the extremes of emotion – acute
bitterness in defeat, arrogant gloating in victory –
provoked purely on the basis that one team had trounced
another, however closely competitive or historically
deep the rivalry between them. It made no sense to him
that Newcastle v Sunderland or Rangers v Celtic was
hyped up as murderously as Corleone v Tattaglia. 'How
can I hate Celtic,' he used to ask, 'when Jimmy Johnstone

plays for them?' Johnstone, tiny enough to fit into a cathedral niche, asserted himself so masterfully and had such a vivid appeal that my father thought the cliché about 'running rings around defenders' had been invented strictly for him. Johnstone was like a free verse poet, always going where his instinct took him. My father would gladly have paid double at the gate to see one of those baroque runs, which involved beating everyone at least twice. The fact Johnstone wore green and white hoops was immaterial to him. The fact Celtic were the Catholic team was immaterial to him also. The religious prejudices he'd witnessed as a boy made him agnostic. He wanted Celtic to lose only because he wanted Rangers to win. But he despised no one if that scenario was reversed; and there was no ulterior motive in his celebrations if it wasn't. Which is why, of all the things Baxter said to my father, the most resonant was this: 'I loved beating Celtic more than anyone else. But some of my best mates play for them . . . some of my best nights out have been with them . . . and, while I wouldn't give them a bloody corner in an Old Firm derby, I'd do anything else for them.' My father knew then that he liked Baxter as much as a person as he admired him as a player. His sole complaint – and he was far from alone in making it – was that Baxter had been so wanton in his self-destruction.

Genius is rare. But the genius to handle genius is rarer still. Baxter was deficient only in the fact he had the first but wasn't blessed with the second. At one stage, without prompting, Baxter said flatly to my father that he was fond of a 'good time too much', a clumsy phrase but which contained, subliminally, a confession about being his own worst enemy; the acceptance, too, that he'd willingly co-operated in his own downfall and spilled out his talent in bars rather than on pitches. Now it was unrecoverable. Squandering this wealth of skill saddened my father more after he listened to Baxter's laid-back acceptance of it, as though he'd lost nothing more than a 10 shilling note from his back pocket. Baxter knew no one else was to blame and he wasn't in conflict with himself about it. He didn't come across to my father as sombre or melancholic. And he didn't seem to nurture the fantasy – prevalent in others facing hard times – that his luck would eventually turn; that he'd soon be flourishing again. 'You know,' my father used to say as he recalled that evening 'it wasn't as though he regretted it. He'd had a lot of money – and spent it. He'd had a lot of drinks pushed his way – and he'd drunk them. But there was nothing he could do about changing himself or his situation. Everything was too far gone and there was no point in moaning about it. He seemed grateful for what he'd already had.' As if he was adding an explanatory footnote for me, my father said: 'It's just as well. If he thought too much about what he might have done with that talent I'm sure he'd have driven himself mad.'

In Nottingham it was a daily occurrence for Baxter to fall into and out of the pubs, bars, clubs and gambling dens. There were murky episodes for him in what passed for its louche underworld. Where alcohol was concerned he was compulsively promiscuous – he'd drink anywhere. Aware the experience of Baxter's company in a bar wasn't unique, my father was sure every landlord in the county had a story about him. 'Probably some of them carried him home,' he said. In one city-centre pub he got tangled up in a fight, the drunken Baxter versus three far brawnier opponents. He finished up in the street sprawled, face-down and almost unconscious in the road. His face was cut badly. His nose was bloody. His ribs and back were bruised by elbows, slaps, clenched-fist punches and indiscriminate kicking. Nothing, however, could jolt Baxter out of his wild ways, which began and persisted because of Rangers' indulgence of him. In a hotel in Glasgow's Argyll Street, the Baxter of his handsome heyday was able to drink however much his young stomach could take and send the tab to Ibrox with impunity. No one queried the cost; not even when multiple bottles of champagne were listed on the bill. Baxter learnt he could take liberties and so took them on the basis that his salary – a basic £25 to £35 a week – was a paltry return for the entertainment he provided. What Baxter needed was a set of steely rules and a Jimmy Reid-like lecture on 'no bevvying'. What he got from Rangers was a see-and-hear-no-evil tolerance of his devout Epicurean life-style, which went beyond the nocturnal since it began shortly after the chimes of noon and petered out only in the wee small hours.

Usually, as Baxter arrived at Ibrox on a Saturday afternoon, the Rangers management were able to guess from the pallor of his skin and the cobweb of red veins in his eyes where he'd been on Friday night and most of Saturday morning. Nothing prompted Rangers to curtail or end the amount he was drinking and efforts to discipline him were tame and wishy-washy. If he trained at all, Baxter did so in a lacklustre manner which made plain his distaste for the treadmill of hard miles. Rangers asked him, as if pleading, to do a 'wee bit' for appearances' sake. But to retain his Saturday freshness Baxter said he sought to do 'fuck all' from Monday to Wednesday and 'almost nothing' on Thursday and Friday.

The extraordinary latitude he received – and the leniency towards alcohol – may have seemed like a good idea at the time; Rangers placating Baxter to keep him sweet. But ignoring his excesses is the worst thing the club did on his behalf. It imbued Baxter with the cock-eyed belief that his immense natural talent would always be sufficient to overcome any demands made of him on the pitch – despite the atrophying processes going on in his internal organs, which were drink-soaked. He thought he could both play successfully and drink prodigiously. He also thought he was taking a drink when, in truth, the drink was taking him. Too late, he realised the opposite was true – but drank on regardless. In a twist on Socrates, Baxter decided the non-drinking life was not worth living and went out to prove it, as if the point needed emphasising. Another inveterate boozer,

Lord Byron, used to itemise his daily consumption for his own amusement. If Baxter had done so only a notebook as elephantine in bulk as the Glasgow Telephone Directory would have been fit for purpose.

Oddly enough, given the amount of days and nights he devoted to it, the drinking didn't begin to slur the fascinating things his feet were saying until after he said goodbye to Ibrox. He spoke to my father about that parting. His defining moment wasn't a Championship medal or a Cup win at Hampden, a Scottish international or an 8–0 carving up of Borussia Moenchengladbach, against whom he scored one of the goals and created the other seven. It was a broken leg against Rapid Vienna in 1965. 'I wasn't really the same player afterwards,' said Baxter. It was the occasion, my father told me, that he looked forsaken and sorry for himself. Rangers and he were then already locked in a squabbling marriage. Baxter nagged for an improved salary; Rangers, worn down by his wanderings, at last nagged him to become fitter and to drink less. Neither could give what the other wanted, and so divorce – which Rangers initiated and Baxter accepted – followed. My father heard Baxter say that 'if Rangers had paid me better, I'd still be there' and he didn't doubt it. 'Baxter belonged there, or in London. He looked out of place in Nottingham,' my father said, intimating that its streets were too small for such a big personality.

At Rangers there was a beauty about Baxter. He moved with elegance and his left foot could land the ball on a silver dollar from 60 yards or more. And, whether using the outside or inside of that foot – and frequently the heel – he could curve, push or nudge passes wherever he chose. A pass from him was like turning a key; doors opened for Rangers because of it. He not only set the tempo of the game as choreographer and conductor, but also shaped the spaces in which it was played. When my father encountered Baxter, he noted his restlessness. Seldom still, he fidgeted this way and that and strolled around the bar, a refreshed drink in his hand. He did much the same thing on the pitch; he roamed across it nomadically. Since he had the blessed ability to be experimental and spontaneous, Baxter regularly used it, looping the loop on a run for no reason other than the joy of doing so, unnecessarily clinging to the ball and mentally timing the length of his possession. He superfluously nutmegged players to please himself and annoy them. These were his tinselled party-pieces and, at his peak, he never failed to decorate a match with them.

When I first saw him on television – against England in 1967 – I wasn't aware that his dominating performance at Wembley that afternoon came at the end of a sub-standard season at Sunderland, where he'd been abjectly off form. I assumed his brilliance was the norm. For Baxter, the international was a release; both a means of escape from the League, and the grand stage to show the English First Division what he could *really* do. Leaving Scotland and heading south had been the natural and lucrative route for Baxter's fellow country-men, who established themselves in England and never went home again. But one of the most gifted Scots of his generation – and most others too – didn't make a success of his border-crossing because he signed for Sunderland on the downward slope. Baxter wasn't indifferent to his English reputation. He was aware, as he told my father, that there were people in England who 'think I can't play'. Wembley '67 proved otherwise.

It was the first game my father and I prepared for together. Its importance was stressed to me as a Home International decider *and* a European Championship qualifier *and* the Unofficial World Championship. Fed by his enthusiasm, I became utterly engrossed and read the morning and evening newspapers for team news. The Saturday match wasn't shown live on television. It was broadcast on radio's Third Network. The game was screened the following afternoon, and my father decided we shouldn't see, hear or be told the result until then. Comic art later imitated our life that weekend. An episode of *The Likely Lads*, called *No Hiding Place*, has the Geordie friends Bob and Terry desperate to avoid the score of England against Bulgaria before watching the evening highlights. They turn off the TV and radio. They take the phone off the hook. They even hide in a church. We didn't have a phone. We did, however, avoid the news bulletins on TV and radio. My mother answered the door in case one of his friends or mine arrived on the doorstep to blab the score. On Sunday morning she took the newspapers off the mat and made a show of laying them on top of the wardrobe. Sealed off and silent in my own world, I sat on the sofa ignorant of what was to come on *Star Soccer*. At the time, I had no knowledge of formations, tactics or the minutiae of football theory. But I was conscious of ball skill, which Baxter abundantly possessed – a fact even a novice like me deduced as soon as he appeared. The pictures came to us in black and white; but every time Baxter got the ball it was as if he shone in full colour. It was impossible not to be dazzled.

I knew where the family obligation lay; I supported Scotland for my father's sake. As if feeling the need to legitimise my choice, he told me that our genealogic line included, albeit very distantly, a Scottish international. His name was Robert (Cumming) Hamilton, a Highlander. As a youngster, my father met Hamilton when he gave a lecture in Stirling. By then he was an educationalist rather than a centre forward and my father had only the haziest memory of gently shaking his smooth right hand. He couldn't remember either what Hamilton said to him or what he looked like. What he did remember was that Hamilton's tweed suit reeked of other pipe-smokers' tobacco and the way in which he removed, with a flourish, a gold hunter watch from his pocket and allowed him to hold it. My father was still able to feel the weight of the watch, and he formed a cup with his palm and fingers to show me how he cradled it. Hamilton allowed him to pull back the lid-hinge and look at the white face with its skinny hands and Roman numerals. The inside of the case was inscribed:

To Robert Cumming Hamilton

Scottish FA Cup Winner

1903

My father guessed the watch was a token of thanks from Glasgow Rangers, for whom Hamilton played in two spells – from 1897 to 1906 and then 1907 to 1908. The 1903 Scottish Cup Final dragged on. It took three matches for Rangers to beat Hearts 2–0. Much later I discovered this wasn't the culmination of Hamilton's career, which was studded with medals, but merely a side-bar to it. He won four League titles, another Cup, 11 Scottish caps and scored 36 times in Old Firm games. In 1898–99 he captained Rangers during an unbeaten season. Of his 15 international goals, four came in the 11–0 dismantling of Ireland in 1901. On the rampage, Hamilton was described contemporaneously as 'like a mountain torrent in flood'. Other accounts make it sound as though the power in his shots was sufficient to punch a hole through a titanium plate. He was inducted into Rangers' Hall of Fame in 2011. My father knew Hamilton was tenuously linked to him through a cousin. But, when I eventually saw a photograph of him, I felt the physical jolt of recognition, as if someone I knew was staring back at me. Hamilton had inky black hair, parted on the left, a long jawbone and a narrow mouth and a blade nose. I thought I was looking at a picture I'd seen before: my father's father on his wedding day. I almost dropped the book I was holding with the shock of the resemblance between them.*

On its own the story of Hamilton, his watch and the Cup Final was seductive enough to convert me to Scotland's cause. But my father pressed on, sharing his own childhood with me. He fell in love with Newcastle, he said, long before he saw the city because of Hughie Gallacher, scorer of more than 400 goals. Off the field Gallacher, always snazzily attired, looked like a prosperous businessman about to close a deal: white spats, a bowler hat, a silk tie and button-down collar, a double-breasted waistcoat, a handkerchief water-falling from the breast pocket of his jacket and a flower pinned to his lapel. On the field he looked like a street fighter: fists clenched, eyes as hard as flints, shoulders aggressively hunched and legs scarred and pitted by defenders' studs, which were regularly raked down his flesh. Gallacher, only 5ft 5in tall and wearing size 6 boots, scored with bang-bang swiftness – 39 times in Newcastle's 1927 Championship win – and established himself in my father's early life because he was a Wembley Wizard.

* For reasons never explained to me, the watch was passed to the family before mysteriously vanishing – pawned and never reclaimed, I suppose – and I spent some of my early life naively searching for it in relatives' cupboards and wardrobes before the hopelessness of the task dawned on me.

On a saturated pitch Scotland tore through England, winning 5–1 in 1928. The performance was described as an exhibition of scientific football. Sportingly *The Scotsman* refused to gloat. The first two decks of the headline above its match report were to the point.

IRRESISTIBLE DISPLAY
ENGLAND OUTPLAYED

Gallacher didn't score; he did, however, 'make the whole thing possible', according to my father. 'He was the puppeteer. Everybody talked about Gallacher afterwards. Because of that, I scanned the papers every day to find his name. I was given a Players' cigarette card of him in a black and white shirt.' The Wembley Wizards were 'immortals', he added. 'I heard about them before I heard about Robert the Bruce or the Bonnie Prince.' My father was taken to the cinema to watch the brief newsreel of the match to mark his sixth birthday. He sat on the front row, legs outstretched. On the screen he saw Scottish supporters in tam o' shanters and tartan scarves. Gallacher's collar was upturned and my father glimpsed him in small excerpts of the game, which were captured from behind the goal. No one could judge Scotland's achievement, or how comprehensively England had lost, from these fragments. But my father always said: 'If there's one game I wish I'd seen, it's the Wizards.' Convinced there would never be another Scottish side to match them at Wembley, he glumly prepared me for defeat before the kick off.

'We' weren't expected to win, he said. 'We' were without Jimmy Johnstone, who was *hors de combat*. 'We' weren't, he suspected, 'on form' anyway. 'They,' he added of England, were World Cup holders after all, and the team contained ten of the players which won it (Jimmy Greaves replacing Roger Hunt). 'I suppose a draw is the best we can hope for,' he said, making it seem as though the Scots were carrying a tattered banner on a doomed journey.

Wembley was washed in bright sunshine, the curved shadow of the stand and its block of floodlights shaded the left touchline. I know this because I decided to watch the game again and appreciated the profound impact Jim Baxter made on it – a performance from almost half a century ago that confirmed as true everything my father said of him. He floats through the international, as if it is a practice session on the training ground. The overriding impression is of someone exquisitely poised – so confident and in such absolute command that he doesn't feel the urgency to run because he knows no one can dispossess him anyway. As though responding to the rhythms of a band's slow march, he seldom breaks into a trot and never into a sprint. Baxter strolls with the ball, as if he's taking it for a walk. He gives and receives passes in such a languid manner that, at any moment, I expected him to stroke the ball on and then lie down on the grass – casually resting his hands behind his head like a pillow – until he is needed again. He taunts England in slow-motion, dragging them towards him and pointing towards the gaps in which he is about to play the ball. He is manipulative and technically impeccable. He takes possession on his chest and releases a 40-yard pass that finds the target perfectly. He propels a short, diagonal ball, which leaves his boot like the flick of a whip.

Beforehand, as he sat in the dressing room with a copy of *The Sporting Life*, Baxter had urged those around him to 'take the piss' out of England. For Baxter, it didn't equate to heavy scoring. It meant demonstrating that Scotland were superior in technique. His lone and deadly purpose was to show off, teasing and embarrassing England so the 3–2 defeat he inflicted on them would always be regarded as ignominious. The Scotland trainer had tried to persuade him to warm up. Baxter laid down his racing paper. He stretched his right leg and then his left. 'There,' he said insolently 'I'm warmed up.' His whole display is like this – colossal arrogance and apparent nonchalance are its hallmarks. But everything about Baxter and his emotions is firmly focused. The laid-back style is bespoke for the occasion because he wants to mock England. And he does – repeatedly and unambiguously. He hugs the touchline and is never hemmed in. He pirouettes past one tackle, side-steps and twists his hip around another and dips his shoulder to avoid the next. He is capable of doing anything – however outrageous or anarchic. He plays, too, with a sense of his own posterity.

In the closing minutes, socks jammed around his

ankles and shirt hanging loose over his shorts, Baxter's radicalised approach to 90 minutes of football culminates in his mini, ad-libbed game of 'keepy up'. The provocation is blazingly emblematic of what he means by 'taking the piss'. Near the left touchline, and mid-way in England's half, he collects a back-heeled pass from Denis Law, which itself is executed as an act of airy contempt towards the World Cup winners. Baxter scrutinises the space invitingly spread in front of him. With England on the retreat, as if afraid of him, Baxter instinctively juggles the ball towards them on his left foot – once, twice, a third and then a fourth time. He travels ten yards this way, across the tightly cut stripes of the pitch, before the final flourish. He kills the ball before scooping it up and over the defence – a gentle lob, which Law takes inside the box. The moment of England's humbling – from Law's back-heel to Baxter's release of the ball – lasts less than ten seconds. But superlatives are still summoned to describe it; pub conversations are still generated because of it; and Baxter's spirit is still roused by recollection of it.

Baxter maintained that he was better against England in '63. But to many, like my father, he was always recalled first within the gilded frame of this one match because the context mattered more and so heightened the achievement considerably. No one thinking of it fails to think of Baxter. He is embedded in any memory of the game. He *was* outstanding in '63; but the mesmerising spectacle of '67 made that performance look merely impressive by comparison. Frequently football's capacity to establish national identity is overstated. And too often, before the heat of a match begins to cool, exaggerated claims are made for its social meaning. My father thought this game was different. He was never a nationalist. He was, however, a patriot; and the win for him was wound together with the rhetoric of patriotism. He considered it therapeutic too. Scotland felt better because it gained a renewed sense of self and a '*This Land is Your Land*' sort of pride through the result. It could be argued – though my father would never hear of it – that mitigating circumstances contributed to England's defeat: an injury to Jack Charlton, forcing him up front, another to Greaves and the tepid contribution of Geoff Hurst. But to press the claim too hard insults Baxter, who made those competing against him seem good-to-adequate second raters. Nor did Scotland ever look like losing. Not after Law poached them an early lead. Not after Bobby Lennox's 82nd-minute hooked goal and Jim McCalliog's driven-in shot shortly after it. Not even when England claimed two consolation goals in a three-minute flurry. Baxter called it 'the biggest 3–2 hammering ever seen' and the recorded version proves his analysis accurate. Scotland power through it, and their hunger and artistry make England look sterile.

Long afterwards, I realised my father had broken the embargo on the result. Either that, or the near exactitude of knowing what was about to happen counts as clairvoyance. He could predict when Baxter was about to make an opening for Law; or when Scotland were about to score a goal. It was a benign deception. His way of involving me in the game.

I soon learnt that allegiance to Scotland came with a caveat: I had to be comfortable with acute disappointment. The lows would outnumber the highs. There was the unbeaten, near-and-yet-so-far World Cup of 1974 in West Germany, and the rush of optimism and euphoria surrounding the trek to Argentina four years later. Bloated claims were made for that team. The manager, Ally MacLeod, was consistent in shouting favourable odds and spoke as though just turning up with clean boots would guarantee our glory. The belated face-saving win over Holland, and Archie Gemmill's unforgettable goal against them, weren't sufficient to obscure the sorry outcome of the tournament. MacLeod became a pilloried figure, easily caricaturable. But, in his cups, my father consoled himself with the thought of Baxter at Wembley – though it seemed, even then, to have happened so long ago as to be prelapsarian.

Baxter never caught alight in the same way again. He played his last international less than six months later. What followed were déjà-vu moments – the repeated, compulsive cycle of drinking, betting and carousing, which incrementally robbed him of health and fitness and finally self-belief. He looked lethargic, and struggled for the extra yard that his wasted legs could no longer give him. In a football sense, he grew old too quickly. The talent dwindled and died; and Baxter was aware of that dying. He confessed it in a song. The lyrics were a requiem to the skills he once had. As Nottingham Forest were about to face Manchester United at Old Trafford – who were then only eight weeks away from winning the European Cup – Baxter's boss Johnny Carey, tired of saying the same futile things time and again, tried to drag a positive response out of him. The appeal he made was to Baxter's vanity. He talked about the crowd, the low buzz and hum of 61,000 audible inside the dressing room, and the gauntlet-throwing challenge of pitting himself against Charlton and Best. This is your stage, he said to Baxter, and this your kind of match. The Baxter of the early and mid-60s would have found Carey's oratory patronising. He'd have expected the opposition, however glittering, to be fretting about him. The Baxter of 1968 reacted to it painfully aware of his limitations. He planted one boot on the bench beneath the peg where his clothes hung, spread his arms wide and began to sing:

> *Those were the days my friend*
> *We thought they'd never end*

This was Baxter's nostalgic lament for his former self. He just couldn't do what Carey wanted of him. Halfway decent games were all he could manage. It was pointless, as Carey finally accepted, to ask for more.

'We skelped their arses,' said Baxter, using quaint Scottish slang, after my father asked him about '67. 'Oh, the night we had afterwards. I think it lasted three days.' He was still on his own at the bar. The bottle of Bacardi was empty, and Baxter asked my father to top up his glass. Finally irritated that his friend hadn't arrived, he changed a note and walked off to use the pay phone near the entrance. Despite the amount he'd drunk, there was no wobble in his gait. But he fumbled with the coins, dropping them on to the floor and cursed as he scrambled on all fours to retrieve them. He returned exasperated, a handful of those coins still jangling in his hand. There'd been no answer from the number he'd rung.

My father was due to clock off – in preparation for the following day's shift at the colliery – and hand over to his replacement. Baxter asked whether he might cadge a lift. 'Of course,' my father said, knowing he'd be dining out on the anecdote of being Baxter's chauffeur. Baxter asked to be dropped near Trent Bridge and wound down the passenger window to take in some fresh air. On the way he began talking about himself in the third person. 'It was Jim Baxter this and Jim Baxter that,' said my father, 'but he wasn't full of his own importance except when he said that he only had to wave at a waiter and say "A drink for Mr Baxter, please" for that drink to come to him on a tray. I suppose someone ought to have said no to him. But I couldn't – even after that first bottle of Bacardi – so how could anyone else?'

Before getting out of the car Baxter insisted my father take a £5 note – the equivalent of £50 today – for both his hospitality and the inconvenience of driving out of his way. For a while, until financial need over-rode sentiment, he refused to spend it. It was still raining, and Baxter disappeared into the night holding his jacket over his head as a makeshift umbrella. He headed towards the tall grey block of the Bridgford Hotel, which loomed over the City Ground. My father never saw him again except from the terraces.

If there's an irony, it is this: my father never got to run a pub. Baxter did, however, which was dangerous in the extreme for someone whose knowledge of the brewery industry was based on taste and who preferred to consume the product rather than sell it. As his biographer, Ken Gallacher, pointed out, Baxter was 'his own best customer'. Aged 30, his career was over because of drink and he fell hard. Rangers gave him a free transfer. Refusing demotion to the draughty halls of the lower divisions, he retired and established his bar – for sensible commercial purposes named Jim Baxter's – close enough to Ibrox to hear the chants from the Copland Road. Aged 55, he underwent two liver transplants. Aged 61 – in 2001 – he died of pancreatic cancer.

Baxter knew he was killing himself one drink at a time, and yet the knowledge didn't persuade him to stop. Abstinence was impossible for such a hardened imbiber. Even moderation was rejected out of hand because of the excuse Baxter invented for his behaviour: 'Moderation,' he said, 'is for moderate people.' As a quotation it is good enough to be one of Oscar Wilde's. As a piece of thinking it is infantile. Another warped argument was used to justify his financial profligacy: 'I made a lot of money. I spent a lot of money and I lost a lot of money,' he said. If you sense a 'but' coming, you'd be right. 'But if I *was* a fool to myself,' added Baxter, 'I was at least my own fool.' The italicised 'was' that Baxter chose is designed to dismiss as unsound the evidence of his guilt. Though it tries to do the opposite, the claim only reinforces the calamity he made of things and the mishmash and balls-up his career became. Baxter was an awful warning of what happens when someone measures out their life in empty bottles. But its sad end partly conceals – but can never destroy – the monument of his early career at Rangers. In every creative aspect of the game he was precociously and richly endowed. There was a sculptured grace about him. This picture of Baxter remains uppermost in the mind because the scarcest talent, which he possessed, always endures. Those who went to see him at Ibrox swore that as soon as he gathered a pass everyone around him was as insubstantial as a shadow. 'The players he was about to bring into the game didn't exist until he let go of the ball,' my father said.

He was devoted to Baxter. Whenever he told the story of his encounter with him, he would imitate Baxter's walk, his accent and the way he lifted his glass, the elbow of his drinking arm still on the bar. He talked about him as if complicity existed between them and the pair were bosom buddies. But then, for two hours on a rainy night in Nottingham, they had been.

5

Reading Minds and Stopping Time

Even now – more than four decades after discovering it – I still stare at one photograph with incredulity, as though the camera is surely lying to me.

The square, black and white image appeared in one of those ubiquitous but now defunct annuals, the *International Football Book*. I remember how the photograph astonished me at the time; and I also remember the way in which the sense of wonder it stirred in me enhanced my then nascent love of, and fascination for, football. If it was published in one of today's glossy magazines or newspapers, I'd mistrust it. I'd assume the picture had been digitally altered and dismiss it, supposing that someone expert in the art of Photoshop had manipulated it to fool the reader. But this shot was taken in October 1966 – Newcastle United verses Liverpool at St James' Park – and there was no enhancement. The unknown photographer, sitting beside the goal mouth, caught exactly what he saw in front of him. The accompanying caption fails to convey its visual impact, as if the writer was either blind to something so apparent to me or could not find the words to match the glory of it. In thin italics, it reads:

Wyn Davies of Newcastle – surely one of the game's most photogenic movers? – leaves the Liverpool defence standing, but his header was wide.

I've never understood the need for the question mark, which the photograph makes superfluous. Davies is unquestionably photogenic. Other than to identify the participants, there isn't the need for a caption anyway because the photograph is self-labelling. Davies is in mid-air. His head is craning to the right after making contact with the ball, which is directly above him at the very top of the frame. His left arm is stretched horizontally from his shoulder and his right is held slightly away from his body to retain his balance. Both of his legs are bent 45 degrees at the knee. In this balletic pose, Davies resembles a stage dancer – a kind of young Nureyev at the Kirov. What took my breath away wasn't his posture, but the height Davies attains. Draw a line with your eyes from the waistband of Davies' black shorts and you'll see it crosses six inches to a foot *above* the head of Liverpool's captain and centre half Ron Yates. Next, remember two things. Firstly, Yates is almost on his points, the toe of his right boot is noticeably angled into the turf. Secondly, he is 6ft 2in tall. Even taking into account minor deceptions of perspective, Davies is three feet higher than Yates. Looking at the photograph, it was hard to decide whether he had descended from the belt of grey cloud above him or levitated vertically from the thickish grass beneath; both options seemed possible purely because a further two were so implausible that I dismissed them: Davies had been swung there on a theatrical wire attached from the Main Stand or he had scrambled up an invisible ladder. Whatever the reason for his mastery of the air, he seemed to have defied gravitational law to achieve it.

At the time I was reading the Marvel comics featuring those invincible, Super Hero do-gooders – immortal, costumed and masked men who could walk through walls or leap high buildings in a single bound, turn themselves into flame or ice at will or were faster than a speeding bullet. But I knew each of them was only a coloured drawing. Davies was conspicuously flesh and blood. It didn't matter to me that he hadn't managed to direct his header on target. The fact he was soaring above Yates in the first place was incredible enough. It was like a magic trick of a type so baffling that I could not conceive any rational solution. I took the photograph to my father and asked him to explain how someone human could jump so high. He examined it and replied with the deadpan: 'Don't you know? Wyn Davies is the footballer who can fly.'

By then my father's entertaining, if fantastical, descriptions of players were already familiar to me. He spoke of them as if each one represented the gospel truth. He told me Leeds' John Charles had a forehead made out of brick, which meant he could head a ball into the top corner from 30 yards. 'I've seen him do it,' he said. He insisted – as if I were too naïve to suppose otherwise – that Tom Finney was capable of retaining possession for 90 minutes 'because he had magnetic feet and the ball sticks to his instep'. And he described Newcastle's (and then Celtic's) goalkeeper Ronnie Simpson as someone with arms twice as long as his small body. 'He could stand in the centre of the goal and touch both posts,' he said. 'When a centre forward came towards him, he must have looked unbeatable.' Whenever I see Anthony Gormley's rust-coloured sculpture *The Angel of the North* – bolt upright and with its phenomenal, ribbed wings embracing Gateshead – I think of it as sculpted in homage to Simpson. Or at least the way in which my father saw him.

Belief is always more interesting than disbelief. When I was originally told these tall tales, I was sufficiently impressionable to believe Charles could head in a goal from fabulously long distances and that Finney was capable of clinging to the ball indefinitely. Given the fact Simpson was so diminutive for a goalkeeper – only 5ft 9in tall – I also half-accepted that his reach must have been extraordinarily long. But I didn't believe Davies possessed a birdlike ability to fly. I did think his legs must be coiled springs instead of thigh and calf, bone and muscle. It seemed as if he knew something about aerial dynamics that no one else understood.

Often I'd take the book down from the shelf in my bedroom and look at the photograph again. I'd stare beyond Davies and into the densely packed terraces behind him – row upon row of featureless faces massed from the touchline and receding into the semi-blackness at the back of the stand. Had any of them been conscious of Davies' feat as he accomplished it? Or spoke of it afterwards? Or had it passed too fleetingly to be caught with the eye and register itself on the mind? At least the camera preserved the majesty of it; one shutter-click and Davies is there for ever – in his prime and suspended between Heaven and earth, as if his body is weightless.

I hadn't yet been to a live match; but the sight of Wyn Davies in that photograph made me long to go to one more than ever. I wanted to see him take off.

Throughout the late 1940s and 1950s my father went to St James' Park almost every Saturday when Newcastle United were at home. The distinct pattern of those days became habit forming. But going to the match was always about more than the match itself. My father enjoyed the camaraderie as much as the game and each stage of his preparation for it was conducted with the same solemnly rigid structure as a Japanese tea ceremony. Watches were synchronised and customs maintained.

There were the lunchtime pints and the tap-room debate about what he'd describe to me as 'the afternoon's prospects'. There was the slow walk to Strawberry Place, which skirted St James' Park and always sounded to me to be pastoral rather than urban. There was the crowd, though pure North East in attitude and tone, which moved through the streeets exactly like those in any Lowry landscape of the North West: dark figures in scarves with heads slightly bowed and shoulders stooped, hands in pockets and cigarettes bobbing from the corner of the mouth as conversation was exchanged. There was the push and shove in the raggedly lined queue for the turnstiles and the jeering of men impatient for the operators to work faster. There was the crack and creak of those turnstiles and the relief at the pushed effort of getting through them. There was the sprint to the top of the terraces for the best view, where everything – the pitch, the other three sides of the ground and the landscape of the city itself – was partly visible: the solid square blocks of factories and distant chimneys from which coal smoke spiralled and blackened the white sky, the fumes spreading across the horizon like a thumb-smudge. Long before the health and safety laws were laid down, there were those who would shin up the floodlights, clinging to its vertical girders or sitting on the horizontal supporters. There were the bluer fumes from freshly lit fags, the misty, competing plumes of Woodbines, Player's Navy Cut and Capstan Full Strength mingling together and then settling over the heads of the men in stratocumulus-like clouds; for nearly everyone puffed away in a grey haze and coughed dryly afterwards from their own and others' intrusive tobacco. They left behind the detritus of smoking too – ash crushed underfoot, spent matches and dead butts or those still faintly sparking. There was the noise – the constant drum and thrum of a mass of people and then the throaty roars, and the crescendo of oohs and aahs and boos in response to goals scored and narrow misses and referees who were chastised for being incompetent, biased or myopic. And, afterwards, there was another pint in a different pub as my father waited for *The Pink* to emerge, still wet on thin paper, from the *Evening Chronicle* presses. He bought it for League tables, the other scores and scorers and the kick-by-kick description of the match he had just watched. After reading, he'd fold the edition three times and slide it into one of the side pockets of his coat, the edges of its pages becoming quickly frayed. Whenever he reopened *The Pink*, the headline ink of one page left an outline of stray letters on the other facing it; and there was more ink on my father's hands too. He swore he could read the match report on his palm. He'd return home to wash and change – sharp suit, white shirt and tie – before an evening spent discussing the result again.

When I heard him speak about all this, I wanted to experience it too; especially so when he told me about the first match he'd ever seen – King's Park versus Bathgate in the first round of the Scottish Cup in 1930.

Bathgate were non-League; King's Park were competing for promotion into the First Division. Earlier in the month The Park crushed Forfar Athletic 12–2 and a debutant called Jim Dyet claimed eight of the goals. 'Dyet was suddenly the new hero,' said my father.

The *Dundee Courier and Advertiser* took such a charitable view of Forfar's defeat, which it complained was inflicted in 'ankle deep mud' and without a first choice defence, that the headline above its report suggests a sub-editor in denial.

FORFAR'S UNLUCKY DAY
But no Reason to be Downhearted

Dyet, though born in Ayrshire, was considered the local boy, then just 21 years old. The Park, which was owned by a coal merchant, had unexpectedly recruited him from my father's team, Cowie. My father saw him carry his kit in a string-drawn duffel bag. He was described as stocky and rugged-looking in a street-wise way, as if he'd know how to take care of himself in a brawl. Dyet had jet black hair without a parting and finely chiselled features, which gave him a Latin-like appearance not dissimilar to Rudolph Valentino's, according to my father. For those who saw his goals against Forfar, it was love at first sight. For those who didn't, it compelled them to head for Forthbank as soon as possible. My father begged his own father to take him. 'He only gave in because I nagged him every day for a week.'

King's Park beat Bathgate 6–2 at Forthbank. A torren-
tial downpour the previous day made the pitch sticky
in most places and a quagmire in others. The ball was
carried across it like a heavy load. It was common practice for the men to pass down the boys to the perimeter
wall and allow them an unobstructed view. The crowd
was over 3,000. My father recalled standing behind one
of the goals, where he was lifted by the torso over the
heads of the adults, one pair of hands replacing another
until he reached the front. He was close enough to hear
the dull thud as the Bathgate goalkeeper kicked his
boots against the base of the wooden post to loosen
mud from his studs and see him repeatedly spit into
his bare hands to clean them. At every corner, he could
hear the swearing and muttered oaths of the two rivals
as the ball was headed or hacked at and bobbed around
the box before The Park forced it into the net. Early on
Dyet scored – a tap-in which my father said he celebrated as though it was Scotland's goal of the century.
As he would frequently point out to me, the irony of
the match was that both King's Park and Bathgate soon
became extinct. Bathgate were gone before the Second
World War began because of financial difficulties and
ever-dwindling interest. King's Park's demise began
during it. The Luftwaffe dropped a Hermann bomb on
to the ground in the summer of 1940. The bomb turned
the Main Stand into a smouldering, skeletal wreck. The
roof was ripped away and the long benches beneath
were charred and broken. Some pivotal supporting

props remained, holding up nothing except fresh air. Splintered, torn-out sticks of wood stood desolately beside the crater which the explosion left. It looked deep enough to be classified as a valley. The ground eventually became a cigarette factory and King's Park were reborn as Stirling Albion; though my father always looked for 'The Park's' result, as if the old club still existed and the new one was an impostor masquerading in the same clothes.

I used my father's own tactics to persuade him to take me to my first game – Nottingham Forest against Leeds United – in late August 1968. I nagged him remorselessly. Though the season had barely hit its stride, Leeds were beginning to look unbeatable. Their first major trophy – the League Cup – had been claimed in a scrappily bad-tempered game against Arsenal at Wembley the previous March. At the beginning of August, the Hungarians Ferencvaros had been beaten in the opening leg of the Inter-Cities Fairs Cup final at Elland Road; and, 18 days after I saw them at Forest, Leeds would hold on grimly in the return. The following April the Championship would belong to them too – only two matches lost and a record 67 points gained. Billy Bremner was my equivalent of Jim Dyet. And, like my father, Bremner was from Stirling, a fact I used as emotional leverage. I pleaded to see him as much as he had once pleaded to see Dyet.

What drew me as a boy to Bremner was his pugnaciousness and his passionate heart. He was a clenched fist, incessantly battling bad loser. To tangle with him was like falling into a thorn bush. In the years to come I would realise that Johnny Giles, rather than Bremner, was the organising brain of the team. But then his robust energy seemed to me to be nuclear-driven and also inexhaustible, as if the secret of perpetual motion existed within him. I saw no minute in a game when Bremner relaxed or rested, or ceased to be anywhere but in the absolute thick of it. Even if his legs were momentarily still, his tongue continued to work at piston-speed. He was constantly directing, gesticulating as he did so as frenetically as a tic-tac bookmaker.

My father thought Leeds were a nasty lot, the Dark Star of the 1960s. 'You don't want to get interested in them,' he said, afraid my early infatuation – even the investment of a Leeds shoulder bag – would turn into unquestioning, life-long support, and already worried that Bremner and Hunter, Jones and Giles were posters on my wall. He argued his case long before allegations of bribery, tapping up and attempted match fixing were publicly attached to Don Revie. He came to dislike Revie because of the manager's neuroses and paranoia. Worry is always rust on the blade and Revie was a fretful and nervous boss – rigid, dossier-driven, superstitious about lucky suits and unlucky colours and always waiting for the worst to happen. Meticulous planning and attention to detail started off as his core strength. They then became his most noticeable weakness because he didn't know when to stop. He mistook windmills for giants.

Even the lowliest of opposition were treated as if the Real Madrid of Di Stefano and Puskas was turning up in disguise. The manager's fear of defeat inhibited Leeds, who regularly choked because of it – runners-up 11 times under Revie in four different competitions. 'I like it when Leeds lose,' my father said scornfully of them. He also thought that in bruising opponents Bremner bruised his own reputation and contributed to the view of Leeds as cynically dirty. 'Admiring Leeds is like admiring bullfighting,' he said. 'There's no virtue in it. The end is always bloody.'

As exhibit *A* he highlighted one of English football's most seminal images, far more famous than Wyn Davies soaring into space. It is of two Scots; one of them is Bremner. Dave Mackay, then at Tottenham, grips the scruff of his shirt at the neckline. It's as if he's about to lift Bremner up and then toss him over his broad shoulders like a Highland caber. With his right sleeve rolled to the elbow, revealing a powerful forearm, he has taken a long stride towards Bremner and is leaning into him. He locks him in a hostile, granite gaze – eyeball to eyeball. His teeth are clenched and bared and the strong jaw-line and chin are as prominent as Desperate Dan's on the front of *The Beano*. In self-defence Bremner sensibly opts for the pose of mock surrender. His body language and his expression are both passive. He is apologetic and pretends to be nonplussed by Mackay's rage. The arms are outstretched. The open palms are his plea of innocence. So is the puzzled, what-did-I-do?

look Bremner tries to pretend he's the victim of a misunderstanding to which he can offer a perfectly rational explanation. As a pugilist, Bremner was always willing to fight above his weight division. But he also hit below the belt. These were not minor or accidental breakages of the chivalric Queensberry rules. Some of his aggression was pernicious and premeditated. The pummelling foul on Mackay was committed after only three minutes of the match. Mackay reacted so volcanically to it because Bremner went for the leg which had only recently healed after being broken. Of course, the tackle could just have been a coincidence.

I didn't listen to my father's nay-saying about Leeds. The competitive, feisty Bremner was the player I went to watch at the City Ground. The game I saw could not have been more memorable; albeit for the wrong reasons.

As ever, my father put on his suit and tie for the occasion. We squeezed into the terracing below the weathered planks in the Main Stand. I can bring the sensation of it back whenever I read Arnold Bennett's novel *The Matador of the Five Towns*. The wonderful, jostling chaos, which Bennett recounted and based on his own experience, was published in 1912. It resonates still. I saw what he did: 'The men whose eyes were fixed, with an unconscious but intense effort, on a common object . . . the wide border of pale faces rising in tiers . . . the shriek of the whistle . . . the uneasy murmuring from the immense multitude . . . the great voices behind me bellowing with an incredible volume of sound . . . the vast field . . . the ball in the air.'

I was absorbed in the electrifying thrill of the moment and the rippled wave of the crowd beneath the roofed Trent End away to our left.

Wary and stubborn, I wouldn't let my father begin the chain that would pass me down for a worm's eye view of the pitch. I didn't want to leave him and, as a consequence, I saw no more than flashes of the match as it sped by me – the occasional glint of Bremner in Leeds' milk-white shirt and a glimpse of a mustard-coloured ball in spinning flight. It was like watching a scene through the slats of a wooden blind. At one stage my father precariously rested me on his left shoulder. I was suddenly more than 7ft tall and able to see the length and breadth of the pitch, still fresh and vividly green near the end of summer, and the masses surrounding me in red and white scarves. I could feel my father's hands against my thin ribs and trusted him not to drop me. For a few seconds only I spotted Bremner – easy to locate because of his carrot-coloured hair – as he played a pass from midfield to the far touchline and then sped forward into the Forest half. But the crowd swayed and my father was obliged to put me down for safety's sake. I stood again, clinging help-lessly to the hem of his brown jacket, and poked my head as best I could between the raised arms and bulging bellies of the cheering, jeering men clustered in front of me. I followed most of the game through sounds the

crowd made in response to it. At half time, still refusing
to move down the terraces because I was scared of being
parted from my father, we glumly decided to head home.
To stay would have been pointless. I didn't think –
because it never occurred to me – of the money my
father had spent on our tickets; money I know now he
could not afford. There were huge television trucks
parked nearby and my father said without rebuke on
the way out: 'Never mind. You can see the whole thing
tomorrow.'

We worked towards the exit and began to approach
the cark park in silence. I heard the tannoy blaring out
chart music. We'd gone beyond the back of the Main
Stand – and were looking down the architectural line
of it – when we first saw the smoke. It curled into the
air and bunched into black, oily-looking clouds. My
father picked me up. I thought he was going to put me
on his shoulder again for a better look. Instead, he began
to run, his arms looped beneath mine. I remember
looking down and seeing the pendulum swing of my
legs. The heels of my buckled sandals rapped against
his shins. We reached the gated entrance – a safe distance
from the smoke – and stopped beside its tall pillars. My
father was out of breath and relieved not to find a crowd
of agitated people behind us. He slowly lowered me on
to the pavement and we turned together to look at the
Main Stand. In less than a minute the smoke had
become much thicker. It had all but obscured the rear
centre section. The smoke began to billow and break

apart and gather above us, floating across the blue sky. It gave off a pungent scent. My father began to peer intently into it, waiting for the first, rapid burst of flame. But then he saw others had begun to follow us: shouting, pointing, waving us on and away. He swept me up and we headed for the main road. 'I thought there'd be a stampede,' he explained to me years later. 'I wanted to get us well away before it happened.' He'd been taught to act this way in the mines, where trouble underground meant a rush to the surface. The fire cracked brickwork, burnt wood and twisted girders and, according to the *Nottingham Evening Post*, turned Forest's 'cups and treasured trophies to molten metal' in the rooms below. The fire brigade used 400 gallons of water to douse it. 'A Soccer City's Saddest of Days', said the *Post* beside a front-page photograph of the gutted cinder box that the Main Stand became. The area where my father and I had stood was a ruin. *Goal* had previewed the match with a prophetic headline:

LEEDS READY TO SET FOREST ON FIRE

The real cause was more prosaic – a faulty heating system. The following week *Goal* published a flippant apology – 'Sorry,' it said, 'we'll try not to be so accurate in future' – alongside a picture of the Main Stand ablaze as those who'd occupied it huddled together on the pitch, watching the yellow-orange lick of the flames and some of them feeling the heat of the fire prickle their skin. Somehow there were no fatalities. Perverse though it sounds, I came to regret that my father and I had made our escape before we knew the fire had broken out. I looked regretfully at the magazine. If I'd been braver, and gone down to the white-washed wall before kick off, I would have had to climb over it as soon as the blaze began. I'd have found myself on the pitch beside the goal that only minutes earlier Bremner had been attacking.

On Sunday afternoon *Star Soccer* – with almost an hour to fill – replayed the whole of the first half before a voice explained why there was nothing else to screen. 'At this point Hugh Johns was forced to abandon his commentary position because of a fire,' its owner said sombrely and as if it was breaking news.

Often I think of that match and the playground bragging rights of 'I was there' which it brought me. More than a decade later, waiting for a flight out of those anonymous and austere airports behind the Iron Curtain, I unexpectedly relived it again in the small hours of a freezing morning. The previous night Forest had won another European Cup tie. Hugh Johns was sitting on a hard bench in a boxy room near the departure lounge. The Communists regarded it as the VIP section. Johns was directly below a circular ceiling light, so harsh that he seemed about to undergo interrogation. It gave his round face, striated with cracks, a weary appearance and accentuated the heavily lidded eyes and the pendulous folds of skin around the chin and neck.

He was wearing a camel coat and the toes of his black shoes tapped against large, stark-white floor tiles. His briefcase stood beside the bench.

Johns' commentary of the 1966 World Cup Final on the commercial channel was eclipsed by Kenneth Wolstenholme's 'They think it's all over' spontaneity for the BBC. 'Here's Hurst,' Johns shouted in simultaneous reaction to the same unforgettable moment, which is always replayed without his description to accompany it. 'He might make it three. He has! He has! So that's it.' It wasn't a dud response; but comparison made it sound flatly banal and disappointing. The rival phrase had wings. It came to define Wolstenholme, who was able to shape his subsequent career around a 14-word ad lib still so well known that no one has to allude to either source or occasion to understand what is being conveyed and why. Johns had the more mellifluous tone, and the solemn power of his voice was heard during a handful of other Cup Finals. Wolstenholme, however, had the one killer line and most of us can hear him saying it, which is why we remember him. Johns didn't and so is recalled dimly, if at all. He was the regular commentator on *Star Soccer*, the highlights programme of the Midlands, and his commentaries were the soundtrack of my Sundays. He broadcast from places, such as Filbert Street, Highfield Road and the Baseball Ground, which are now referred to poignantly as among The Lost Grounds. Johns was concise and authoritative. He didn't, as so many contemporary commentators do, feel the need to fill every crowded minute. His silences allowed the viewer to carry on his or her own internal monologue about the match without constant inter-ruption. Nor did he give the egotistical impression that what he thought about a game counted more than the game itself. It is a compliment to describe him as an old-fashioned commentator.

Our charter plane home had been delayed. I went to sit near Johns and we began talking about the match we'd just seen. When the conversation ran out, I told him we had one thing in common: the Forest fire. Johns' features contracted, making the age-lines harder, straighter, deeper. 'Those were the early days of *Star Soccer*,' he said, leaning forward and turning his head cautiously towards me, as if he'd prefer to discuss anything else. 'If circumstances had been different I might not have seen any more matches.' Johns clasped his chubby hands together, as though he was about to fall to his knees and give thanks for his salvation. 'It's a long way down from that gantry,' he said. He began to add something to the statement before hesitating and leaving it unfinished. He spoke instead about the orderly way in which the crowd dispersed from the Main Stand and on to the pitch. 'There was no alarm,' he said, 'and no crush. Everything was done without hysteria.' I had naïve supplementary questions – how frightened had he been, for instance, and had he feared death? – but I had no chance to ask them. The flight was called. Johns collected his briefcase and made his excuses. Only years later did I comprehend the terror he must have experienced; a terror which he either couldn't or didn't want to mention to me. I reread the postscript he gave to *Goal*. There was just one route to and from the gantry – an ordinary looking 40-odd-rung ladder which he and his cameraman used. 'If the crowd had charged out of the grandstand and knocked the ladder away we would have been stranded up there,' said Johns.

I reported back to my father. I told him I'd spoken to Hugh Johns about the fire and I mentioned his reticence about elaborating on it. Perhaps, I said, he still had occasional nightmares about what happened. 'I used to have one of those and it was always the same,' my father replied. 'You've been passed to the front and I can't find you in the crowd.' Like Johns, my father abruptly stopped, aware he had said enough, and so the conclusion to this bad dream always remained unknown, like the last page of a book torn out, its ending lost and unrecoverable.

In the final week of the 1960s, my father took me to St James' Park for the first time. We followed the route he'd always taken, swopping Iron-Bru and Tizer for the alcohol he usually drank. He sacrificed an afternoon in the Gallowgate End for one in the West Stand. Its redeeming feature was the corrugated outer façade. It was painted battleship grey with the words NEWCASTLE UNITED grandly stencilled across it in white, 50-foot-high capital letters. This time I went uncomplainingly to the perimeter wall and stood without him. Behind me, the men who usually smoked cigarettes from packets puffed on miniature cigars from shiny tins, which had been given to them as Christmas presents. They wore new sweaters or scarves and drank spirits from fake silver hip flasks.

Newcastle were coincidentally playing Leeds and I soon found Billy Bremner lying in front of me in the mud. His socks, knees and the side of his face were caked in it. It even clogged and stiffened strands of his hair. He looked as though he had been buried alive and then dug up again. His limbs were awkwardly splayed, and he gave a groaning cough before his mouth opened and closed around a rebuke to the tackler which I could not hear. Bremner boiled at a particularly low temperature and was eventually booked in search of retribution. Another round of invective followed. It was a pointless protest, which ended when he wiped a splattering of mud from his shirt and bad-temperedly hurled it on to the floor, like a child throwing away a toy which had displeased him. Newcastle won 2–1 and Wyn Davies claimed the first goal. He did not fly to score it. Near the end of the first half Davies came over to the touch-line to take a quick throw in and I looked at his legs to judge whether the muscles were dramatically pronounced. His calves were solid and well curved. The other muscles didn't seem anatomically different from anyone else's on the pitch. But, near the end, I did see him climb to an extraordinary height at the far post, his header scraping against the side-netting. It was the year of the Apollo moon landing and the technical jargon of the space race was common parlance. I saw Davies and thought of booster rockets and vertical thrust. He did more than out-jump Jack Charlton. The man Newcastle called 'The Leap' or 'The Mighty Wyn' made Charlton – like any other defender he took on in aerial combat – look Lilliputian. Davies doesn't know how he managed to propel himself effortlessly upwards in this way. 'It was just something I could do,' he says, the secret as much of a conundrum to him as it was to those who faced him. Even as a schoolboy, his proficiency was obvious. A coach suspended a ball from a high ceiling and he reached it 'easily'. The scale of Davies' ability was measured by Malcolm Allison, who tested him from stationary start and saw he could attain, without much stretching effort, the awesome height demonstrated in the photograph. 'I was blessed,' says Davies, now 70 years old.

That photograph still beguiles and animates me. I only have to see it to be transported back to the 60s. To the old terraces. To scarred pitches. To the World Cup. And to the sight of Davies as I first saw him, able to rise as if wings in his boots allowed him to hang motionless in the air. 'Whenever I show anyone the photograph I'm always asked: "How did you do it? How did you get so high?" They're in awe of it,' says Davies. I would go further. In an unarguable sentence, the writer Roland Barthes once defined the spontaneity of photography as repeating 'to infinity [what] has occurred only once'. I know what Barthes means because the photograph of Davies has a life beyond the moment it records. But Barthes, who studied and wrote essays on the art of photography, also asked: 'Is one not in love with certain photographs?'

I am. I am in love with this one.

The 1960s only look glamorous to me now through football. Nearly everything else about it seems in retrospect excessively hyped. Principally those years shone because the decade preceding it was class conformist and coated in imperial pomp. Its elders were wary of Bill Haley and Elvis, crepe-shoed Teddy Boys and teenage rebellion. And the one after it was fractious, as if society was irreparably splintering in 1970s angst and perpetual industrial unrest. There were more angry young men – and middle-aged men too – than ever before. But much of what was sandwiched in between, the 60s pop art culture and razzle-dazzle, was specious, superficial or overstated. People like my parents only read about, or saw on a black and white TV screen, the minuscule geographical area in which it was played out and the coterie of celebrities at its centre. Hedonism's worst excesses gate-crashed the home only when the *News of the World* juicily reported on them. In 1966 *Time* declared London 'the *fin de siècle* city of the world'. The magazine believed the capital defined the 60s in the same way Paris defined the jazz age of the 1920s. It was 'switched on' and 'pulsing with half a dozen separate veins of excitement', it said, breathlessly. But in the places I knew best – Newcastle and Nottingham – the carnival parade of the 60s passed through without stopping for long. There were certainly new clothes hung on pegs in High Street shops and new clubs and bars to listen to the music. But poverty in Newcastle was so conspicuous that, after filming *Get Carter* in and around it, Michael Caine admitted: 'I've always gone on about the working-class image I've got . . . now I've been to Newcastle I realise I'm middle-class.' Nottingham was a landscape of dingy terraces, its streets certainly neither fab nor particularly groovy. The colour-scheme was muted, beige or grey, rather than psychedelic.

Ken Loach's *The Golden Vision,* a film intercutting fact and fiction to convey the nature of football fanaticism, is a window on the sort of 1960s which my father experienced. Its 75 minutes combine Loach's fly-on-the-wall documentary about Everton, then managed by Harry Catterick, and a fictional hardcore Evertonian family, whose working men subordinate everything to Saturday afternoon and whose women tolerate it under sufferance. 'It's football, football, football,' moans one of the wives with a stare of bitter contempt. With justification, she is angry and jealous at the intrusions it makes on her life. A husband disappears to watch Everton at Highbury on the day his wife is due to give birth. A best man abandons the nuptials as soon as the ceremony's final words are spoken and heads for

Goodison Park in his wedding suit, the carnation still in his buttonhole. An ailing old stager with a faraway expression is warmed by memories. Without them, what would he own? 'I can't remember much about yesterday,' he says, 'but I'll never forget the 1906 FA Cup Final.' To these men football is responsible for motivating and sustaining them, perhaps atavistically, in the factory. It is the purpose of living. In these Liverpudlians I see bits of my father.

There is no Mersey beat in *The Golden Vision*, and no sign either that it exists, let alone flourished; not even on the juke box. Like the barber's customers in Penny Lane, the Beatles have already come and gone, decamping to Abbey Road. Beneath those blue suburban skies scruffy youngsters kick a ball across waste ground that still looks war-ravaged. The houses around them await demolition.

What was considered affluent and trendy then also looks ridiculously Spartan in hindsight. Try making a case for the social revolution when the things representing it include prawn cocktail starters, the transistor radio, audio tapes and Tupperware in the kitchen. But football did give off a white heat, and Loach's film transmits it. Its title comes from the sobriquet Evertonians gave to Alex Young, and clips of it prove the claim authentic. Young doesn't run; he glides, gorgeously. He is slender and so blond his hair looks bleached. He sways one way and then the next like a sheaf of corn bowed by a gentle wind; a Golden Vision undeniably.

'Most of the players were just like us – working folk at heart,' my father used to tell me. Loach supports the assertion. He catches Ray Wilson sitting on a train with a cigarette burning between the first two fingers of his right hand. He shows Catterick wearing a tweed jacket, which makes him look like a country solicitor in a dowdy practice. The private view of Young constantly reminds you of how differently the footballers of that era thought and lived and also the precariousness of choosing football for a living. At one point Young, past 30 and knowing retirement isn't far off, admits: 'I don't know any professional footballer who feels absolutely secure . . . we all feel very insecure.' At another he confesses that football is 'a hard grind' before adding: 'After a few years, when you weigh it up, you think, well, maybe there's something better you can do.' Young is seen at home, which is on a typical 60s estate of three up and two down houses made of fresh orange brick. He lives beside some of the people who watch him. He drives a two-door Austin Farina that has seen better days and he is anything but a dedicated follower of fashion; his clothes come off the peg from the High Street.

The Golden Vision was screened in 1968, the year that Bobby Charlton earned more from playing than he'd done before or would do again. It was £15,000. Qualifying as a handsomely paid footballer meant earning £100 per week. That was considerably more than anyone who wore overalls, but not enough to bring home the bling

– and nowhere near enough to guarantee financial independence at the end of a career. Photographed with their wives for *The Football League Review*, the players neither appeared particularly affluent nor much different from their white-collar neighbours. Their living rooms had Constable prints on the walls, ships in bottles on the mantelpiece, a vase of flowers placed on a doily on top of the television. Net curtains hung at the window. The life-style was unflashy but the football was vibrant, and the centre-piece was England's World Cup win over West Germany.

Is it possible to write any more words about that game? Repetition dulls. That '66 final is replayed so often that we look at it without interpretation. The scenes – and the order of them – are familiar, stripping them of uniqueness. We see only what we have seen before; and though we retain the meaning we lose the context, which is like having latitude without longitude. But on that late-July afternoon of sun and showers football finally reached beyond its natural constituency. Patriotism was the obvious reason. The less obvious one was the way the competing forces of the 60s – the pull back towards the past versus the counter-pull towards the future – both got something out of it. The achievement was favourably, if egregiously, compared to former glories: VE Day, Dunkirk and even the siege of Mafeking. But it was also used as proof of the hope of what seemed possible if change continued. The journalist Bernard Levin unjustly called the small, winged trophy 'one of the most hideous artefacts Western Man has ever produced in his long history of bad taste'. He added cynically that in the 'dry-mouthed hour before the dawn, many must have realised that nothing had changed, that nothing was better for England because the World Cup had been won'. He missed the point. Something had changed. As it progressed the World Cup became a TV event. Less than an hour before England's opening Monday-night match, against Uruguay, it was possible to walk up to Wembley and buy a ticket for it. Less than three weeks later football was in vogue even among those who had previously paid it no attention. The World Cup converted unbelievers. Even highbrow commentators such as Levin were obliged to write about its cultural impact.

In recalling it to me, my father said that he came across people incapable of 'telling the difference between Jack and Bobby Charlton' who were suddenly debating tactics. Apart from what he described as 'the bloody obvious' – the very fact England were triumphant – he believed it was because of the appealing figure of Bobby Moore. The *Guardian*'s David Lacey wrote perceptively that Moore 'managed to embody the spirit of an age without abandoning the values of its predecessor'. He added: 'The footballer was a child of the fifties and he never lost the simple dignity with which the best players of that era are endowed.' In a much more basic way, this is the theory my father explained to me. 'He was the son every parent wanted,' he said. 'He had all the glamour and none of the big-headedness. When you heard him speak, he didn't alienate anyone – not the old, the middle-aged, the young.' Moore was recognisably a leader; and he also fitted the zeitgeist of that blossoming, very different age – confident and dashing in appearance. In my youthful eyes Moore was the only figure who held the attention as much as George Best, whose crazy superstardom saw women felled with emotion simply at the sight of him.

At the beginning of the 1966–67 season *Match of the Day* promised to explain the game's technicalities to the new and novice audience attracted to it. To continue the World Cup theme, the first game it chose was West Ham against Chelsea. Moore walks on to the sunlit pitch as if there's a ribbon of red carpet beneath his feet. Probably there should have been. He ran and tackled without ever looking dishevelled and left the field the way he'd gone on to it: virtually unblemished and with barely a crease or muddy mark on his shirt. If Wyn Davies could fly, then I was willing to believe Moore was born with extrasensory perception or could stop or slow Time without the rest of us realising it. Even the explanation that Moore saw the game unfold in front of him with a near-scientific exactitude seemed inadequate in accounting for his anticipation and positioning, both of which seemed spookily other-worldly. I thought Moore could read minds. It was as if he knew where the ball was going before the player in possession knew it himself. This way of seeing detail is the rarest of abilities. It enabled Moore to visualise and measure the shape an attack was about to take. His legs lacked pace. His brain, however, computed things at warp speed and mapped the pitch like a grid. Effortlessly Moore moved from one square to the next, clearing up trouble which his meticulous observation picked out well before it had registered with anyone else. Whatever he did was finessed and gracefully languorous. Done as it was in such a nonchalant and unhurried manner, Moore seemed to have been inoculated against feelings of strain or pressure; partly because his footballing precognition gave him a calm space in which to work. Nothing fazed him. If an earthquake had burst the grassy earth in front of him, I'm sure Moore wouldn't have blinked. He'd have strolled along the seam of the split and simply passed the ball on. He made good players – and great ones – look only minimally gifted in his company.

Evocations of Moore almost always begin with his tackle on Jairzinho in the 1970 World Cup. The Brazilian's breakaway run in the broiling heat takes him at full, powerful pelt from the half way line to three feet inside England's area. Moore tracks Jairzinho the way the hunter tracks the gazelle. He holds him in his sights for nearly 40 yards. He knows he has only one shot to stop him. The challenge Moore makes – off the 'wrong' right foot as Jairzinho tries to cut around him – is a triumph of patience and timing and nerve. But for me the quintessential Moore is found in another piece of defending four minutes from the end of normal time during the

'66 Final. England, clinging on at 2–1, flock to defend a Franz Beckenbauer corner, which is so skewed it skims well wide of the six-yard box. Moore is running parallel with Wolfgang Weber and beats him to the ball by half a stride. Shaking Weber off, he shields it inside the angle of the area. The foremost thought in the mind of most defenders – especially in the circumstances – would be row Z. Whether the ball was thumped or shanked there would be immaterial; it would just be got rid of. Moore, however, turns back towards his own goal-line, Weber lurking on his heels. Moore is unconcerned, as if he's on Chadwell Heath, West Ham's training ground. There's even a minor, almost Best-like body swerve as he dummies to go to his left and then turns in a counter-clockwise movement which outwits and wrong-foots Weber and makes him look hopelessly slow. Closer still to the line, he checks again. Another subtle twitch of the shoulders confuses Weber further. Moore is hemmed tight against the line and less than ten feet from the corner flag. But, as Weber lunges towards him, he casually flicks a short pass to Martin Peters with the outside of his boot. Weber turns, utterly defeated, and makes a dismayed, capitulatory gesture; Moore unflappably jogs back into position as England counter-attack. The moment – which goes unreported – involves only nine touches of the ball. All his class and patrician ways are distilled in it nonetheless. We know what happens next: Weber's revenge at the last gasp and England's recovery from it during the extra half hour. The story of the final is Geoff Hurst's hat-trick. But one of the sub-plots is Moore's creation of two of the goals with perfect placement and flight.

Sometimes the iron in Moore was also overlooked because he usually applied no more force than was necessary and seemed to rob attackers courteously, like a polite bandit. He didn't scramble either, as if to do so would be undignified or unsightly. I once saw him slip, arms flailing, on the wet turf of St James' Park. Momentarily he looked like an abandoned puppet. As his left leg slid away from him, he stuck out his hand to break the fall and managed to hook his right foot around the ball to retain it as he did so. He was instantly upright and perfectly composed before passing. That pass left Moore's boot as if his foot and ankle were the spring-release that sends the silver pinball on its way. Only a defender such as Moore could have turned an ugly error into an act of grace. Standing on Newcastle's Gallowgate End, I heard the voice beside me. 'That was bloody genius,' said my father above the sound of hands clapping. He had taken me to the match purely so we could watch Moore together. At one point, recognising the futility of trying to out-jump Wyn Davies, he telegraphed in advance where his skimming header was sure to land and blocked it on his thigh before cracking a 40-yard pass to the right wing. 'I bet he knows where Davies will be a week next Wednesday,' said my father as we left St James' still admiring Moore's anticipation.

I once asked Bobby Moore whether, rather than hindering him, his lack of speed had actually sharpened his senses as a matter of survival. 'The advantage of not having pace was not losing it as I got older,' he replied, good-naturedly. Moore was already dreadfully ill with cancer – the face gaunt, the pallor of the skin worryingly white, like fresh chalk. Less than six months later he died, aged 51.

But I don't have to believe it if I don't want to . . .

6

The Boy from Beatrice Street

The game was 72 minutes old, and the white number 12 on the scarlet shirt in front of me stood out to the extent that it seemed to have been artificially lit. Its wearer jogged lightly on the spot near the half way flag. Waiting for the ball to go out of play, and the referee to beckon him on, he began to stretch out his arms, the way a swimmer does before diving into a pool.

He responded to the chanting of his name with a raised left hand and a modest, snappish nod of acknowledgement, as if – half-embarrassed by the spontaneous rush of attention and flattery – he wanted the moment to pass quickly. He made a semi-turn and I caught him in profile – the roundness of the chin and the steep line of the nose, the high curve and bald, shiny dome of his head. The wind caught the long thin strands of his hair, combed over from just above the left ear, and I watched him make a token attempt to push them back into place before accepting the pointlessness of the gesture. He was dapper-looking. His shirt was tucked tightly into his shorts. The top of his socks were immaculately turned, the roll of red, black and white bands perfectly matching in height. Even though it was only October, and each club's League matches for the season scarcely totalled double figures, the touchline at St James' Park was already worn. Skinny patches of smooth mud ran parallel with the lines. The turf was soft too, and his boots left the imprint of each small stud in the dark soil. I remember he stood close to me for what seemed well over a minute, flexing his muscles and kicking his heels, before his chance came.

He sprinted on to the pitch, as if late for an appointment, and the noise which marked the simple act was loud enough to have shaken every window-frame in Gallowgate. Someone leaning over the perimeter wall waved a wooden rattle – an object rare even then and shortly to become extinct along with silk rosettes. The clack-clack sound of the rattle, like an early Victorian textile machine, still echoed after the original burst of shouting for him had stopped. He went on to the opposite wing from me and almost immediately made one of his trademark runs – arms slightly crooked at the elbow, cheeks puffed out and his left shoulder tilting to the left. He swept speedily past one man, going around him in a wide arc, and then played a one–two. As the pass was returned to him, he shaped to drive it first time. The entire crowd craned forward in anticipation, waiting to track the line of the ball from his boot towards the top corner. For once, he misfired. He got under the shot rather than on top of it. The ball sliced off his left foot, drifting away from the goal like a child's let-go balloon. Had it been anyone else, the mistake would have been an excuse for jeering and mockery. But for him there was only more applause – sincere in the sympathy and encouragement it offered.

For this was Bobby Charlton.

Earlier that month, in the autumn of 1972, Charlton had turned 35. Some thought he would imitate Stanley Matthews and carry on playing until he was nearer 50 than 40. Manchester United would never force him to go and, compared to Matthews, who claimed he quit 'too early' – aged 50 years and five days – Charlton was almost a whippersnapper. But my father was certain that Charlton – even if he hadn't accepted it himself – was saying his farewells one ground at a time that season. He'd been given a testimonial, against Celtic, at Old Trafford. And he wasn't able to clear tackles as effortlessly as he'd once done or consistently make those decisively surging runs which had been a feature of the 1960s. The blazing shots were rarer too. The game was getting quicker; Charlton was getting slower. He wasn't guaranteed to start a match any longer. Even if he did, he might not finish it. My father felt Charlton would take stock and come to the conclusion that nothing in his extraordinary career should become him like his leaving of it. He based his theory on Charlton's character. 'He's a proud man,' he said to me. 'He won't want to let himself down by hanging around half a season too long. And he won't want to be remembered as someone who gets a place in the team simply because of who he used to be.' Unequivocally certain that Charlton wouldn't be back at St James' Park again, my father saw this game as his farewell to the Tyne. 'If we miss it,' he'd said, 'we won't catch him again. I want to be able to say I saw the last ball he ever kicked in Newcastle. I want you to be able to say you saw it too.'

This need stemmed from the fact that only Jackie Milburn ranked higher in his affections than Charlton. He believed that Milburn and Charlton shared more than the bloodline and kinship of being second cousins, each born and bred among the headstocks, the coal, the allotments and pigeon lofts of Ashington. As my father saw it, Charlton *was* Milburn – raised in his image and identical in almost every aspect because of it. He was dignified and unshowy, scrupulously dedicated and loyally decent. Just as Milburn had carried an air of noble intention about him, so did Charlton. Just as Milburn had been a staunch one-club man, so was Charlton. And just as Milburn had been the model professional, so Charlton had inherited and carried the mantle. The unfortunate circumstance of not being born had denied me any sight of Milburn as a player. Taking me to watch Charlton, my father said, was partly compensation for it. I know he'd have paid to see him take the field alone that afternoon and practise pot shots at an empty net.

On our way to St James' Park, he spoke of no one but Charlton. There was the young Charlton – slimmer and blonder, the features of his face much sharper, as he released drives of such enormous power or guilefully splayed an intelligent pass. There was the Charlton of the 1966 World Cup – that right-foot shot against Mexico, the pale yellow ball moving fast enough through the summer air to rock the goal. There was the Charlton of the European Cup Final against Benfica – the grazed, flicked header off his glistening pate and the way he heaved the bulbous trophy aloft on his shoulder afterwards, revealing the butterfly-shaped sweat stains on his Cyanine blue shirt.

My father believed he could date and time the decline in English football. The seminal shift had occurred on 14 June 1970 in the 69th minute of the World Cup quarter-final against West Germany. England, 2–0 ahead and looking impregnable, had just leaked a goal to Franz Beckenbauer. In the heat of that Leonian sun, as furnace-hot as Hell's breath, Sir Alf Ramsey miscalculated, hauling Charlton off to save him for a semi-final which England never reached as a consequence of that decision. Unshackled from his gaoler, Beckenbauer revelled in the freedom, and England lost raggedly, moving too slowly in the heat. 'The saddest score in English football because it was so avoidable,' my father said. Sadder still was that Charlton didn't kick a ball for England after it.

As he walked towards the bench, clots of hair plastered solidly to his skull, Ramsey waited solicitously for him. Charlton's head was slightly bowed and he pursed his lips, as if there was something meaningful he wanted to say to his manager, but decorum prevented him from speaking it. 'Coasting with him and beaten without him,' my father explained far later, seeing in it the beginning of the long malaise that followed: a failure to qualify for the 1974 and 1978 World Cups, Ramsey's ignominious removal and Don Revie's disastrous tenure. 'Charlton would have won that match if Ramsey had let well alone,' he added.

My father's chief regret was that Charlton had revealed none of his skills in Newcastle's black and white. 'You can't blame him for picking Manchester United,' he said, unaware then that Milburn had altruistically nudged him towards Old Trafford because of the haphazardness of Newcastle's own youth policy in the 1950s. Whenever Charlton came to St James', it always reminded my father of what Newcastle had missed. He saw as many of those games as he could and went to each of them with a sense of expectation that seldom went unfulfilled. 'I don't think he's ever disappointed me,' he said. 'There's always a shot or pass that I think no one else could have done.'

I'll always remember the prediction he made to me as we went our separate ways before kick off – my father towards the Gallowgate End with his friends and me towards the main stand to meet mine. The lengthening queues sloped away from the turnstiles, the programme sellers moving along them with money-pouches bulging with coins. 'He'll do something you'll remember,' my father shouted above the din. 'He'll make you glad you came.'

I didn't properly appreciate Bobby Charlton until the clock was running down on his career. Until a few minutes before the European Cup Final, I didn't even realise he was a Geordie. Of all the players, my father told me to watch him in particular because of our shared roots. To someone as young as I was then, Charlton seemed to belong to a much earlier era. I thought he and Jackie Milburn had been playing contemporaries. It was difficult for me to believe that Charlton had once been Matt Busby's 'new Babe', which is the way one newspaper headline described him in black block capitals after an impressive, two-goal debut for Manchester United at Old Trafford in 1956 – an afternoon when Charlton the player upstaged Charlton Athletic the team. My crass notions about him stemmed entirely from his appearance. His lack of hair made him look as old as my father, who already seemed antique to me.

It was said of George Best that his play mirrored his personality – carefree, insouciant and risky. If character did equal expression, I was certain it applied to Charlton too – safe, deadly serious and slightly staid in his work; until, of course, he released one of those firecracker shots, which I mistakenly thought counted as his only virtue. My father made sure I saw everyone he thought mattered: The World Cup winners in their club colours, plus Jimmy Greaves and Denis Law, so cheekily alive; and others – such as Colin Bell and Mike Summerbee, Howard Kendall, Ian St John and Eddie Gray – who were compelling enough that I willed them to get the ball. His preference was always for those he rated as artists rather than artisans. My father argued that he didn't hand over his colliery wages to see Ron Harris or Peter Storey 'crush some poor beggar into the cinder track'. To the point of tedium, he also kept telling me that Charlton – not Best – was the premier player. To hear him talk, you'd think Charlton had never played badly. By then, my fascination for Best was limitless and all-consuming to the extent that Charlton barely registered with me. Best played on a whim, improvising as he went along. Charlton looked to be in a planned, settled groove. Apart from his shooting, there didn't appear to be anything dazzling or impulsive about his approach. At the time I no more understood the magnificent range of Charlton's abilities than I could fathom the abstractness of Picasso. Blinded by Best, I failed to see Charlton in his own right; probably because he didn't have the rebellious zest of Best or his casual, cocky assurance. He lacked his handsomeness and glamour. Best was the epitome of the youth movement, and prone to its mistakes and fixations. But he seemed more relevant to me and to modernism. I could never imagine Charlton dressed in the clothes Best wore: the llama coats, flowery or swirly patterned shirts in primary colours or the plush velveteen jackets and fashionable turtle neck sweaters. Charlton was a suit, tie and sensible shoes sort of man. Even in interviews Best was the more articulate and engaging. Ever the diplomat, Charlton came across as diffident and sometimes a little awkward on television. Conscious of his position and responsibilities, he chose words with elaborate care, as if afraid the wrong one would wound. Now I know the generational gap between Charlton and Best was too wide ever to be satisfactorily bridged. As personalities they were polar opposites. As people they represented things which were wholly different – pre- and post-war, the sedateness of the 1950s and the whirligig of the 1960s, the cigarette card and the glossy wall poster. Charlton was married with young children. Best was single and bed-hopped. To expect Charlton to be more like Best was as fatuous as expecting Bing Crosby to be more like Mick Jagger.

Arthur Hopcraft wrote of him: 'The flowing line of Charlton's football has no disfiguring barbs in it . . . It is the combination of the graceful and the dramatic which makes him so special . . . He is never clumsy or desperate in movement; he can rise very close to the athletic ideal.' Eventually I saw it as well, and knew Hopcraft was also right when he described a typical Charlton shot as 'one of the great events of the sport'. Charlton scored as easily from 30 yards as Greaves tapped in from two. A season or two before his retirement I remember the BBC marking one of the numerous records Charlton had broken. The compilation of clips was dominated by his sensational shooting. Asked why he didn't *look* as fast retrospectively, whenever film of his bowling was re-run on screen, the England pace bowler Fred Trueman used to complain gruffly: 'You always looked slower in black and white.' Not so in Charlton's case. In every reel the ball zoomed in.

In one international – against Northern Ireland – Charlton kills a pass and then dispatches it below the angle of post and bar from the edge of the area. The suddenness of the accomplishment stuns the muddy defenders in front of him. Their eyes search hopefully for the ball, almost refusing to believe that it is already in the net. In an FA Cup tie at Coventry City, Charlton takes a throw-in and controls the return. He sets off on an angled run across the box, glances up and whips the ball into the top corner with the nonchalance of someone used to doing this sort of thing routinely. He achieves it on a pitch – sticky, clinging and rutted – that looks as though a farmer has ploughed it in preparation to plant a potato crop. Against Spurs at White Hart Lane, Charlton is better still. The film is hazy, but you can gauge the immense speed of the final shot nonetheless. Charlton begins the move mid-way in his own half and joins it again ten yards into the opposition's. He imperiously flicks the ball knee high and takes five short touches to get himself into range. Spurs allow him space, which is the equivalent of writing a suicide note. Charlton feints to go one way, and then goes the other.

If the netting hadn't held the shot – arrowed into it from 35 yards – you can bet someone behind the goal would have been decapitated. This was a more reserved era and Charlton reveals almost no emotion afterwards. He doesn't – as the modern player does – dive on to the grass with his arms and legs outstretched. He doesn't flamboyantly kiss the badge on his shirt. He doesn't slide on his knees and punch the air. Or dance around the corner flag. Or bang his fist on his jutted-out chest. He simply turns and walks back to the centre circle with his head lowered, as if he's done nothing more than what was expected of him and is impatient to move on. United were being well beaten that day, and Charlton saw nothing to celebrate.

What became my favourite Charlton moment – at Anfield – wasn't shown for good reason. It had yet to occur. Best is weaving his way towards the Kop when he either sees or senses the white-shirted Charlton wide to his left. Charlton meets the lofted pass Best flawlessly delivers to him. The finish is quintessential Charlton. Liverpool's defenders are on the half turn, still watching the loop and spin of Best's delivery, as the goal is scored. What impresses me most is the tremendous force of Charlton's diagonal shot. But, curiously, the ball appears to me to glide inside the far post, as if only the merest pressure has been applied to it. Its pure, smooth power stems from Charlton's sublime timing. The strike is clean and economical; there isn't even much of a back-lift. He was able to do this with either foot, so no one could pick which was naturally the stronger before constant practice made the other its equal.

This shooting was barely the half of it. Though never fabulously creative – as Best proved to be – Charlton seldom misplaced a pass. He had an awareness of where everyone was on the pitch and where he ought to go himself. He also had a noticeable gear-shift. This change of pace was used in devastating tandem with a body swerve on the run, which made defenders look darned fools. Charlton could do it because of balance and co-ordination. The minor blemish was his heading, which was coincidentally almost as weak as Milburn's. But he made up for it in other ways. Like everyone else, he was thuggishly hacked and shoved and occasionally left flat on his back or face after pedestrian defenders purposefully went after him. It was simpler to cut Charlton down with a trailing leg than dispossess him. Charlton accepted it as an occupational hazard. But, since players then didn't peel off their shirts as part of exuberant goal celebrations, I had no idea that he'd developed a body-builder's physique to withstand the punishments he took. In kit, he looked almost weedy to me. Only as Charlton swopped shirts at the end of a game did I become aware of how he'd survived the batterings regularly meted out to him. The shoulders, the upper traps, the pectorals, triceps and biceps and abdomen were prominent and taut. Cotton hid solid muscle beneath it. The man I originally didn't consider an athlete at all was actually a superb one, and also self-made. I should have realised it without the need for the pictorial evidence. For no one could have withstood what Charlton did without rigorous physical conditioning. He scored so many goals because he played so many matches; and he was able to do that because he took care of his body.

When the reality of his talent dawned on me so belatedly, I put together the first of several Bobby Charlton scrapbooks. Most of the photographs, which I saved from smudgy newsprint or the back copies of *Goal* and *Shoot*, caught Charlton on the point of shooting or a nanosecond after the ball has left his boot. His hair flops over his face. The veins and muscles in his neck and thigh bulge prominently at the point of impact. The position of his arms looks as though he is about to cartwheel across the pitch. On several occasions Charlton is two inches above the grass as the thrust of his own momentum carries him upwards. What appeared poetic from a distance seems anatomically stressful close-up, as if every sinew is being pulled to its limit and every blood vessel is fully pumped. Sometimes Charlton was criticised for lifting his head too soon. But the camera more often than not reveals technical perfection. The Football Association's coaching manuals could use most of these images to demonstrate the fundamentals of good shooting. One classic photograph of Charlton, taken in April 1965 at Blackburn's Ewood Park, demonstrates the wasp-sting of his shots. The viewer peers through the sagging, bowed squares of the net and registers the brown ball first because it is captured against the skeletal trunk of a floodlight pylon. The goalkeeper's left hand – the fingers parted – is stretched to within touching distance of the ball. He's looking at the shot, but already aware that the dive he's making in an effort to stop it is pointless. Charlton is on the fringe of the box, standing in an ankle-high billow of dust created from the shot he's just fired. The dust reminds me of gun-smoke. Whoever looks at it can't fail to imagine the frame which must have followed – the shot slapping against the net, the goalkeeper prone and beaten on the turf, Charlton turning to face a crowd rising to salute him. The photograph is so evocative that I can *hear* the throaty roar of that crowd and the thud of the ball on Charlton's boot and the rasping sound it makes against the nylon netting.

The footballs Charlton hit in the 60s and early 70s were appreciably lighter than those used in the 50s when the inflatable bladder counted as cutting-edge technology. But, compared to today's innovative moulds, panels and groove-textured thermoplastic polyurethanes, what Charlton kicked was still weightier than two copies of *Whittaker's Almanac*. The damage he could have done with the World Cup's Jubulani or the Champions League's Finale Capitano would have frightened goalkeepers half to death. Those Charlton beat in his prime only had to worry about the speed he generated; he was essentially a straight-shooter. But, if Ryan Giggs or Paul Scholes set him up now, the swerve and banana bend he'd get without trying from improved aerodynamics would make most of his shots unreadable and unreachable. Given his devotion to practice, he'd have taught himself to control and exploit the vagaries and lightness of the modern ball.

'He's some player,' my father once said to me 'you just don't appreciate him.' Finally, I had to agree he was right.

Early on I was taken to the two spots in Northumberland which my father regarded as historically most important. The first was Jarrow, from where 200 impoverished workers foot-slogged 300 miles to London to protest against the town's extreme poverty, mass unemployment and industrial depression in 1936. The Jarrow shipyard was redundant and rusting in a filthy, dirty, falling down and consumptive area. The out-of-work in the 30s were as T. S. Eliot contemporaneously described them in Choruses from 'The Rock' – shuffling, bored and destitute on street corners, and living in cold, dark rooms because heat and light were luxuries to them. Eliot gave them a voice, and this is what it said:

> *Our life is unwelcome, our death*
> *Unmentioned in 'The Times'.*

The Conservative Prime Minister, Stanley Baldwin, refused to see or speak to the Jarrow marchers, originally claiming he was 'too busy' and then bleating about the precedent it would set. The marchers went home without achieving the practical change the Crusade had sought to make. But the image of the march itself – desperate men with grey pinched faces carrying banners, playing harmonicas and shielding themselves from October rain – finally did stir *The Times*. They did not go unmentioned in its pages after all. In its obituary of 93-year-old Con Whalen, who had been the last surviving marcher, the newspaper conceded: 'Poorly clad, peaceable and yet somehow heroic in the very hopelessness of its cause [the march] has come to symbolise human dignity.' My father took me to Jarrow because the Crusade, which he and his own father followed in the evening newspapers, turned him implacably Socialist. But politics still meant less to him than football. Which is why we went to Ashington too.

It was a drowsy and sluggish summer Sabbath in the early 1970s. Your daytime entertainment came from reading the Sunday newspapers or listening to the radio. No shops were open. With the new season weeks away, there were no highlights of the previous afternoon's football on television to wait for either. My father decided he'd break the monotony. We'd go to Ashington in the claret and cream Wolseley, another car which he briefly owned before our finances dwindled to near-nought and it was sold to meet bills.

Jarrow represented the mind and conscience of Newcastle for him. But he believed Ashington was its heart. He called the town 'the football factory', and I'd read so much about it that, irrationally, I expected the description to be glaringly apparent as soon as I got there. In my mind's eye I saw a kick-about on every street corner and a vast chessboard of pitches similar to those on Hackney Marshes.

It was a warm, blue-sky morning. The fake-leather upholstery of the car seat was already hot to the touch. Ten miles separated my grandfather's house from Ashington, and my father drove there in a hesitant, stop–start way. We drove close enough to the coast for me to catch sight of the North Sea, which was like a bar of blue light. Once we reached Ashington, my father knew exactly where to go. It was as though he'd made the journey previously without me. The town was representative of the wider North East insofar as it was dominated by mining and football (today, there's no working pit – only a mine as a museum – in what was once the biggest colliery village in the world). We passed one mine and my father said he'd almost moved there shortly after the war. 'I could have worked with the Charltons and the Milburns around me,' he said. I saw in Ashington what I was used to seeing elsewhere – slate roofs and chimneys coughing out smoke. Off-duty miners were heading for the traditional lunchtime pint in the Welfare, where dominoes were shuffled, or a working-men's club, where sing-songs took place around out-of-tune pianos. All the men wore Sunday best suits and big, clomping boots. Some carried folded up newspapers. The scene fitted the stereotypical image that southerners have of the North

East: flat caps and white mufflers and whippets on short, tight leads to stop them from chasing ahead. The windows of the stores were tired-looking. The goods inside seemed sparse. The streets were long, and each council home was almost identical to the next: two first-floor windows, another wider one downstairs and doors with ribbed glass. We found a park where a makeshift match was taking place without posts. The ball was perpetually whacked up-field, huge kicks carrying it from one end to the next, and it bounced awkwardly on the dust dry surface after landing. My father parked the car and we walked on to an apron of grass. He convinced me that Bobby Charlton had played there regularly as a boy, gesturing towards the full expanse of sun-browned parkland as if he was showing me the battlefields of Bannockburn or Bosworth Field.

Bobby and his brother Jack were raised at 114 Beatrice Street, which like others parallel or close to it – Rosalind Street, Portia Street, Juliet Street – was named after a Shakespearean heroine. My father didn't often refer to Jack. To him Bobby came first; he was smitten by his skill rather than the no-nonsense roughness his brother demonstrated regularly on behalf of Leeds United. Jack was all sharp edges – knees and elbows and studs. Bobby was a ship in full sail. It seemed hard for my father to think of Bobby as being Jack's 'wor kid' at all because – apart from the shape of the nose and other facial likenesses – the two of them seemed as fundamentally different from one another as Dostoyevsky's Aleksey and Ivan Karamazov. Indeed, if my father thought of Bobby as being close to anyone at all, it was Duncan Edwards. He saw them as spiritual brothers long after Edwards died in that Munich hospital.

We went silently along Beatrice Street, aware we were walking where Charlton had once walked. We stopped two houses short of number 114 and stared at Charlton's one-time home self-consciously, like a pair of gawking tourists. The front door of the house was painted Manchester City blue. The small front garden was bordered on three sides by a low wooden fence. Change came gradually to the North East, my father quietly explained as we moved closer into the shadow of the house. Though more than 20 years separated Charlton from me, he added that the place in which I was born, as well as the streets around it, were so like Ashington's as to be practically the same. I knew what he meant. One of the photographs in my scrapbook showed Charlton strolling along Ashington's back alleys, which had high brick walls. The entrance to each cement back-yard was through a tall, press-latched wooden gate, and every home had a coal hatch and bunker. It reminded me of the first house I remember living in. There was another picture of the inside of the Charltons' home. The rectangular living room contained things familiar to our own: heavily patterned curtains and wallpaper, dark furniture, the odd ornament, figurine and ornately framed photograph and a radiogram with black dials, its wiring encased in teak. When I saw it I could almost smell the wax polish necessary to keep everything spic.

I think my father respected Charlton so much not only because of what he'd become, but also because of what he'd overcome. Charlton had shown immense mental strength by playing again so soon after the Munich crash. When it happened, he was 21 – far too young, my father thought, to be reminded of your mortality. My father speculated on how it must have aged Charlton prematurely and entirely altered his view of a world which offered limitless adventure before Munich and grim reality after it. As a teenager, my father lost a friend, who drowned in a swimming accident as he tried to save him. Afterwards his friend's mother always crossed the street to avoid him. Every sight of my father reminded the mother of her dead son. Though he seldom spoke of it, I know he carried that death with him all his life, which is why I'm sure something he said to me – 'you can't know how much Bobby Charlton must miss Duncan Edwards' – related as much to himself and his dead friend as to Charlton and Edwards.

As human beings we like to see traits in others that we think we possess ourselves. My father identified Charlton as a romantic because he saw himself this way where the game was concerned. The tone in which Charlton spoke about football was endearing. It meant everything to him the way it meant everything to my father. He also believed Charlton had a lot to teach me; most notably the fact that you either possessed at birth, or taught yourself through studious application, something useful to avoid working down the pit. But it was much more than that. 'If you behave like him,' he said 'you won't go far wrong.' The virtues he most cherished he also attributed to Charlton: duty, chivalry and modesty.

My father thought it was 'too easy to get carried away watching football'. In the frenzy of a match you could be fooled into thinking that nothing else – not even food, drink, light and heat – mattered as much as the result. A player's behaviour, he said, influenced the reactions of those watching him. It could be transmitted, like an electric charge, from pitch to terrace and mistaken loyalty could boil into verbal abuse or hooliganism because of an injustice that was real, imagined or manufactured as an excuse to release pent-up emotion. Charlton's conduct was exemplary. He was kicked, but didn't kick back. He didn't start fights; he broke them apart. He wasn't provocative or bullying. He didn't commit cheap fouls or trick referees. Rules were sacrosanct and he obeyed them without demur. All this was an integral part of Charlton's nature. 'Football owes a lot to him,' my father impressed on me, conscious when he said it of the shift of attitudes on the terraces, which made him uncomfortable.

The game then was beginning to attract the unsavoury individuals who came with the purpose of causing trouble and would blight the 1970s. Their allegiance was to violence, often physical – fists, bottles or whatever hard or breakable object came to hand. On the way out of one match he'd protected me from a head-butting contest between two so-called 'fans' who had doughy faces and the meaty build of Sumo wrestlers, an over-pouring of flesh bulging from beneath their shirts. On the way out of another we passed a supporter whose face was smothered in blood. He'd stripped off his white T-shirt and was holding it to staunch the bleeding from a slashed cut between his left ear and eye.

Brawls and shouted threats, outside and inside grounds, were occurring too frequently for my father's liking. He traced the connection to the rising level of friction between players and referees. My father remembered aspects of the game in an affectionate glow; sometimes in the same idealistic way that Britain was recalled in the last Edwardian summer before the Great War. His views were unquestionably coloured by idealism and sentimentality. I didn't believe the teams of the 1930s, the 1940s and the 1950s were blessed with purity of thought towards officials or the opposition and always behaved angelically. Every bad trait existed then too: diving, feigning injury, low-and high-grade gamesmanship, back-chatting the referee. But my father had a point when he reckoned hostility on the pitch was more overt and intimidating. A different breed of player was emerging, he said: someone ruthlessly blatant or loutish in his tactics, who sought to gain an underhand advantage irrespective of the consequences, and in doing so despoiled the matches. The more my father saw of it, the more virtuous Charlton became to him. He upheld the values of an earlier, better age. He was

The Last Sportsman, and my father genuinely saw Charlton's retirement as the end of an era. He couldn't conceive of the First Division without him.

Bobby Charlton's last appearance at Newcastle warranted the marching brass band and the bunting associated with those celebratory, high summer miners' galas of the North East.

But it was a dank and distinctly autumnal day, the sky was dismal-looking. Not even the newspaper bills, tied to lampposts with knotted white string or leaning against outside walls, mentioned his name. St James' Park was undergoing renovation too, so there were only 38,000 of us inside. There had always been a shabby magnificence about the place. The brickwork was crumbling. The stone terraces were chipped and split. The metal barriers were badly in need of paint. It was a ramshackle ground sliding slowly into decay and decrepitude. But at last something was being done about it. The East Stand was a building site of stacked wood and concrete blocks, the flat and pointed roofs of the city spread across the far horizon, which was obscured by thin fingers of mist. Wooden ladders were propped up against the half finished, blank construction and a pair of cranes were lowered before the match. I still have my programme, which cost 7 pence. On the cover is an artist's pen and ink impression of the stand, which wasn't completed for another five months. The quaintly titled 'Pen Pictures of the Players' on page six read as though Charles Pooter wrote them. The anonymous author focuses on the banal, pointing out that Best 'cost no fee' and Charlton 'holds the club appearance record'. An article called 'Welcome to Manchester United' surmises that under Frank O'Farrell 'one has the feeling [the team] is once more preparing to stagger the football world with their power and skill'. United, enduring a laboured transformation, were second from bottom of the table. Eight weeks later O'Farrell was sacked; he still had three and a half years left on his contract. It seemed unimaginable then, but another 21 years would pass before United took the Championship again. After O'Farrell came the garrulous Tommy Docherty, and then Dave Sexton and Ron Atkinson, before United found in Alex Ferguson the successor to Matt Busby that it had been searching for all along.

On that afternoon, however, it seemed as though United's inconsistency was a temporary aberration. Best and David Sadler were still only 26. The goalkeeper, Alex Stepney, hadn't reached 30. Around them was the decent-looking frame of a new United: Martin Buchan, Willie Morgan, Ian Storey-Moore.

Newcastle were already 2–0 ahead before Charlton came off the bench to revive them. And my father was right: he did do something I'd remember, leaving it like a going away gift. Within three minutes he'd sent a shot from 30 yards which skimmed over the bar. Inside another five he struck the bottom of a post. Two minutes from the end he gave me a goal. Long after it was scored my father and I described in swopped dialogue what our eyes still saw. Best gets possession in midfield and instinctively runs at the defence. He motions to take the ball on the inside, but actually moves outside the confused, rushed challenge of Frank Clark, whose right leg collapses beneath him because of the rapid change in direction which Best initiates with a nudge of his foot. The panicky Newcastle defence loses its shape, contracting in the faint and false hope that Best will be daunted by the number of bodies positioned between him and the goal and so lose his composure. Instead he is aware of the gap on the left flank, which Charlton is running into. Best glances up and floats the ball into it, clipping the pass to Charlton off his instep. Charlton dashes on to it, knowing what he will do the moment he sees the ball coming towards him. He doesn't break his stride and thumps it on the half-volley. He is 16 yards out and on the angle. The shot thunders inside the near post. It qualifies as a Charlton Special.

The Newcastle crowd had repeatedly shouted 'Bobby is a Geordie' and at the end Charlton motioned towards the three full stands and held up an arm in gratitude for it.

Afterwards I waited with my black-covered auto-graph book at the bottom of the 11 wide stone steps which led from the car park to the main entrance. There was such a jam of hangers-on, well-wishers and rival autograph hunters that first Best and then Charlton disappeared into it, as if swallowed up by the waves of crowd. I couldn't get close enough to either of them.

The buff-coloured page I had saved for Charlton went unsigned. At my grandfather's house I found my father already sitting by the fireside studying that night's League tables in the newspaper. 'Told you,' he said, the edge of triumph in his voice as soon as I walked into the room. 'I knew he'd score. I knew where that ball was going as soon as he hit it. Just beautiful, wasn't it? Did you get his autograph?' I shook my head and my father said: 'You saw the goal – that's what really counts.'

Less than six months later, Charlton formally announced his retirement and I watched the news footage of him emerging alone from the Old Trafford tunnel before standing on the pitch where he accepted Manchester United's official farewell gift of a silver tray. He was appointed manager of Preston North End. I wrote him a letter and received a photostatted reply on the club's embossed white notepaper. My name, like thousands of others, had been poorly typed after the word 'Dear' and was followed by two standard paragraphs – 'many thanks . . . very kind of you to take the trouble to write'. The 'yours sincerely' was followed by a faint, facsimile signature and beneath it the word 'Manager'. I had expected something in his own hand. A signature in Biro or fountain pen ink. 'It's not real,' I said dejectedly to my father. 'Never mind,' he replied, striving to be optimistic. 'You'll get his autograph one day.'

As in most other things, my father was right. Eventually, I did; but it was far into the future and in a way I could never have imagined.

PART THREE

A Corner Where Past And Present Meet

7

Several Shades of
Bloody Red

The television crew were packing their things away before the rain returned: a camera on its spindly tripod, a long microphone that was the colour of seaside rock, a loop of thick cable and a huge circular light, the bulbs of which had glowed almost phosphorescently through the murk of a late-January afternoon. Its white brightness had revealed every groove and fissure on Bill Shankly's face – the wrinkly bags beneath his eyes, the deep fold lines from his broken boxer's nose to the corner of his mouth and the wavy furrows stretching across his forehead. His skin resembled the craquelure of an old painting. His hair was grey and bristly too, shaved so close on the crown that the pale skin of the scalp was visible. It accentuated the jutting boniness of his cheeks and jaw and the hooded eye-sockets.

A few yards away, holding my hard-covered reporter's

notebook, I watched him being interviewed. He wasn't far from the place where those wrought-iron gates now bear his name and the simple tenet of his and Liverpool's faith: YOU'LL NEVER WALK ALONE. I'd gone to gather material before the League Cup semi-final in 1980. Around me were a dozen or so middle-aged and elderly men who, reluctant to intrude, loitered at a respectful distance from Shankly. Liverpool was miserable-looking that day. The sky was smothered by white-grey cloud, which refused to break. Wispy mist stretched like a dirty veil over the high peaks of the city, and a prolonged shower during the morning had given the roads a dark sheen. All of us wore coats and tightly knotted scarves to shut out the cold and damp. But not Shankly, who seemed immune from them. He was impeccably natty and groomed in a dark grey suit and a purple shirt and tie combination. The sharp tip of a red handkerchief poked from the top pocket of his jacket. He looked like a guest at a wedding.

The film crew were from Italy and had come to make a programme about why English football was dominating Europe. Liverpool was one of several ports of call; I'd seen them in Nottingham earlier in the week talking to a reluctant Peter Taylor, who disliked the cameras. Brian Clough had refused to talk to them, telling Taylor: 'It's your turn,' before driving off in his Mercedes. Taylor the late substitute endured ten minutes of questioning, often staring around him as if searching for an escape route.

Shankly was supposed to explain the roots of the

game in blue-collar cities such as Liverpool, which his interviewer sneeringly implied had nothing to recommend it other than success in the European Cup. Neither the skyline of the city nor the Mersey ferries had charmed him. He looked at Liverpool dismissively from beneath the brim of a wide dark hat, and said to Shankly in preparation that Merseyside was hardly picturesque. Shankly gave him the basilisk eye in return for that statement, which he heard as an insult. For him the remark was as heinous as impugning the legitimacy of his parentage and calling him a bastard child. Or of saying that coalmining didn't count as an honourable job. Devoted to every aspect of the city, except for the square acreage of Everton's Goodison Park, Shankly wouldn't allow the slur to stand.

All of us strained to hear what he was saying over the blow and whip of the winter wind. Stray phrases blew my way only because he said each of them with such admonitory force. Riled by the interviewer, Shankly was in his element. Here was someone who cannily understood how to make language work for him. His sentences were poetically crafted for effect. The cadence and rhythm of each one were beautifully conveyed by the raspy growl of the voice. Through its measured rise and fall, he was able to take the rough edges off his accent and make it sound almost mellifluent. He knew where the stresses should go too. It was if certain words left his lips already italicised. There was an actorly poise about Shankly, evidenced in every line. I heard him say and then wrote down:

> There's an *intense* and very powerful passion for football in Liverpool that you find *nowhere* else except Glasgow. That's because it comes from the *heart* here and flows in the blood.
>
> You can't *make* a football club without the ordinary working man. He *is* the club. And *football* is the working-man's sport.
>
> What we do on Saturday provides a purpose and a focus for the *people*. You cannot cheat them. Or you'll be found *out*.
>
> If the people *trust* you they will follow you. And they will follow a *team* which they recognise as being committed to *them*. That's why there is a fervour and pride here.

After so many decades, I still think about the responsibility of translating the tone of these sentences; how, specifically, any translator could have accurately conveyed the lilt of the voice, the impact of words delivered like short, hard blows and the way in which Shankly treated the interview as if it was armed combat. His gusto shook the smoothly assured interviewer, taken aback by the speed of the speech. Shankly described Liverpool as a kind of working-class Arcadia, and did it convincingly enough to suggest this was established fact rather than subjective opinion. He made it sound as much of a movable feast as Hemingway's Paris.

And he made it plain that the interviewer was privileged to walk on Scouse soil.

At the start of the interview Shankly stood perfectly still. He was straight-backed. His chin was prominently raised. One hand was locked stiffly into the other at waist height and his toes pointed at ten-to-two. He appeared to be on military parade, awaiting inspection. But, as he became more animated, there were expressive gestures synchronised to match the things he said. Whenever Shankly used the word 'heart', he laid the flat of his right hand across his breastbone. When he talked about 'the team' he jabbed a forefinger finger towards Anfield. When he referred to 'the people', he pointed towards me and the gaggle of men nearby. And when he used the phrase 'fervour and pride' he clenched his fist. I saw Shankly glare into the camera unsmilingly, as if the grimness of his expression doubly underlined the seriousness of his convictions. To him all this was clearly unchallengeable. He suddenly looked formidably intimidating. In that moment I imagined Shankly's response to anyone who disputed his views always beginning with this kind of stony front: a withering stare, which – because the recipient was unable to see what Shankly plainly saw – contained within it an amalgam of incredulity, incomprehension and pity. Shankly, it seemed to me, expressed every opinion equally cogently. If he'd been asked about the weather in Liverpool, Shankly would have come back with a soliloquy. The interviewer finally managed to interrupt him long enough to meekly enquire whether the rest of Liverpool was as passionate as him about football and its heritage. 'Go into the city. Talk to the men and women who live here,' replied Shankly tartly. 'You'll see then.'

After the questions were over he nodded to indicate his departure and began to glance around him, as if unsure about what to do next. With the spotlight off, Shankly's shoulders drooped slightly and he flattened his hair with the palm of his right hand. One of the men near me – flabbily overweight and with round, flushed features – broke away from the other admirers and approached him. The man untied his scarf, bunched beneath the raised collar of his coat, and showed Shankly his tie. It was in Liverpool red with a white Liver Bird in the centre. The tie was clearly a souvenir of another decade – probably the mid-60s – because its colour had faded after what I supposed were several machine washes. I watched him offer a handshake to Shankly, who willingly took it and laid his other hand on the man's shoulder. Eventually the man shyly produced a scrappy piece of paper and a ballpoint pen and Shankly signed an autograph for him. The other men, warily at first, went up to him too before fanning into a crescent. Among them was a stubby-framed business-type, incongruously tugging on the peak of a tweed flat cap; a rumpled chap with hair like gorse, who looked old enough to remember Keir Hardie; and a sallow-skinned man in his mid-20s with heavy black spectacles, who was determined to be heard. He kept asking Shankly, parrot-fashion: 'You know you're a genius, don't you?' Shankly, clearly embarrassed, all but ignored him. A young boy, nervous among the grown-ups, tagged silently alongside him, his mouth agape. He was finally introduced to Shankly and told to shake his hand; Shankly solicitously got down on his haunches to meet him at eye level.

Slowly I walked around the group, positioning myself so I could look at both it and Shankly side-on. I can still see now what I saw then: the stage performer – the role which came naturally to Shankly – and his eager audience. The attention re-invigorated him, as if the television crew's light was shining on him once more. Again, he relied on his hands for emphasis and effect. Asked about tactics and Liverpool's form he made three chopping motions with his hands to block off defence, midfield and attack. He then spread them wide before drawing his fingers together into a point and stabbing the air to illustrate the channels which forwards could profitably exploit. He drew an upward semi-circle with his right forefinger. It was sign-language for the long ball. His open palm, pushed like a southpaw's jab, demonstrated the short pass. On several occasions Shankly seemed to be playing in the match which his imagination had conjured. He could have been on Anfield's pitch rather than the pavement beyond its brick walls, which were smeared by spray-paint graffiti proclaiming ungrammatically in capital letters and with twin exclamation marks: LIVERPOOL KINGS THE

TRUTH!! Shankly turned first one foot and then the other, and simultaneously dipped his left shoulder too, like Steve Heighway or Peter Thompson on a touchline run or Kenny Dalglish sliding sinuously past a defender. Shankly looked around him, swivelling his head, as if he was about to effortlessly clip the ball 40 yards cross-field. He simulated a goalkeeper's dive and demonstrated the block tackle. At one point he jumped an inch or two in the air and gave a flick of his head. As I witnessed all this two images of Shankly in markedly different circumstances came to mind.

In the first, during the 1974 FA Cup Final, he was sitting on the managers' crimson leather benches. Liverpool did not so much beat Newcastle that afternoon as bury their bones beneath Wembley's grass and then dance across them. The final score was 3–0. It could have been six-nil. Or ten. Or anything Liverpool wanted it to be. As the passes fizzed around them, Newcastle were dazed spectators – always in pursuit of, but never possessing, the ball. From his touchline seat Shankly began to orchestrate Liverpool's attacking raids, the line and angle effortlessly switched from one flank to the other. The Newcastle defence was stretched until it broke apart. With extravagant but rhythmic sideways and back movements of his hands, Shankly looked as though he was pulling the strings of an invisible cat's cradle controlling the tempo and direction of what Liverpool were doing.

My father watched the final in the hope that it would recapture the flavour of the early 1950s for him. I watched it in the hope Malcolm Macdonald would emerge as a garlanded Cup hero in the charismatic mould of Jackie Milburn. Milburn scored after 53 seconds of the 1955 Final against Manchester City – the fastest goal ever claimed at Wembley until Roberto Di Matteo struck from 30 yards in only 42 seconds for Chelsea against Middlesboro in 1997. Macdonald didn't muster a shot against Liverpool until the 77th minute. Soon resigned to both Newcastle's demolition and Macdonald's anonymity, we sat back and admired the parade of Liverpool's far superior skills. My father had a theory anyway that, as a people, Geordies and Scousers were twinned. He'd list what he believed to be the proof: the distinctive and instantly recognisable accents and the same darkly self-deprecating humour; the coastal geography of the two working cities, which were each struggling to recover from 1970s unemployment and the economic hardships caused by industrial decline; the tendency towards insularity and introspection; the role of football in establishing reputation, core beliefs and a streak of independence. 'The same folk in different clothes,' he'd say, set apart from Manchester, which he thought was 'swanky', and the spread of the Midlands, where he felt the landscape and the people were uniform. He felt an affinity to Liverpool. It wasn't as wounding to lose to them as it would have been to Arsenal or Tottenham with whom he felt nothing in common.

Also, he put his North East partisanship aside because of Shankly and his charm. My father adored Shankly.

After all, Shankly was another miner, born and brought up in a pitman's cottage in the West of Scotland coal-fields, where Matt Busby and Jock Stein had also toiled with a pick. He liked his unpretentiousness. He liked the way the feelings and opinions of other, ordinary people – men like my father – mattered to him. He also liked the way Shankly spoke, as if always addressing a mass meeting. He wouldn't tolerate poseurs, schemers or opportunists, which suited my father too. 'If you have to be beaten,' he said to me consolingly as the whistle released Newcastle from their torment, 'it may as well be against Shankly. He's impossible to dislike.'

With Kevin Keegan, scorer of two of the goals, Shankly's Liverpool had the potential to control much more than a Cup Final. There was an unshakeable assurance about them. It stemmed from the manager's belief that he'd either bought or found the best and could let them loose against all comers at home or abroad. Although never reticent to talk up his team, Shankly went further. He spoke afterwards of a 'new' Liverpool, capable of winning the League and Cup Double. Out of anyone else's mouth, the claim would have sounded arrogantly boastful and premature. From Shankly, who repeated it with a matter-of-fact dryness, the forecast seemed a mere formality. All he needed was Time to hurry along and prove him right. No one then imagined Liverpool's future would not include Shankly. But his prediction was also his valediction; for less than ten weeks later he was gone from Anfield after resigning.

The definition of purgatory for Shankly was always the close season. Liverpool were his magnificent obsession, and to give them up voluntarily went so dramatically against the grain of his being that the act was scarcely believable; indeed, some didn't believe it – even when the inky headlines in Liverpool's *Post* or *Echo* made denial ridiculous. My father called it 'The Abdication'.

My second image of Shankly is during his retirement. On a humid September evening in 1978 he was working as a radio analyst and sitting behind me in the press box at the City Ground during Nottingham Forest's first round, first leg European Cup tie against Liverpool. Shankly was hunched in his seat, a pair of small black headphones tightly pressed to his ears. Liverpool, defending the Cup for the second successive season, were beaten 2–0. Afterwards I found him wandering disconsolately in the semi-darkness beneath the Main Stand. Moving distractedly in these half-shadows, he seemed a shrunken figure; someone who looked as though he didn't have a genuine purpose for being there. To thoughtfully interpret what he'd seen for radio was never going to be a satisfactory substitute for influencing it from the dugout. There was the vigorous Shankly in football management and the forlorn Shankly out of it, who seemed haunted in his isolation. This is the Shankly I saw. What I recall with most pain were the hollow eyes. There was an aching, bewildered sadness behind them. Shankly said he quit Liverpool essentially because he felt too fatigued to tackle another great burst of work;

but he was diminished and lost without this labour. What he'd given up he could never have again; and the regret and dejection was all too apparent. The best known and most reproduced photograph of Shankly captures him in front of the swaying Kop – arms aloft, fists firmly clenched, silk Liverpool scarf around his neck – after his testimonial match in 1975. But another photograph, taken before the kick off, is more revealing to me. Shankly is on the pitch. He has a sombre and faraway look about him, as if he's projecting the noise and drama of other nights on to the stands around him.

I went up to Shankly and asked him whether he thought Liverpool would recover in the second leg against Forest. He gave me one of his falcon-fierce looks and began to stroke his chin. His fingers were thick and knotty. 'Of course,' he said, slightly irritably, as if simply asking the question established me as imbecilic. 'There's the Kop, you see,' he added without feeling the need to say any more. 'It'll be a different sort of game there – more intense.' (Forest stifled Liverpool at Anfield; a goalless draw there led to two European Cups for Brian Clough.) I dutifully filed Shankly's thoughts for my employers on the night, the Press Association. I relied on the lazy tabloid approach for my opening line: 'Bill Shankly has warned Brian Clough etc, etc.' I left Shankly reluctantly, aware of his loneliness. He moved away from me and I saw him walk slowly down the stone steps, which led into an L-shaped car park. He clutched the metal handrail and glanced at his feet. At the bottom of the steps he found a group of autograph collectors and appreciably brightened. He was still nattering to them ten minutes later. I suspected that only hunger or the chimes of midnight would force him home. For all Shankly ever needed was a live crowd.

With crass naivety, which now makes me blush whenever I think of it, I once asked Brian Clough in casual conversation whether – apart from the financial liberation Leeds' cheque guaranteed him – there were any 'highlights' during his calamitous 44 days at Elland Road in 1974. We were travelling together on a tedious coach journey in the mid-1980s, well before what happened to him there became familiar in the novel and subsequent film, *The Damned United*. Clough dropped his chin to his chest and looked at me contemptuously, as if I was wearing the pointy cone of the dunce's hat. His reply was something about not being there long enough to find out where to take a piss. Or, if he had, where to wash his hands afterwards. He turned away from me, pretending to study passing traffic from the window. I assumed discussion about Leeds was strictly off-limits. An uncomfortable silence settled between us, which Clough finally ended with a vignette. 'If you really want to know, I got to walk out at Wembley with Bill Shankly and then sit next to him,' he said, promptly adding the caveat. 'I say that only with hindsight – since I didn't want to be bloody well there myself.'

Liverpool let Shankly take charge during the Charity Shield as his reward for bringing back the FA Cup, which allowed him to say an appropriately public goodbye. The match fell on Clough's 11th day at Leeds. The week and a half before had been harrowing for him. The fault was entirely his own. He'd alienated the players, inherited from Don Revie, with that provocative opening speech to them that in *The Damned United* Michael Sheen, as Clough, delivers with a pointed finger. 'Chuck your medals in the bin – 'cos you won 'em by cheating.' The atmosphere between Clough and his team turned sulphurous. Mistakes and misjudgements were frequent, each fresh error exacerbating the previous one. He telephoned Revie to ask him to take Leeds on the pitch at Wembley, an offer ostensibly made out of generosity and the desire to acknowledge Revie's achievement of winning the Championship. In reality Clough was so estranged from the side he was supposed to be managing that he didn't want to do the task himself. 'I tried to be clever and appeal to Revie's vanity,' Clough told me. 'I wasn't thinking 'cos he saw it a mile off. He knew why I was asking. He knew everything I did and said in that club. He also knew that if he did it he'd be letting me off the hook. And he certainly didn't want to do that, the bastard. I was bonkers to ask him in the first place. Revie was never going to do me a favour.' Revie, he added, used the invitation against him. 'He was able to say I was getting along so badly with the players that I didn't even want to lead them out. Mind you, he was right.' Shown live on television for the first time, the game was marred by fisticuffs between Billy

Bremner and Kevin Keegan – a scuffling, handbags affair – that led to both of them being sent off. And then Leeds lost on penalties.

Of those memories, most of which I think he'd striven to suppress, Clough retained a clear picture of Shankly wringing his hands together outside the dressing-room doors, which faced one another at the bottom of the gloomy, high-walled tunnel. He began to button and re-button his jacket and then pulled at the sleeves and continually adjusted the Windsor knot in his blue striped tie, as if it might come loose. What Clough recognised in that fidgeting was Shankly's apprehension, which seemed strange in someone of his stature. He saw the conflicting emotions spinning through him: the realisation that *his* players – who still called him 'boss' – now belonged to someone else; and that *his* team were about to play a match in which his own role was fundamentally ceremonial. One thought occurred to Clough. Only as the two of them stood side-by-side, waiting for the signal to start walking into the oblong of sunlight at the head of the tunnel, did Shankly begin to consciously understand the full implications of his decision to go. 'I looked at Bill and I knew he was already regretting what he'd done. I asked him what he was going to do all season.' The answer Clough received – 'I'll be busy enough' – was sufficiently nebulous to convince him of Shankly's desolation. 'It was going to be bloody torture for him – absolute bloody torture,' said Clough. 'He was aware he'd dropped a clanger and there was nothing he could do to correct it. He just tried to pretend it didn't matter.' The coach we were travelling in rolled on through the night and a couple of minutes had passed before Clough, still thinking about Shankly, added distractedly: 'I applauded him on to the pitch. You know, I respected him so much that I used to call him Mr Shankly.'

In the year Shankly died, aged 68 in September 1981, I'd heard the last two sentences of a telephone call between him and Clough. I have no idea who rang the other. I do know that the promise Clough made would have been fulfilled without question: 'Anything you ever want Bill is yours if I can provide it. As Lauren Bacall said to Humphrey Bogart . . . all you have to do is whistle.' Clough put down the phone and I heard him say, as much to himself as the rest of us in the room: 'He won't do it. He's a stubborn bugger. He doesn't like to ask for things – even tickets. But oh, I do love him.'

With hindsight I am sure Clough's managerial style and philosophy owed much to Shankly. Out of it he made something bespoke for himself. Shankly was already an established professional by 1934, the year of Clough's birth. He won an FA Cup winners' medal before Clough outgrew short trousers. He'd already claimed a Championship and a Cup at Liverpool before Clough became manager of his first club, Hartlepool, in 1965. Clough insisted he learnt the fundamentals of what he referred to as 'his trade' from Alan Brown, his boss and sergeant-major mentor at Sunderland. But I think he picked up a lot from observing Shankly and reading about him; certainly more than he ever let on. One committed Socialist, maverick and rigid disciplinarian recognised the strengths of another and borrowed from him. Imitation was certainly flattery.

Clough doesn't dwell on Shankly in either of his autobiographies. He appears only briefly in the index. He nevertheless made reference to him regularly during the day-to-day running of Nottingham Forest. He would quote from Shankly, beginning anecdotes with 'as Bill used to say . . .' or 'what Bill did was this . . .' He was tender in discussing Shankly, as if affectionately referring to an idiosyncratic but favourite uncle, someone who influenced him from afar. Shankly's quixotic nature, intelligence and razor wit appealed to Clough. 'He was crafty too,' he said. 'When I was a young gaffer, wet behind the lugs, he used to invite me into the boot room. He'd give me a beer and some soft soap before a game. He'd pick my brains and his team would pick our pockets on the pitch. Eventually I learnt to go into that place only *after* matches.' Clough added: 'If you went to Liverpool, you knew who was in charge. He was everywhere all at once. He dominated the place.' Clough got the feeling that Liverpool's board couldn't rehang a picture without consulting Shankly first. He admired such authority.

Much of Clough's approach matched Shankly's exactly, as if he was following the template the older man had cut. In retrospect the parallels are clear. Shankly believed in the importance of recruiting what he called a 'spine' for his team – goalkeeper, centre half, centre forward. So did Clough; he even used the same phrase to describe it. Shankly preached the mantra of 'clean sheets' – 'if you don't concede goals you won't lose matches.' So did Clough; and, again, his language was identical and frequently used. Publicly at least, Shankly seldom bothered about the opposition, focusing instead on preparing and motivating his own side. So did Clough; motivation was the stamp of his career. Shankly took a stand against on-the-pitch gamesmanship, such as back-chatting officials, shirt-tugging, diving or time-wasting. Players who cheated referees, he said, would cheat themselves and also try to cheat their manager eventually. Clough agreed; his players were rarely petu-lant on the field because his wrath towards them was worse than the Football Association's could ever be. Clough was Shankly's philosophic kith and kin too. Disliking authority and interference from directors, Shankly dismissed them as peripheral to the success of the side except in one regard. He argued there was a 'Holy Trinity' comprising players, the manager and the supporters. 'Directors don't come into it,' he claimed. 'They are only there to sign the cheques.' In Liverpool's boardroom, Shankly recalled, the mood was attritional. 'I used to fight and argue and fight and argue and fight and argue,' he said. Clough spent his entire career fighting and arguing against those he belittled as 'busy-body, know nothing' directors and treated most of them with outright disdain.

To him Shankly represented his ideal of what a manager should be. Clough adhered to Shankly's purist vision of how the game ought to be played; there was no reliance on an arrow-shower of long balls for them. Tactics were unfussy too. 'The system and the language should always be kept simple,' said Shankly. Clough in this regard out-sang him: 'The game isn't complicated. It comes down to controlling a ball and passing it to a bloke in the same-coloured shirt. That is the first and last principle of football.' Shankly disliked orthodox coaching, and Clough concurred. Coaching for him meant improving on the basics. He revelled in the story of Shankly attending a Football Association course at Lilleshall and leaving almost as soon as he arrived. The jargon he heard had the same effect on him as chloroform. 'Of course, he used tactics,' said Clough. 'So did I. But neither of us overdid it. We taught the game sensibly and in our own ways, not caring what the manuals said. And his team talks – about being able to throw 11 red shirts on the pitch because he thought the other lot were crap – worked because he knew his players and he knew what to say to them. I knew that too.' The other gift Shankly and Clough shared was being able to use words as effortlessly as Turner used paint. But knowing how and when to employ them was more complex. Often what appeared casual, off-the-cuff remarks from Shankly – what he actually called 'bombs' to enliven newspaper back pages or to spark his players – were carefully thought out and sharp-ened at the point of delivery. Clough also came out with ostensibly ad-libbed one-liners – designed to provoke, cajole or gain a psychological advantage of some sort – which in practice had gone through several drafts in his mind before he spoke them.

This headline-making and attention-grabbing enabled Shankly and Clough to create personas for themselves; and, once these images were established, both found themselves obliged to live up to the typecasting. Shankly always had to behave like the toughly irascible Scot with a streak of romanticism beneath his iron exterior. And he always had to say something Shanklian. Clough had to be the Clough which the wider public imagined him to be – loudly brash and belligerent. There was also something wonderfully crazy about the pair, who were wily, contrary and bewilderingly complex. Saying the wrong thing to either of them was like flicking a lighted match into a box of rockets. But they were also compassionate, kindly and extraordinarily loyal. No wonder each found the other companionable.

The two men were alike in one final way. Shankly, especially during the 1960s, harped on about resignation to the degree that Liverpool's board stopped taking the prospect seriously. Clough, at both Derby County and Forest, seemed on the point of departure almost on a fortnightly basis. In both cases the threats were more about gaining power than serious declarations of intent. But when Clough did go from Derby in 1973 – gambling it all on being indispensable – recrimination over the rash miscalculation remained with him for ever. Since he felt more for Derby than for Forest – Clough was like a twice-married man still inconsolable over divorcing the first wife – his thoughts turned to them often. A scene in the film *Save the Tiger* evokes Clough for me. Jack Lemmon won an Oscar for his portrayal of a middle-aged businessman always harking back on roads taken and not taken. At one stage he wistfully recites the names of his boyhood baseball heroes, the New York Yankees. Whenever I see it I think of Clough nostalgically listing the team he left behind at the Baseball Ground: 'Hinton . . . Hector . . . McFarland . . . Todd'. Like Lemmon's character, he could neither stop pining for the past nor resist the urge to try to reclaim something long since out of his reach. Had Clough not abandoned them, he was adamant that Derby, not Liverpool, would have been masters of the mid-to-late 1970s and early 1980s. The Liverpool of which he spoke was Shankly's team. Derby beat them 3–1 less than a month before Clough left.

What Clough did at Derby held him back from resigning impulsively again. What he saw Shankly do at Liverpool persuaded him against early retirement. Clough would talk about the allure of the garden and the sunny beach, and shedding the pressures of Saturday afternoons. But he resisted the temptation to embrace them full-time because of his concern about becoming a second Shankly. Surface engagement with football wasn't sufficient for Shankly, and Clough saw him struggle to fill the vacuum in his life where the game had once been. Not wanting to go through the same agonies, Clough clung on until his dependency on drink decided the issue for him. Whenever retirement was mentioned to him I knew Clough was conscious of Shankly. 'We all know Bill retired too soon,' he'd say. 'He wasn't even old enough to qualify for a state pension.'

What Shankly perceived as sleights stayed with him like scarring; the tough guy bruised easily in this regard. But the grievance I detected most strongly in Shankly was the one he felt with himself at quitting prematurely. He thought the board had been ungrateful and contemptibly guilty of disrespect after his career at Anfield ended, cutting him adrift as if he was a nuisance. But, hearing the stories of Shankly turning up at Liverpool's training ground because he missed everything about the job he'd just relinquished, Clough conceded: 'Bill hung around afterwards and that was difficult for everyone – including him.' I know, however, that Clough never thought less of him because of it. His respect for Shankly manifested itself in a way that only those who came across him daily and close up would have registered. I never saw him try to kiss Shankly the way he kissed everyone else. He was even wary of half-hugging him in case it caused offence.

It was possible to ring Shankly at home after his retirement. His number was widely available and he didn't mind talking; in fact, I think he wanted to talk. I rang him on half a dozen or so occasions and for a few years after he died, I refused to scribble his name and number out of my contacts book. After Clough, he was the manager I most wanted to cover. I think the experience would have been similar – except, of course, I'd have drunk cups of tea instead of glasses of whisky.

I often imagine Bill Shankly in the Premier League. He was a modern manager in the 1960s, a tracksuit on the training pitch when most of his contemporaries dressed in lounge suits from John Collier. As football changed, Shankly had the sense to change almost imperceptibly with it. Were he managing now, he'd ignore, as best he could, the unnecessary flummery and frills accompanying the Premiership. He'd be a slightly different Shankly, of course: forced to consider the repercussions of a drop in the club's stock market value; forced to tolerate the whims and vanities of wealthy overseas owners; forced to accommodate – through gritted teeth, no doubt – the rapaciousness of exploitive agents and the oily slickness of marketing men. He'd still be a players' manager; a boss who stuck up for the workers – even when he saw those workers arrive for their shift in a Bugatti or a Ferrari and wearing a watch worth more than he paid for the whole of his 1963 Championship winning team. 'What?' I can imagine Shankly saying, this shocked exclamation rising and crackling in his voice. 'You're wearing jewellery that cost more than Ron Yeats.' He'd tolerate squad numbers and adjust his eyes to the constantly changing electronic advertising boards. He'd become used – eventually – to calling a linesman an assistant referee. He'd patrol the box of his technical area, his grimaces and semaphore a prominent side-show of *Super Sunday*. His press conferences would make *Sky Sports News* unmissable and generate YouTube hits around the globe. He'd find efficient uses for the computerised data of *ProZone*, blinking at its graphs and coloured arrows, the tracking lines and charts of possession won and lost, the miles run and the tackles completed. But it would complement – though never come near to replacing – his gut instinct and the penetrating wisdom accumulated from compulsively watching football at every level.

I once heard Sir Alf Ramsey repeat what he'd once said about the vagaries of management. He was standing in the slender corridor at the City Ground, where most press conferences took place. Reporters were clustered around him, and Sir Alf looked uneasy, as if he was feeling claustrophobic. He backed off until he leant against the corridor's dimpled windows, which were beside a double set of swing doors. He hardly moved his mouth to speak. I thought he resembled a ventrilo-quist's dummy – the head only occasionally turning on a thick neck, the lips narrow, the black brows theatrically high, as if painted on, and the eyes wide and looking glassily ahead. He was enduring a dreadful but merci-fully brief period as caretaker of Birmingham City, a side hovering between the lower and nether regions of the First Division. On a reconnaissance mission – against the odds Forest, freshly promoted, were then sweeping towards the Championship – Sir Alf left the wood-panelled directors' room and walked into an interrogation. What he'd achieved in the past offered only the flimsiest protection against criticism in the present. The 1966 World Cup, despite being won only a dozen years earlier, seemed long ago. Sir Alf was straining to live up to his reputation at Birmingham, where he scarcely made a difference. His only defence was: 'I have told you before, gentlemen, that managers get too much praise when things go well and too much criticism when things go badly. That is the nature of the beast.' It came out in his familiar clipped, terse tone, which sounded like a rebuke. But what Ramsey said remains valid.

The cult of the manager is usually overstated and overrated. The fact it wasn't in Shankly's case reminds us of what and how much he gave to Liverpool. He saw them win three European Cups, one Uefa Cup, four Championships and one League Cup in the six full seasons between his retirement and his death. But he was the principal begetter of that success. What Liverpool did under Bob Paisley wouldn't have been achievable without the sweat Shankly shed first. Anfield wasn't even a desirable piece of property when he took over in 1959. The gabled Main Stand was decrepit, the rest of the ground depressing. So it is not mythologizing Shankly to insist he did more than animate Liverpool; he rescued them and then shaped them in his likeness over the next 15 years. Nor is it glib to say that Liverpool has never forgotten the debt it owes him. Nowhere, I believe, is emotional reverence to a manager greater or more tangible than it is in Liverpool for Shankly.

On one of my first visits to Old Trafford I took a wrong turning and fortuitously found myself in a plushly carpeted and crowded room where Sir Matt Busby, holding a china white tea cup and saucer, was framed by a floor-to-ceiling glass cabinet, which contained shelves of polished trophies. With affection, Busby was called 'The Old Man'; and so he appeared to me in that moment. I knew – and I had frequently seen photographs and film to prove it – that, aged 25, he had won the FA Cup with Manchester City in 1934 when George V was King, Ramsay MacDonald Prime Minister and United were Manchester's impoverished relations, 12th in the Second Division. To me he nonetheless seemed to have been born old, like Benjamin Button, and remained old; probably because I originally (and erroneously) perceived Busby in the same way that I perceived my grandfather – someone already too old to die young. I lingered in the doorway, which made the fact I didn't belong there all the more conspicuous. In the minute or two's grace I was given to study Busby before being moved on, I was instantly aware of his magnetism. After Busby's death in 1994, Hugh McIlvanney wrote memorably of him: 'If Busby had stood dressed for the pit, and somebody alongside him in the room had worn ermine, there would have been no difficulty about deciding who was special.' When I read it, I immediately experienced the flashback of the

Busby I saw at Old Trafford; and I knew the claim made on his behalf was true.

I interviewed Don Revie during the turbulence of his England years. He met me wearing his navy Football Association blazer and tie and took me into an office that – though I appreciated it only years later – mirrored his mind and personality. Everything about it was precise and scrupulously ordered, as if the objects on and around the desk had been arranged with geometric calculation. Resting on its polished teak were a small stack of opened letters, each one perfectly aligned with the top left-hand corner of the next. There were sharpened, blue-stemmed pencils bunched in a neat vertical row. A few pens were pushed together horizontally beside them. The other things on the desk – a wooden box of paperclips and matching tray, a flat glass paperweight and a paper knife – all had their specific place. Nothing was askew or looked as though it had been left there absent-mindedly. It dawned on me that Revie – known for his tremendous exactness and his fetishness for just-so detail – probably measured the distances between them every morning. Even four low-backed chairs, which stood in front of the desk, seemed to have been evenly spaced to the last milli-metre. Waiting to be hung were framed photographs of Leeds United's two Championship winning teams. It occurred to me that Revie was still thinking of the road home to West Yorkshire.

I remember the immense dignity of 'The Big Man', Jock Stein, who filled a room simply by entering it and whose leaving made it feel bare and empty again. Stein was so imposing – the solid head, the wide shoulders, the hard hands which had hacked out tons of coal – that it wasn't necessary to know of his achievements with Celtic to be aware of the greatness alive within him. Even with those miner's hands buried inside the pockets of his brown suit, Stein exuded an authority that identified him indisputably as one of those men you'd follow into battle without bothering to ask why. In listening to him talk, Stein made you think you were sharing discoveries with him rather than being lectured at. My father's allegiance to the blue half of Glasgow never prejudicially blinded him to Stein's qualities. In fact, his appreciation of Stein went beyond just admiring him as a manager. He used to say that if Scotland ever decided to reintroduce royalty of its own, there was no doubt who ought to be the monarch. The only question, he added, was whether to hold the coronation at Celtic Park or Hampden Park.

Busby built what Manchester United became out of the wreckage of the Second World War and then rebuilt them after the catastrophe of Munich. Revie took a scruffy club from one of the dirty and unfashionable industrial heartlands of the North and dressed them in Real Madrid white. Stein turned Celtic into an irresistible force capable of pushing aside previously irremovable objects; and he did it with players born just a corner kick from his office desk. Brian Clough turned the drab provincialism of Nottingham into one of football's

capital cities. Busby claimed eight major pieces of silverware; Stein collected a phenomenal 26, including nine
consecutive Scottish titles; Revie picked up six; Clough
had eight to his credit. If this was an official League
table, Shankly would be at the bottom of it. He won
only six trophies: three Championships, two FA Cups
and a Uefa Cup. But the flat statistics of straightforward
profit and loss accountancy don't reflect the depth and
breadth of the impact a seminal character such as
Shankly made. Or the warmth and regard for him.

For Shankly, the ceaseless grafter, there was always a
duty to be completed and a role to be fulfilled, and he
went about them with an enormous sense of obligation
to his adopted city. He gave a voice to a club which had
been lacking one and he came to see the world in only
three colours: everything was black and white to him,
signifying the absolute sureness of his convictions,
unless it was Liverpool red. He never had to pick a scarf
from the rack in the club shop and wear it, like a fashion
accessory, in a pretentious and ostentatious show of
commitment. Most often Shankly is recalled through
his most famous phrase about football being more
important than life or death. Some thought then, and
still think now, it was another Shanklyism, uttered with
his tongue pressed firmly into his cheek. It doesn't seem
so when you see him deliver it. Shankly is jabbing the
air with his finger to emphasise what managing
Liverpool had meant to him. The epigram was still
unnecessary because his love for them was demonstrable

in whatever he did. He breathed for Liverpool, and anyone who supported them was family to Shankly; each a brother or sister. He devoted his life to them and got in return a level of devotion and adoration that no other manager of my experience has ever matched.

It endures posthumously. To think of Liverpool is to think of him, and vice versa. Walk through the city streets now (even on non-match days) and you'll see, as I did not so long ago, broad and bulky men with Shankly's face spread on the front of T-shirts; and young boys, born 20 years too late to have seen him in the rugged flesh, decked in scarves stitched with one of those choice Shankly quotations. In the pubs there are Shankly photographs and Shankly mirrors and Shankly slogans fixed to the wall; and beneath them there is talk of what Shankly did and would have done if he were here today. Had someone arrived in Liverpool without prior knowledge of the team or Shankly, the assumption would have been made that he was still in charge of it. In one bar I found a pop-art print of Shankly painted entirely in variegated, bloody reds – almost every shade available on an artist's palette: brick red, deep red, Indian red, flame red and burgundy among them. Here was a study in scarlet. I also found a willowy, loose-limbed man in a Liverpool baseball cap drinking beer from a glass too large for his small hands. When I asked him what he thought about Shankly, he said: 'He is Liverpool,' a reply notable for the use of the present tense more than a quarter of a century after the manager's ashes were scattered on the Anfield pitch.

Shankly had – and always retained – the common touch because he possessed an imperishable common decency. Regarding them as equals, he never separated himself from the supporters or talked down to them. I saw the evidence of it on that rain-splattered day outside Anfield. What struck me as Shankly spoke were the facial expressions of those disparate men and the wide-eyed glances passed discreetly between them. It is no exaggeration to claim each felt blessed and could not quite believe that serendipity had placed them in Shankly's company; or that Shankly was talking to them. I reckoned for each man it constituted the defining quarter of an hour of his life and would be replayed – in pubs and bars, on the steeply banked Kop and during family gatherings – as long as that life lasted. They were awed by his physical presence and looked at Shankly as if he was much more than a man. But the privilege of being there was as much his as theirs. He passed on his expertise willingly and as seriously as if he were sitting in Anfield's boot room instead of standing on a blowy street corner.

As the television crew were packing up, I remember Shankly collaring the interviewer who had been so condescending about Liverpool. He wanted the last word. 'Come back soon,' he said. 'The air is much sweeter here, son, and the people are real.' The interviewer slunk away, not knowing how to reply.

As my father said to me when I told him about it: 'It was hard enough to win a match against Shankly. But you'll never win an argument.'

8

Home of the Unlikely Hero

The previous season had ended weeks before and the next was so far off that no one spoke of it much. Football was on its holidays; Test cricket filled the sports pages. It was one of those summer's afternoons without blemish. The pavements were hot and heat haze quivered and broke the horizon of the surrounding farm land, its enamelled brightness stretching flatly towards the sea. There was no breeze to bring relief from the full sun – rare on the North East coast – and the shadows cast were pit-black and resembled solid objects.

No one casually passing would have paid much attention to the scene. There were four figures on the pitch – three youngsters and a man who was passing a ball between them. The grass was well shorn and smooth. Only the faintest trace of old, burnt-brown touchline markings were visible. The goals were imaginary – no coats or bags to take the place of the posts and nets, which had been pulled up and stored away, leaving deep square holes in the ground and a slightly worn patch that identified where the dead-centre of the six-yard box had been. The ball was light and as shinily grey-white as a pearl. It was the sort of ball that you could buy cheaply in Woolworth's or from any newsagent's shop and it moved extravagantly through the warm air. There was a Brazilian swerve, dip and bend to every shot. The youngsters, a year or two older than me, had trouble mastering its flight. But the man I was watching always had it under his command. He flicked the ball up, bounced it off his head and shoulders and chested it from one knee to the other before side-footing or back-heeling a pass. Sometimes he crouched, letting the ball lie on the nape of his neck before pushing it forward with a muscular heave and then killing it with a trap as it fell. When the ball left either foot it made a solid sound, as if he'd found its sweet spot.

What comes to mind when I think of him now is the artist Salvator Rosa's self-portrait – dark eyes and dark curls and a Mediterranean complexion. He was olive-skinned and strong-looking. He was also inappropriately dressed for a park kick-around – formal polished shoes, a pair of dark maroon trousers with wide flares and a patterned shirt with huge, stiff collars. His hair was black and fashionably long. His sideburns were cut straight but grown wide, finishing level with the lower curve of his cheekbones. The most impressive thing about him was his powerful shape. He was big-boned and substantial, his bullishly fit physique made for heavy lifting. The scale of his arm, chest and thigh muscles were traceable through the lines of his close-fitting clothes.

My grandfather and I were nearing the end of our daily walk. At some stage we always came to the field. We sat on one of the bleached benches that were dotted along the edge of the football pitch. The benches were elephant-grey and the wood was scarred with proclamations of love or lone names, which had been gouged out with a penknife. In summer the football pitch became part of the cricket club's boundary. The fenced-in field was overlooked by a row of thin trees, a line of modern housing and the low Wesleyan Chapel, where I'd been baptised. We followed the ball as it was hoofed upwards, climbing into the postcard blue of the sky. The man positioned himself beneath it, waiting with his left foot outstretched and slightly hooked to cushion the impact of the drop. He took the ball flawlessly, the way a juggler takes an object thrown at him and incorporates it effortlessly into his act. One of the youngsters tried to tackle the man, who held him off with a simple twist of his body before the other two came to jostle and outnumber him. The man got stabbed in the calf with the sharp toe of a boot and appealed for a free kick, holding up his hand as though a referee might appear and whistle for the foul. He soon reclaimed the ball and began to dribble it in giant strides. Finally, he volleyed it into the far corner and began a chase, deliberately slowing and losing the race. The weary youngsters came to a breathless halt, panting in the heat.

The man, who had done almost all the fetching and carrying, showed no sign of fatigue. As the youngsters rested, one of them sitting on the ball, the man glanced up and saw my grandfather. He gave him a wave of acknowledgement. My grandfather held up a hand in return and waited until the man had turned away again before he lowered his head towards mine. 'You know who that is, don't you?' he asked, aware the question was superfluous. Of course, I knew. I must have looked like a cartoon character – my bulging eyes on stalks, my jaw slack and my mouth gaping open.

My father told me about an impromptu game he'd once seen on the Town Moor during the Hoppings, the enormous fair held annually in Newcastle and which brought with it the Big Wheel and the Hall of Mirrors, a Wild West attraction with pretend cowboys and a boxing ring, a seven-and-a-half-foot 'giant', a dwarf acrobatic troop and the standard Bearded Lady. In one tent there was a menagerie of exotic creatures, including poisonous snakes, their bodies as thick as a man's arm. In the early 1950s three of Newcastle's FA Cup winners made a sober promotional appearance among the sideshows and circus attractions. Afterwards my father watched as Charlie Crowe, Bobby Mitchell and Joe Harvey, Newcastle's captain, were persuaded to demonstrate the skills which team responsibility had stopped them from performing at Wembley. The players found an oblong of grass on the periphery of the Moor, well away from the painted booths and garishly signed frontages. Each of them took off and gently folded his club blazer and tucked his tie into his shirt front. The crowd stood back to give them room. For half an hour, as the fair's hurdy-gurdy machines blared in loud competition with one another, Crowe, Mitchell and Harvey played for fun. 'They were like ordinary lads practising on a street corner,' my father said. 'They were using a big, panelled ball,' he added, 'but it went back and forth as though it weighed nothing at all.' This level of skill, observed in microcosm, taught my father the difference between a good amateur and a professional. Mitchell was especially impressive. For minutes at a time he was able to stand statue-still on one foot and hold the ball on the other without tipping over. Mitchell retained full control even when he nudged it only an inch or two upwards. At one point he unlaced his shoes, peeled off his socks and turned up the bottom of his grey flannels to perform the same tricks barefoot. My father described the exhibition as 'the best free show I ever saw'. I thought my free show was better. I still think so because, as pictures of it were forming in my mind, I recognised it as an imperishable memory.

'It's Ray Kennedy,' I replied to my grandfather, still looking at Kennedy as he took the ball on another run, knocking it from one foot to the next as though he was playing hopscotch. Kennedy was then 21 – seven years my elder. He'd already won the Double with Arsenal and a European medal as well. My father and I had seen him from the terraces and from our armchairs. On every occasion he had said the same thing to me, as if

I might have forgotten that Kennedy was the local hero. 'Here's our Seaton Delaval lad.'

I felt a particular affinity with Kennedy. The terrace house of his birth and the home in which I was brought up were less than a quarter of a mile apart. As a child Kennedy and I did the same things. We kicked a ball repeatedly against the coal-house door. We followed the line of the burn through the woods and berried hedges of Holywell Dene. We went to Wheatridge Park, where the local team had been playing since before the Great War and where Hughie Gallacher once drew a crowd that stood 20-deep to see him. Kennedy's father had worked in the same three-shaft pit as mine. In Seaton Delaval, it didn't matter whether you supported Newcastle or Sunderland. You also supported Kennedy.

Until he began his career at Highbury, my village was anonymous – a distant dot on a map. There was nothing much to commend or promote it either. If it had a reputation, it was for dreariness and insignificance. The poet Ivor Gurney, gassed facing the Passchendaele Ridge in 1917, was placed on a signalling course at Seaton Delaval as part of his recuperation. He found it a 'freezing, ugly, uncomfortable Hell of a Hole'. The village, then as later, was reliant on coal for its vitality. When its lattice-work of seams were sealed off and the pit closed in 1960, eventually forcing men like my father southward for survival's sake, the place was destitute. It wasn't so much a case of living as hanging on. At the beginning of 1964 more than 7 per cent of the North East's workforce was unemployed.

The national average was 1.9 per cent. In Seaton Delaval the figure was 8.8 per cent – the highest in the region. The Beeching Report isolated it still further, closing its railway station and uprooting and hauling away the tracks. Its middle-aged men – their prominent facial veins already a tell-tale blue from the coal dust lurking beneath the skin – were idle and doleful. The village soon began to collapse in on itself. Houses became run-down or partly ruined. Shops were boarded up. Small pyramids of colliery slag remained because no one bothered to clear them, and the rubble-strewn streets resembled 1930s Jarrow. Writing contemporaneously about the North East during the 60s, Geoffrey Moorhouse said parts of it looked 'as if Doomsday has already been and gone'. It was true in Seaton Delaval. The village's only virtue was Delaval Hall, the Geordie Versailles and the masterpiece of Sir John Vanbrugh, also the architect of Blenheim Palace and Castle Howard. Close to the miners' cottages Vanbrugh's creation rose incongruously in the landscape, aloof in every way from the grimy poverty encircling it. Coming across the Hall's beauty unexpectedly was like finding a cut ruby in a coal tip. Vanbrugh designed it in English baroque: decorative Doric columns and pediments, Roman military insignia fastidiously chiselled on metopes, serliana-form windows in the towers and grand statues set in tall wall niches. John Piper painted it in ochre and used loaded brushes of rose madder and cadmium yellow to add shocks of colour. The Hall he turned into a canvas made the village seem bleaker than ever. When Kennedy became its lone standard-bearer, the disappointments of one decade had spilled into another and Seaton Delaval was still staggering slowly and pessimistically through the process of recovery. He was the only reason my village was ever mentioned outside its borders.

I remember Kennedy, pictured in his Arsenal kit, answering the life-style questionnaire that appeared weekly in *Shoot*. The replies he gave didn't point to an over-luxurious existence. His car was a Ford Capri. His favourite food was his wife's hot-pot. His favourite singers were Neil Diamond and The Temptations. Asked what he'd be if wasn't a footballer, Kennedy replied with the blank confession: 'I don't know.' But, as far as I was concerned, his most significant answer recorded the purely factual because I felt pride as I read and re-read the name of my village in print.

Birthplace: Seaton Delaval, Northumberland.

Unhappy is the land without a hero; and unhappy is a land that needs one. But Seaton Delaval needed Kennedy. He restored its self-respect. The village felt good about itself again because he was its son. For a while, he represented the only worthwhile thing in it.

Football was always taken seriously there. Those miners unable to afford the fare or the entrance admission to St James' Park or Roker Park went to Wheatridge Park instead. Between the wars several thousand walked there on Saturdays to see matches in the North Eastern League, where the amateurs would play the reserve teams of Newcastle United, Sunderland and Middlesbrough and local rivals such as Blyth Spartans. The men hugged the touchline or stood in orderly tiers on the bank beside the sharply pitched roof of a slatted cabin, which housed the rudimentary dressing and committee rooms and were as cold as Captain Scott's hut. From behind the goal, you could see the chimneys of tiny, brick-block houses sloping towards the heart of the village. The games at Wheatridge Park relieved tedium. Those who lived in Seaton Delaval worked in it too, and football alone occasionally carried them elsewhere. My grandfather once took me to the empty ground and explained the facts succinctly: 'Without a match, most people had nothing to do,' he said. 'Saturdays here were better than birthdays. The men forgot the pit and the bills and their troubles.' He said it in a slightly choked voice, as if it applied to him also. The village had produced an occasional professional before Kennedy. No one, however, had matched his personal story, which attracted the profile writers because its unorthodox narrative was drenched in working-class romance. When Arsenal claimed the Double in 1971, Kennedy was still a teenager. He went to Highbury from the production line of a sweet factory, where he'd expected to remain. Sir Stanley Matthews, an unimpressive manager of Port Vale, had already taken on and then discarded him, writing unequivocally to his parents:

I now feel that Raymond will have difficulty making the grade in football to take it up as a career . . . I consider he will be wasting his time here when he could be finding alternative employment.

Elsewhere in the letter Matthews said he regarded Kennedy as 'sluggish in his movements', a coded rebuke to his natural bulkiness. As judgements go, it proved as egregious as the verdict of the RKO Pictures executive who damned Fred Astaire in a brief paragraph following his screen test for the studio: 'Can't act. Can't sing. Can dance a little.' Much to his discredit Matthews responded disingenuously to Kennedy's success. He claimed to have released him only because the club was overburdened by debt. Matthews used it as an excuse to conceal his mistake, which hubris wouldn't allow him to admit. Only near the end of his life – reminded of the letter he'd dictated and sent to the Kennedys – did he own up to the untruth of it. Matthews preferred ball-players in his own image rather than sweaty labourers. Probably because of it, he didn't recognise that Kennedy, so markedly different from him, could actually play or was even capable of improvement. Kennedy did more than prove him wrong; he exceeded every expectation – including his own. My grandfather knew of Kennedy long before he met him properly. He watched him play and score regularly for his amateur side, New Hartley, in local leagues where only the resolute were retained. He read the reports about him in weekly newspapers, which lay on the tables of the

Miners' Institute. 'I was waiting for another club to pick him up,' he always maintained, swearing that opinion was formed without the advantage of knowing what came next. The things Matthews saw as weaknesses Arsenal and then Liverpool viewed as strengths. Matthews missed the grace in him. Even at 6ft tall, and weighing over 13 stones, it was evident in a lot of the ostensibly minor things Kennedy did. His first touch was excellent and he learnt to turn sleekly and move well despite his lack of pace. One of the most impressive sights was Kennedy accepting a pass – often with his broad back to goal – and then screening the ball before redistributing it accurately. Another was his chesting down of it, always done with a block or swivel of the torso that would cushion the ball at his feet or lay it in the path of whoever was supporting him. He was astonishingly good in tight spaces where his size ought to have rendered him practically immobile. On the day I saw him close up I marvelled at how fleetly he ran on those trunk-like legs. The contradiction between Kennedy's solid build and his abilities created confusion when it came to describing him. It was as though he defied precise classification. Some said he resembled Tommy Lawton. Others compared him to Bobby Smith. A few more saw elements of Duncan Edwards in Kennedy's bravery and brawn.

One goal, for Arsenal against Wolves at Molineux, reveals his special strength. He's almost 40 yards out when he gets the ball and is facing the half way line. The arc of his turn, however, is slight and he bulldozes past his

marker who neither expects – nor is ready for – this rush
of energy. In full flow, it looks as if only a concrete wall
would stop him. Kennedy could carry the ball further
on. But, after one minimal nudge, he swaps it from his
left foot to his right and thrashes the shot inches inside
the post. Another piece of film highlights a different kind
of skill, wonderful in its vision and consummation for
Liverpool at Aston Villa. It is a two-man move. Kenny
Dalglish begins it with one of those delicately threaded
passes from midfield. The ball bobbles along the roughness of the Villa Park pitch, the sort of appalling surface
that only the arrival of the Premiership eradicated. Sand
smothers the bare morass beneath. But Dalglish is aware
of how to play on it and clearly knows where Kennedy
is heading and what he will do; Kennedy similarly knows
where and when Dalglish will release the ball to him. He
begins his run 15 yards inside his own half and collects
the pass 15 yards inside Villa's. He lets the ball do the
work for him and doesn't snatch at it over-eagerly. But,
from the second he gathers possession, Kennedy looks
sure to score. Suspense is generated only as to the manner
in which the goal will come. Some would have blasted it
early. Others would have sprinted on and tried to slide
it around the goalkeeper. Kennedy is more inventive. He's
travelled 50 yards but taken only two touches. The third
is decisive and comes after no more than a darting glance,
which frames in a very bright eye what is in front of him.
Seeing Jimmy Rimmer outside his six-yard box, Kennedy
takes the most difficult option. He decides to chip. It's

like watching the most gentle of sling-shots, the ball drifting as Kennedy caresses it off his boot. On the half-turn Rimmer begins to aimlessly flap and jerk his arms. He looks like a man trying to catch a butterfly in a gale. The ball drops well beyond him. That goal was the highest expression of Kennedy's self. But despite scoring it for Liverpool, and also despite the fact he spent eight seasons at Anfield where he claimed a further 11 winners' medals, including three European Cups, I always think of him wearing an Arsenal shirt. It is all because of that '71 Double and specifically what it meant to Seaton Delaval.

During a mid-week League Cup tie during 1986 I found myself beside Danny Blanchflower in the press box at Selhurst Park. We occupied seats at the end of the row. He was 60 years old, his face understandably fuller than the photographs I'd seen of him during his Double-winning prime at Tottenham. Blanchflower was nonetheless easily recognisable, his skin remarkably unlined for his age. Still working as a columnist for the *Sunday Express*, he was a fluent raconteur and I was a willing listener.

'I used to play this game once,' Blanchflower said to me with an ever-so-sly wink to open the conversation. He offered me his handshake. 'I heard you were quite good,' I replied, taking it. 'I could pass the ball a little and hold it,' he added.

Blanchflower began to eat a meat pie, a rivulet of gravy dribbling down his chin. He had the blarney without being boastful. He was more entertaining – and definitely more enlightening – than the early scrapping of the match played in front of us on that chilly, floodlit night. He told me the story of the Duchess of Kent, who before the 1961 FA Cup Final said to him half way along the presentation red carpet:

'The other team have their names on their tracksuits.'

'Yes, ma'am,' agreed Blanchflower before adding with a comedian's timing, 'but we know each other.'

He then regaled me with his account of how the manager at Barnsley in 1950 banned the ball from training sessions. He thought it would make the players hungrier for it on a Saturday. But training in those days was an army-style regime of road-walks, the endless dull lapping of the cinder track around the pitch and skipping with a rope, which Blanchflower said made them look like 'schoolgirls in a playground'. 'I told the fella that if I didn't see the ball from Monday to Friday that I probably wouldn't recognise it on Saturday afternoon. We got our ball in the end.' The same boss, Blanchflower went on, threatened to report him to the Football Association as a rebel for refusing to sign a contract until the Players' Union approved the terms. 'He didn't get far with that one either,' he said.

Blanchflower spoke about tactics and management, the end of his career at Spurs and the 1958 World Cup in Sweden, where he captained Northern Ireland with the dictum: 'Try to equalise before they score.' He described the pragmatic Bill Nicholson, who he said was as different in composition from Brian Clough as 'land is from water'. As those words left his lips the green-jerseyed Clough leapt out of his dugout in front of us to point frantically at a player on the far touchline, mercifully unable to hear him yelling like a banshee. The pointing turned into an aggressively waved, balled fist. Clough's complexion was the colour of vintage port, the anger rising inside him and reddening his cheeks because of a misplaced pass and a slovenly tackle that followed it. Blanchflower nodded towards him: 'I don't mind that the fella has a lot to say for himself. Especially when he talks about directors. I share his derision for them. It's a rule of mine to try to avoid the boardroom.'

He answered whatever I cared to ask him and even seemed keen to do so, as if no one else was bothered about his past. Blanchflower kept tugging at the brim of his trilby, pulling it lower across his face, and put his hands in his overcoat pockets to ward off the cold. He grew hunched in his seat. Out of duty I kept a weather eye on the pitch and made the briefest notes of what I saw. I was more concerned about Blanchflower's thoughts on games played 25 years earlier – it was the silver anniversary of Spurs' 1961 Double – than an inconsequential, easily forgettable League Cup tie. Except for the odd goal and few scrambles around the posts, I explained to Blanchflower, half-ashamed by the admission, that I'd seen almost nothing of Spurs' achievement or the team that he captained with such intelligence, eloquence and élan. With his globed, slightly protuberant eyes he looked solicitously at me, as if grieving for my loss. I added that

I could reel off the names of Arsenal's Double team because of Ray Kennedy. I knew of Kennedy's telepathic partnership with John Radford, the rapport transparent in the way each related to the other in complicated crossovers and unselfish spinning off to create angles, the two of them scissoring through defences. I knew of Charlie George with his long straight hair and raffish approach. I knew of George Graham, who with finely calibrated passes polished the industriousness that went on around him. Arsenal were technically textbook and tactically organised. But what they failed to do was to set neutrals' hearts aflutter. Spurs scored 115 League goals in '61; Arsenal mustered only 71 ten years later; and ten of their matches were won 1–0. How did the Spurs team compare?

Blanchflower educated me. The press box became a classroom and he was a footballing Mr Chipps. 'The eras were more different than you might think. We were able to play pretty much as we liked. We weren't restricted by a rigid formula. We found our pattern match-to-match depending on who was on form. A decade later the game was more tactical and defensive-minded. Teams in '61 were concerned about winning. Teams in '71 were concerned about not losing.' He re-created the whole season for me – 11 straight League wins and the Championship all but theirs before the third round Cup ties had begun. He offered pen sketches of those who had taken part in it: the battering ram of Bobby Smith; the artful John White, who moved like drifting silk; the courage of Cliff Jones who, Blanchflower said, 'would have dived in to tackle anybody without a second's hesitation'; and the inexhaustible Terry Dyson, described as 'a marathon performer who was still running half an hour after a match ended'. He also talked about someone who was then a stranger to me: the right back Peter Baker. 'The unsung hero,' said Blanchflower, 'not unsung to me, though . . . he covered my back all season. Without him I couldn't have done half of what I did. He was the pro's pro.' And of Dave Mackay, he recalled: 'He scared the daylights out of us when he tackled. I thought some of the opposition might faint before he got to them.' Blanchflower stopped, as if he could hear what he was about to describe next. 'He had a growl,' he said, 'like a war cry.'

I didn't have to push Blanchflower or steer him much. He volunteered his thoughts, giving them a quarter of a century's perspective and instinctively knew what would interest me. I received a tutorial about the teams who *might* or *should* have won the Double before Spurs: West Bromwich Albion of 1954, who won the Cup but stumbled in the League; Manchester United in 1957, who did the opposite, taking the Championship and then losing at Wembley after Peter McParland floored and left unconscious the goalkeeper Ray Wood with a challenge that would now be classified as assault; and Wolverhampton Wanderers, the Cup winners of 1960, who missed the title by a single point. The fact this triumvirate had come so close made Blanchflower certain that winning the Double was possible rather than impossible. 'I always thought we'd win it that season,' he said. 'I looked around at the team and thought our time had come. I told everyone. I said: "Look, we can meet and make history here. We've got the blend – ball winners and ball players and a goal-scorer and a spirit." No one else believed me, really – at least not until the season was three months old.' Blanchflower began to laugh. 'The experts said the same about the Double as they did about climbing Everest or rocketing to the Moon. That it was out of reach. That it couldn't be done. That you'd kill yourself with the effort. The newspapers thought it was physically and mentally impossible to win those two trophies together. In the modern era we weren't supposed to be able to take the strain.' Here Blanchflower stopped and smiled at the idea that 1961 had once been modern; and that he had once been modern himself. As if I was still too young to fully understand the ageing process, he added: 'Some days it feels as though all that happened a thousand years ago. On nights like this, talking to you, I can see it as freshly as the things I did this morning.'

Sometimes obvious questions elicit the best answers. I asked Blanchflower about his most enduring memory of that season. 'Easy,' he said. 'The end of it. Taking the two trophies down Tottenham High Road on our bus. I thought there'd be a few men with rattles and the odd dog, yawning. But you couldn't move. I looked down on the biggest crowd I'd ever seen. Everyone was waving at us.' As he said it, I knew he was back on the top deck of that bus again – the Cup in one hand, the Championship in the other. I could see it in his eyes, which were misty with reflection. The sound of the game before us had been briefly overwhelmed by the cheering of another Time, another generation of 'Glory, glory Hallelujah'. Only the final whistle applied the full stop to Blanchflower, who, without a report to file, a deadline to meet or a notebook to fill with after-match quotes, tipped his trilby at me and sauntered away, his hands inside his coat pockets. I never met him again and I've always regretted that I didn't write or ring to say thank you. Or, better still, to arrange a reunion. It also only occurred to me afterwards that Blanchflower barely talked about himself, as if his role was unimportant or subservient.

The testimony of others told me he was one of the most precise passers of the ball that the game has ever seen. Brian Glanville wrote of Blanchflower: 'He was indisputably a great player, with a vision of the game which was at once sophisticated yet simple; the qualities of the very best football.' (He even used him as the eponymous footballer – articulate and urbane – in his 1963 novel, *The Rise of Gerry Logan*.) And Blanchflower's friend, the philosopher A. J. Ayer, put aside his usual arguments about logical positivism, verification principle and left-wing politics to write of the Double in the *New Statesman*: 'At his zenith [Blanchflower] is the best wing-half that I have ever seen.'

I hunted out a photograph of the Tottenham coach as it inched along the High Road. Blanchflower's memory was impeccable (though, during the early 1990s he would suffer from Alzheimer's Disease). The coach was Spurs white, a floral badge fixed to the front. The peak-capped driver wore white too; he looked like an ice cream salesman. There were balloons attached to lampposts and twisted streamers sagged like Christmas decorations across the windows and the grille. The coach barely had enough of the road to travel on. The crowds swarmed around it, the people waving just as Blanchflower had remembered.

It made me think of Seaton Delaval during Cup Final week in '71. The window of the newsagent's shop was dominated by two colour pictures of Kennedy. One store was decked in red and white bunting; a crude cardboard cut-out of the trophy wrapped in silver paper was attached to its wall. Another used a portrait of Kennedy as its main display and placed a sign above it written in red chalk: 'Ha'way the Lad'. Someone pinned a row of newspaper headlines on to the felt notice-board in the club where my grandfather drank. These were all about Kennedy and his 88th-minute goal against Tottenham at White Hart Lane. Scored at the start of Cup Final week, it won Arsenal more than a North London derby. It won the Championship too. Spurs, caught ball-watching, didn't see Kennedy lurking near the penalty spot. He took two steps towards a left-wing cross and his header scraped against the underside of the bar so powerfully that I imagined it splintering away some of the wood. In the photograph that accompanied the laudatory words Kennedy looks Lawton-like. The camera nails the forward thrust not only of his head, but also of the whole upper body. The ball leaves his forehead with the force of a heavyweight's punch. With perfect symmetry – 19 goals at 19 years old – he finished as Arsenal's top scorer and achieved more in his first full season than the majority of players expect to gain from an entire career.

At Wembley, Arsenal ought to have beaten Liverpool by three or four goals instead of being dragged into extra time before taking the Cup. Kennedy missed one of the chances, unaccountably failing to connect properly from close range when normally he'd have thumped in – without thinking about it – the pass Radford gave him. That night, after Arsenal's 2–1 win, the club in Seaton Delaval was drunk almost dry of Newcastle Brown Ale and McEwan's Export to toast him. The village drank to Kennedy because he didn't forget where he came from. He had gone to London and came back wearing London clothes. But he was no Cockney. The twang in the accent remained unmistakably Geordie and the affectations and big-headed pretensions of success were alien to him. 'It doesn't matter where I go,' he once said to my grandfather, 'I'll always come home and when I finish playing I'll live here.'

Each summer he returned to Seaton Delaval and sat in that same smoky club – and often at the same small round table – as my grandfather. He quietly supped his ale as the dominoes were shuffled, the cards dealt or the cribbage board arranged. My grandfather and his friends used to josh with Kennedy, telling him he'd never be in the same class as 'the real footballers': Jackie Milburn, Len Shackleton and Raich Carter. Kennedy would listen amiably to stories of glorious goals and performances that only those born shortly before Queen Victoria died could possibly have seen. Like my grand-father, Kennedy was a Sunderland supporter – a minority in a Newcastle heartland. So, whether he wanted to hear them or not, Kennedy was captive to tales of the mous-tachioed Alf Common, the first player to be transferred for £1,000 (as far back as 1905) and Alex Hastings, captain of Sunderland's 1936 League Champions. My grandfather would say to him: 'Those '36 lads . . . now *that* was a team . . . they'd have sorted your lot out.'

He asked Kennedy whether he would bring his Cup and Championship medals to the club to 'show the boys'. The 'boys' were septuagenarians and octogenarians. One was a nonagenarian with a curved spine and pouches beneath his eyes that were the colour of rotten peaches. He had a faint, scratched voice. When he walked, head bowed, he looked like a question mark. My grandfather and each of his friends had ribboned medals of their own as a consequence of a quite different sort of battle: the Star of the Expeditionary Force, the Star Clasp or the War and Allied Victory Medal. These were almost always shut away in sideboards or hidden discreetly in clothes drawers, seldom displayed and never flaunted. Kennedy's kindness allowed the astonished old soldiers to gain brief tenancy of his medals and to pass them from wrinkled hand to wrinkled hand. They did so

gently, as if unwrapping glass, said my father. He reckoned the privilege ranked as one my grandfather's
proudest moments. He removed his fingerprints from
the medals by rubbing them with his polka dot handkerchief before returning them pristinely to Kennedy
with the words: 'You've made us all very happy, son.'

As a voracious reader, I only wish my grandfather had
been alive to pick up J. L. Carr's comic novel *How Steeple
Sinderby Wanderers Won the FA Cup*. It is the story of a
nondescript team from a nondescript village that does what
the book's title says with a set of part-time players, including
a milkman and a vicar. In it I'm sure he'd have seen something of Kennedy's rise – the youth who came from the
dead-end obscurity of that sweet factory to claim almost
everything football had to offer – and Seaton Delaval's part
in it too (in a later edition the cover even depicts Tom
Whittaker's Arsenal). My grandfather was born and raised
in the village, and would also die there shortly after
Kennedy's gesture. But he lived long enough to see 'Seaton
Delaval win the Double', which is how he described
Kennedy's success in his own proudly parochial way.

In a few of the summers that followed, my father sat
where my grandfather had done in the club and Ray
Kennedy, still young and still generous with his reminiscences of the season just gone, would pass ten
minutes with him. My father and I followed his career,
always supporting whoever he played for – unless, of
course, the opposition was Newcastle United.

I find it difficult to comprehend the agonies Kennedy has since endured – and endures still. The medals my grandfather held with such pride were sold in 1993 as part of Kennedy's entire collection. The sale raised £80,369. Nowadays Christie's and Sotheby's glossy brochures regularly include the silver and gold of a footballer's trophy cabinet. There is a queue to sell – albeit reluctantly sometimes – and a relatively flush market to sell into. But giving up what the game gave was a fairly rare sight when Kennedy did it. After paying the auctioneers' commission, he was left with £73,063. By then he needed every pound of it, the fruits of his footballing life spent to maintain his dignity in the purgatorial years following the end of his career.

Illnesses do their early work in secret and so medical science still can't be precise about when Kennedy became a casualty of Parkinson's disease or definitively trace the cause; though the terrifying degenerative disorder of his central nervous system probably began at least five to ten years before its diagnosis, which came in the mid-1980s when Kennedy was only in his mid-30s. The atrophying process of Parkinson's is glacial, the virulent symptoms emerging so slowly that someone such as Kennedy had actually incubated them during his most successful seasons at Liverpool. At first the Parkinson's sufferer is ill at ease with himself without knowing why. There is a disquieting perplexity about the way he or she is feeling. For Kennedy, the involuntary shaking of a finger became the tremor of a hand, which in turn became a rigid right arm and an aching stiffness in his once robust body. He became easily exhausted and maladroit. He broke out in sweats. His facial muscles froze, making him expressionless, and his speech became slurred, which was misinterpreted as drunkenness. The dopamine-containing cells in part of his mid-brain had begun to die. Eventually everything he attempted, even the simplest tasks, was ponderous and terribly difficult – from turning a key to opening a tin can, from holding a pen to holding a conversation and from eating and drinking to walking a few steps.

He was essentially no longer himself. It was as if he'd woken from a fitful sleep and overnight had found himself 40 years older. In that *Shoot* questionnaire which I cut out and saved, Kennedy was asked who he would most like to meet. He replied Cassius Clay, which was curious only because by then Clay had been known as Muhammad Ali for nearly ten years. But be careful what you wish for, lest it come true. Parkinson's made Kennedy's life entwine with Ali's in person and on a charitable poster designed to raise awareness of the disease. In describing himself in 1984 Ali articulated what Kennedy was already experiencing: 'I go to bed and sleep eight, ten hours; and two hours after I get up, I'm tired and drowsy again,' said Ali. 'Sometimes I have trembling in my hands. My speech is slurred.' With Parkinson's in common, Kennedy met Ali privately in London in 1992. Ali signed a book for Kennedy, who had a snapshot of the two of them taken and framed. In it Ali's cheeks are bloated and his arms look limp. Only his eyes are sparky. His disease was then more pronounced than Kennedy's. But the decline Parkinson's causes is generally generic. Among its signposts are nausea, paranoia, hallucination, depression, belligerence and disability; and Kennedy went into the black labyrinth of them all – physical and cognitive. He turned moodily aggressive. He was convinced someone wanted to poison him. His long stride became a hesitant shuffle, always on the edge of falling. Often his left foot was so clawed by cramp that he had to crawl around his home on all fours.

Critical judgement of Kennedy as a player could be softened by sympathy for him. But Kenny Dalglish called him 'one of the best players Liverpool have ever had', and didn't offer it as false flattery. I still believe Kennedy was underrated and under-appreciated as a player except by those, like Dalglish, who played alongside him and recognised his worth. Whether as a striker at Arsenal or as the left-sided midfielder he became at Anfield – Bill Shankly signed him and retired on the same morning – he made and scored goals and counted as a team man. When Bob Paisley saw him anew, and switched him to midfield, Kennedy adjusted and then flourished when others would have floundered and found the new demands alien and disorientating. But the initial consequences of Parkinson's meant his decline was rapid and his departure from the game was swift.

Football moves on constantly. It is never still. One season almost overlaps into the next and players – the genuine geniuses, the crowd-pleasers, the cult heroes and the journeyman pros – come and go alike. Even the seemingly irreplaceable are replaced eventually. To watch a recording from only a decade ago makes you appreciate the never-ending churn. Names and faces reappear like strangers after being half forgotten. If their departure from the game registered at all when it occurred, the memory was soon wiped as another, younger player – unknown and untried – emerged instantly to fill the space on the team sheet and then the columns of back pages too. Age or injury sentences the once brilliant to an overlooked retirement. But Kennedy was felled by something far crueller; something, moreover, that he did not understand and was difficult for him to accept.

Just as he'd promised my grandfather all those years before, Kennedy did come home after his retirement. He still lives less than two miles from the football field where I saw his startling energy in that kick-about. In thinking about Kennedy I always reflect on how football is written and spoken about. The game's language leans heavily on the word tragedy. It is rattled off liberally and frivolously and without thought for real meaning. There is the tragedy of an own goal; the tragedy of defeat; the tragedy of a Cup failure. Each is given equal weight and emphasis; and each wears an impostor's clothes. In the classification of human suffering these are no more than flesh wounds and minor breakages. Football continues to count unlucky mishaps and mild misfortune as tragedy simply because such creative accounting wrings more drama, however spurious, out of its seasons. But real tragedy is what happens to good people like Kennedy, a man once healthy whose days are now measured by the medications he takes and whose future is planned an hour at a time.

On a quiet mid-week in 2002 I spotted him in Whitley Bay. He was sitting alone on a slatted bench in front of a building that I remembered from childhood as being a cinema. He was frail-looking and his shoulders were hunched, as if he was sheltering from something. His hands were interlocked, presumably to prevent them from shaking, and he was rocking his upper body, which was wrapped in a chunky sweater. People passed by without acknowledgement. I walked around Kennedy and began pretending to glance into shop windows as I tried to decide whether to bother him with a greeting. I was still making up my mind when a car pulled parallel to the bench. With difficulty, Kennedy used his weak arms as gentle leverage and climbed up from it, taking nearly a minute to do what anyone healthy would have accomplished without strain and in a second. He leant forward and took vulnerable baby steps, his hand resting on a friend's shoulder, towards the passenger door, which was opened for him. He eased into its leather seat, almost catching his head on the edge of the roof as he lowered himself in. Kennedy sat back and breathed in as the driver buckled the seat belt for him. The car drove off and I watched its left indicator blink as it turned towards the coast road.

He was gone, leaving only a long-ago memory of summer behind him.

9

A 6-shilling Ticket
for the Show

The crawl towards the turnstiles was a fiesta – a procession of banners and flags, the blast of horns and whistles and the competing singing and chanting of rival supporters.

It took me almost half an hour to shuffle from the platform of Wembley Park station, along the bottle-neck congestion of Wembley Way and into Wembley Stadium. I moved in half-strides, as though my ankles were chained, and in the impossible crush of people I found myself briefly buffeted by a potato-faced fan in a floppy sombrero, the size of a dustbin lid, and then sandwiched between two Catalonians, who were each shaped like a sherry cask and wore cardboard Lionel Messi masks. The cut-out eyes of these smiling masks were small – the size of an old sixpence – which made them strangely sinister-looking. The men were dressed in replica

Barcelona shirts, the blue-red stripes of each widening as the shiny fabric stretched and rode across their plump bellies. Messi's name and number were emblazoned on the back of the shirts in yellow and every yard or so the men began shouting and clapping for him at full volume, tilting their heads backwards to scream at the sky. They then stopped and bowed in synchrony towards the lattice arch above the stadium, as if it was an altar, and slowed the crowd behind still further.

After manoeuvring past them, I drew alongside an elderly figure with white hair and enormously bushy black eyebrows, a man who was surely a tottering infant during the Spanish Civil War. I guessed his life was entwined with Barcelona's modern history. He'd have been a teenager when Laszlo Kubala claimed his first goals for them in La Liga and in his early 20s by the time Helenio Herrera became manager in 1958. He'd know, painfully, the period when Barcelona were subservient to Real Madrid and remember, rapturously, the double era of Johan Cruyff; first as player and then as European Cup-winning coach. Smartly dressed in a fawn jacket and cream trousers, he was well-tanned, the colour of strong tea. He stooped slightly but was surprisingly sprightly for someone nearer to 80 than 70 years old. The incongruous thing about him, which is why he stood out, was his sagging, weather-beaten cheeks. Each was covered in a broad swipe of Barcelona's bright war paint – long ribs of blue-red to identify him as one of 'El Cant del Barça's 'blue and red people'. The club's silk scarf hung loosely around the shoulders of his jacket and he walked, arm in arm, with two young boys, who I presumed were his grandsons. One wore the Catalan flag as a cape, knotting the corners around his neck. The other had already slipped a Champions League Final T-shirt over his Barcelona stripes. He began several choruses of '*We have a name everyone knows – Barça, Barça, Barça*' and eventually the elderly man accompanied him too. Ahead of me there were flashes of another thousand Barcelona shirts, almost every one advertising Messi.

Eventually I reached the top of the ramp and paused to stare down on to Wembley Way. I watched the sluggish progress of the crowd and felt privileged to have a seat waiting for me. Outside the tube station I'd passed others who had travelled hopefully; dozens of fans brandishing roughly written, oblong signs that begged for a ticket. 'Willing to Pay Whatever You Want', read one. 'Please – don't let me miss THIS match', appealed another. A third was tantamount to on-your-knees pleading in only four words: 'Take pity on me', it said. But the Manchester United supporter holding that placard high above his head already looked forlorn, aware he was asking the impossible. I saw no one stop and miraculously flourish a spare ticket at him or anyone else. Waiting for my turn through Entrance L, I witnessed another ticketless fan, only two places ahead of me in the queue, trying to vault the narrow barrier, which was built into a cubicle. The security in front of him made the effort futile and he ran off, no doubt to try again elsewhere.

The desperate gesture illustrated how much the final mattered; indeed, how much it meant to be inside Wembley instead of watching what it offered from an armchair or a barstool. Rarely does a match acquire iconic status before a ball is kicked. But Barcelona against United managed it on the premise that it could be The Game of the Decade, The Match of the Century or at the very least qualify as one of those indisputably 'great' European finals, a late May evening for connoisseurs that would live on in the memory and be talked about long after the fact. So those with tickets – a goodly number, like mine, bought at grossly extortionate prices – were never going to part easily with them; and probably not at all.

Palpable in every corner of Wembley as kick off drew closer was a feverish amalgam of anticipation and of expectation, as if the game was guaranteed to fulfil every prediction made about it. This level of optimism was generated almost wholly by thoughts of what Barcelona were capable of achieving through their classical stylists, Messi and Iniesta, Xavi and Villa. But I'll wager that what motivated most neutrals – such as me – to be at Wembley was focused on Messi's talents alone. The Messi who, against Real in the semi-final first leg at the Bernabeu had claimed a goal that counted as a miracle – a simple pass and a simpler return, a pivot, a beautiful body-sway, a gimlet-eye and a sharp and super-fast brain, a crafty touch and a rocket sprint that carried him past five white shirts before the smooth delivery of a slid-in shot. Even though Messi was firmly locked on to Real's radar, his mesmerising close control made intercepting him an impossibility as soon as he picked up the ball mid-way in the half and decided that his rivals' next touch would be to collect it from the back of the net. He bamboozled them with a vigorous grace, the ball affixed to his boot during a solo exhibition. Out of nothing he created something; and that something was so sublime that critical judgement was able to declare it instantly as a stroke of genius without fear of being proved wrong or stupid afterwards. The cameras naturally concentrated on Messi's celebrations. But the most telling scenes were caught behind him and in long shot. Real's defenders were experiencing a level of trauma normally only induced by the most sudden and jolting of shocks to the system. It was written across their blanched faces. Real looked as though the reality of what had just happened to them would take at least another day and a night to sink in; and even then some of them would still refuse to believe it.

My father once told me: 'Don't be lazy. Never miss a chance to see a great player.' He cited one example, which pressed home the point irrefutably. Like almost everyone else, he'd assumed Glasgow Rangers would comfortably dispose of Eintracht Frankfurt in the last four of the 1960 European Cup. He'd already drawn sketchy plans to go to Hampden Park and see the first final ever staged in Britain. He felt sure it would be between Rangers and Real Madrid. When Eintracht humiliated them – beating Rangers 12–4 on aggregate – he abandoned the idea in disgust at the drubbing. But, as the final loomed, and as he waited for one mining job to begin after another had ended, he changed his mind. At the last moment he withdrew some spare beer money, saved in a black tin box, and headed overnight to Glasgow. He travelled with friends in a converted bread van, the men inside rattling along rough roads like bottles in a crate. 'I decided it didn't matter that Rangers had lost,' he said. 'Who cared about club loyalties when you could watch Ferenc Puskas, Alfredo Di Stefano and Francisco Gento?'

Those fans without tickets at Wembley in 2011 would have been astonished to know how straightforward my father found gaining admission to Hampden. The cheapest ticket had a face-value of 5 shillings and got the bearer a crowded spot on uncovered terracing behind the goal. My father had one in his wallet scarcely five minutes after walking into Glasgow's railway station. 'I knew I'd get one there because I had done before,' he said. He paid a tout, loitering near a newspaper kiosk, 6 shillings. From his inside jacket pocket, the tout – wearing a plaid suit and acting like a spiv who still thought nylons were in short supply – approached those he identified as possible customers with a nod, a wink and the whispered question: 'Going to the football?' He produced a wad of tickets as thick as a deck of cards.

The bundle was bound together with an elastic band and he tugged one of the tickets free as surreptitiously as possible and palmed my father's coins on to an associate for safe-keeping. The tout smiled warmly as he handed over the ticket, as if he and my father regularly did business together. In the years that followed, my father would always say: 'Paying that extra shilling seemed a bit extravagant at the time – especially when I found out I could have bought one for 4 shillings outside the ground two hours before kick off.' The thin paper ticket was pale yellow – 'golden', my father said, and added: 'I was a lucky man to have it.'

For those 6 shillings he saw ten goals and a match that overwhelmed him. The performance dominating its 90 minutes was close to perfection, stupendous enough to rank as historically significant while the clock was still ticking on it. Sometimes in remembering it my father would close his eyes, as though in doing so he'd flicked on a projector in his mind which began flipping through slide-show images: Hampden Park sunlit and the corner flags flapping like sails because of a briskish breeze; the immaculate whiteness of Real, moving ghostily across the pitch; Puskas with his sophisticated juggling; the balding Di Stefano, arrogant because he had every right to be; and what my father called the 'old-fashioned, mazy dribbling' of Gento on the left wing. He described the Eintracht goalkeeper, wearing a peaked cloth cap, as 'looking like a pigeon fancier in his lofts'.

As seminal as Hungary's 6–3 embarrassment of England during Coronation year, Real's 7–3 unpicking of Eintracht taught British football a lesson about continental wiles and ways at a stage when Europe, despite the geography, still seemed socially and culturally far away and mysterious to my father and his 'Who won the war?' generation. Misguidedly thinking that 'foreigners' had nothing worthwhile to import, there were rabid isolationists in our island game who disregarded the European Cup as a frippery and European methods as inferior. At Hampden, Real blew away both the haughty notion of British superiority and the smug assumption that the Cup would come to our shores if we simply turned up and competed for it often enough. Some, such as the far-sighted Matt Busby, understood the blatant fallacies of that argument from the outset. Others only recognised it as outdated, like medieval belief in a flat earth, because Real forced them to recognise it. The enlightenment began at Hampden.

My father thought the final was unsurpassable. After the fifth or sixth Real goal, he looked around and noticed the crowd had fallen into two categories. 'There were those who couldn't stop shouting . . . and there were those who could barely speak.' He fell into the second category. He followed the conquest without much of a murmur, entranced by the visual spectacle and knowing Real could have outshone all-comers that night with a display which was both beautiful and clinically businesslike. In discussing it he always made the experience – through tone rather than his choice of language – seem almost spiritual. 'I've got bad news for you,' he once said to me. 'If you're waiting to see a match like that, you'll wait in vain. You won't be so fortunate. *Never.* I promise you. It can't happen again.'

Those words came back to me at Wembley as I slid the electronic bar code on my oversize ticket into the scanning machine and waited for a click and the light to turn green before I pushed through the gleaming steel turnstile. Surely Messi would match Puskas? Surely Barcelona would imitate Real? And surely I would remember 2011 as clearly as my father recalled 1960?

That, after all, was the purpose of being here.

The day before going to Wembley I watched a recording of that Hampden Park final. Though I'd seen all the goals before – four of them from Ferenc Puskas – I'd never sat through the entire match. The idea was to find out whether the game lived up to its billing as *the* classic. It would tell me whether my father had over-mythologised and idealised both it and the Real Madrid he had seen. I also wanted to test the legitimacy of comparisons made between Di Stefano's Real and the current Barcelona.

The BBC's black and white broadcast showed the scars of age. There were needle-thin scratches across sections of the film, and some of the reel was smokily pale, which suggested the stock had faded gradually. Because I take the super-sharpness of High Definition for granted, the recording seemed as ancient to me as one of those early and particularly crackly Hollywood talkies. The programme began with an aerial shot of Hampden Park's oval bowl, the terraces like a series of cliff faces. I froze the picture and looked closely at the end of the ground where I knew my father had stood, his hands and belly pressed against a crash barrier. Each figure in the gently rolling mass of 135,000 was no bigger than a pin-dot.

Nowadays the hour before any major final is accompanied by all sorts of glitzy hoopla. As if fearing the match will fall flat as a spectacle, the organisers wrap fancy packaging around it in the hope no one notices any deficiencies lying beneath. There's always loud, portentous music, which sounds like Wagnerian pastiche, the even louder fizz of fireworks and coloured flares, the sponsors' advertising spread across the pitch and several hundred miles of glittery ribbon and tinsel. Hampden Park didn't have any of this. The build-up there was so low key that it was difficult, at first, to believe anything momentous could come out of such an ordinary-looking and informal occasion. The teams simply came out of the tunnel and kicked off. But, by the end, I was thinking about the sense of wonder my father must have felt as he saw this dream-like match unfold between the bobbing heads and shoulders of those in front of him on the terracing.

I could watch this game time and again and repetition would never dull it. More than that, I think I could find something new in every viewing – especially the infinitesimal things which escaped attention the first time only because there were too many to absorb at one sitting: another of those sly, inside runs that Puskas makes to create space for himself when the route to goal is seemingly impassable; or a clever feint from Gento – a drop of the shoulder so quick as to be almost subliminal to the naked eye and which only the defender reads before making the elementary mistake of believing it; or a previously overlooked moment when the demanding Di Stefano bellows for the ball on the edge of his own area before beginning his cerebral scheming, an expressive wave conducting the entire form, line and tempo of Real's counter-attack over the next 70 yards.

My father had a panoramic view of it that television could never capture; certainly not the BBC of the 60s with its two cameras on a high gantry, which missed more than was filmed. Still, what made it on the screen will never be dismissed as a dusty period piece. Even taking into account the vast differences between the football then and the football now, no one can doubt the purity and weight of Real's achievement over Eintracht. The goals' landslide, which brought them their fifth successive European Cup, is no longer possible. Todays' coaches drill today's teams too well to allow it to happen when a prize such as the Champions League is at stake. Teams are marshalled along rigidly tactical lines. Insofar as tactics existed for the Real of 1960, the primary one was based on the most rudimentary mathematical equation, which is to score more heavily than the opposition. If this happened, nothing else mattered. Real were able to live by this airy philosophy because they had the confidence and talent to make it workable. And never more so than at Hampden Park. True artists in whatever field exert full and discriminating control; that is what Puskas and Di Stefano did – and not only because the two of them shared Real's goals.

Football back then thought anyone still playing at 30 qualified as a pensioner. Puskas was already 33 years old and Di Stefano was about to turn 34, which made them geriatrics. What is more, both looked far older than their years. Or perhaps some kindly registrar had once fiddled with the date on their birth certificates as a favour to them. Puskas was a good advertisement for the fuller figure. Heavy-faced and tubby, he looked over-fond of big breakfasts and gluttonous lunches. Di Stefano's build was rakish, but he had a bald patch as distinctive as a Franciscan monk's and dented features. The topic of age and appearance became irrelevant at Hampden Park only because Puskas and Di Stefano defied convention with such command and aplomb. Puskas was poised, and Di Stefano laid back. Though the Hampden Park pitch was hard and rough, the short, rapid passes each pushed or clipped along it made the surface look smoother than a bowling green. Poor, nonplussed Eigenbrodt of Eintracht. He originally attached himself to Di Stefano and then switched in desperation to tracking Puskas instead. He was equally unsuccessful. Whatever he sought was always just a shadow, and eventually he gave up chasing it.

Odd, that there were no goals before the 18th minute and none after the 76th. Odder still, given the deluge which followed it, that Eintracht should score first. But Real reacted to that goal as if it was a provocation. What followed was the most uneven contest since Captain Ahab took on the Whale. The insoluble problem for Eintracht was trying to retain the whip hand without the ball, which Real refused to give them. If Puskas didn't own it, then Di Stefano did. If neither was in possession, Gento, Canario or Del Sol stretched the Germans with quick footwork or tortured them with party-pieces – nutmegs and back-heels. Once Real got going, Eintracht were like stooges in a variety act. One improvised move comprised 27 consecutive touches – nudges, flicks, three-penny turns – in a 20x20 feet square of turf on the near touchline. This was showing off, and Real did it only to prove it could be done. For me the best of their seven goals was the galloping, breakaway fifth. It was created with spontaneous elegance and team work rather than a blaze of individuality. Only five passes were needed to move the ball – regained after an Eintracht corner – from box to box before Gento crossed it and Puskas plunged his podgy frame forward and headed in from six yards. It doubly underlined not only Real's capacity to score almost at will, but also the uselessness of any attempt on Eintracht's part to stop them. Even then, after less than an hour, the truly merciful would have ended the game and Eintracht's punishment. In search of a modicum of respect, which was the only thing salvageable for them, the Germans ploughed gallantly on nonetheless and managed to score twice more. But by then Real, unassailable and almost bored by their own brilliance, were cooling down and had lost much of their earlier inspiration.

The final left its mark on me for other reasons than establishing Real as upper crust. There wasn't an offside flag until the 70th minute. There was no diving, no rolling, no indignant or heart-on-the-sleeve appeals to the referee to have an opponent booked or sent off. There was no obvious time-wasting and none of the foot-stomping tantrums of dissent that regularly blemish modern matches. Gento, speechless, threw his arms wide after a plaintive appeal for a throw-in went against him; that's about as far as the juvenile pettiness went.

I don't suppose I'll ever forget Puskas. Seldom has beauty been contained within such a peculiar shape. Whether he was icily calm or just insouciant is a moot point, but a penalty he took with no fuss and barely a flicker of emotion remained prominent in my mind afterwards. I still recall it detail by detail, and I can imagine no modern penalty-taker doing what Puskas did. He allowed the referee to place the ball on the spot for him. He didn't dash towards it to check the positioning. He didn't wipe the ball free of dirt or carefully readjust its line by spinning it in his hands. And he didn't attempt to eyeball the goalkeeper or psyche him out with a daggered gaze. In fact he hardly glanced at him, as if his presence was immaterial. There were no displacement actions either. He didn't anxiously scrape the front of his boot against the back of his socks or pick perfunctorily at his laces or tug the front of his shirt to loosen it. There was no trace of nerves in Puskas. He began a seven stride run-up from outside the area and placed his shot inside the goalkeeper's left-hand post. It was all as neat and clean as banging in a nail.

The blinding display Real gave obliged my father to stay for the Cup presentation as a matter of duty. 'It'd have been rude to go without saying thank you,' he explained. The ceremony was unpretentious and un-choreographed. The trophy sat on a small, slender-legged wooden table near the mouth of the players' tunnel. The table was covered by a plain cloth and looked to have been borrowed from someone's kitchen. The dignitary in charge passed the Cup to Real with no more grandeur or solemnity than a headmaster handing out a winner's rosette during school sports day. As the silverware came towards him at the beginning of Real's lap of honour, my father said he waved a white hand-kerchief towards it (for such a reserved man I knew this counted as a show of wild emotion). Afterwards he and his best friend, a Celtic supporter, downed pints beside a half-drunk group of Frenchmen in a run-down pub that ignored licensing hours on account of the fact its publican had suddenly fallen in love. The subject of his affection was Puskas. My father didn't speak French and the Frenchmen barely spoke English and found Scottish colloquialisms impossible to understand. 'It didn't matter much,' my father said. 'We shouted out a name of a Real player and then had a drink. All of us were from Spain that night.'

He disliked hoarding ephemera. He saw programmes, ticket stubs and newspaper cuttings as unnecessary clutter, best dropped into the dustbin once their purpose had been served. So he didn't buy a programme at Hampden Park and he screwed up and threw away his ticket. But he came home late the following day with a copy of that morning's *Glasgow Herald* poking out of his raincoat pocket. My mother eventually used the newspaper to line the top drawer of a little-used chest. For years afterwards, until the print became yellow and dusty, my father would occasionally open that drawer and find the *Herald*'s front page staring back at him again. Beneath the masthead there was a photograph of the crowd making its way into the stadium. 'I'm in there somewhere,' he'd say.

That match was the highlight of his football-watching life. When he tried to replicate it, the unsuccessful attempt gave him a far sharper realisation of his good fortune to have been in Glasgow when aesthetic brilliance lit up its austere surroundings. Believing Eusebio, then a tender 21, might remind him of either Puskas or Di Stefano, he went to Wembley in 1963 for Benfica against Milan. Benfica had won the European Cup in 1961 and then retained it by beating Real 5–3 in Amsterdam 12 months later. As if anointing his heir, Di Stefano had peeled off his shirt and taken Eusebio's in exchange. Were Benfica the next Real?

Sitting in splendid isolation at Wembley – the stadium less than half-full after a boneheaded decision to kick off in the afternoon – my father urged Eusebio through the strapping run that brought him the opening goal. He sat back to wait for lightning to strike again. It never did. Wearied under the sun, Eusebio ran out of puff and Benfica wilted, losing 2–1. The game was worth seeing – but not worth going to see. It convinced him more than ever that he'd never witness another Real.

In advance of every European Cup Final he and I saw together on television, he would say pessimistically: 'Won't be anything like 1960.' It was the safest bet to lodge, which is why no bookmaker would ever have taken the wager if he'd chosen to make one. Some of those finals were so awful that what ought to have been a pleasure became a bitter test of endurance instead. In particular Steaua Bucharest against Barcelona in 1986 and Red Star Belgrade against Marseille in 1991, were so sterile that my father drifted back to Hampden Park to relieve the tedium; the atmosphere, the goals, the parade of the Cup were retrieved from the archive again. He believed Uefa ought to have made that final compulsory viewing for all other finalists. While watching two teams spar cautiously with one another, the flair which got them to the final paralysed because of the dread of defeat, he'd say: 'I'd show them the film of Real Madrid the night before the game and tell them: This is what you've got to live up to. This is what we expect.' A minute or so later he'd add, irritably, 'I'm right, aren't I?'

I'd nod silently at him, as I always did when I knew the argument was unwinnable.

Every final since 1960 has aspired to equal its quality and reputation, and almost all have suffered by comparison to it. The exceptions are contemporary high-dramas: Manchester United, 1–0 down and time already up, beating Bayern Munich 2–1 in 1999; Liverpool, 3–0 behind at half time, overcoming Milan in 2005, a resurrection so improbably stunning that even the combination of film, photographic and printed accounts still persuades you to recheck the evidence to make certain it happened.

Those finals owe their encasement in legend to the crucial element of suspense – the unforeseen twist in the plot. But only as I left Wembley, after watching Barcelona take apart United 3–1, did I properly appreciate what my father must have felt viscerally at Hampden Park more than half a century earlier; and why an attachment to that game never left him. Seldom does history actually seem history when you are living through it; the label is nearly always attached retrospectively. But, at Wembley, the past and present met and what the eye saw the brain immediately recognised as setting down an historical marker. What Barcelona provided was a celebrity exhibition as divine as Real's in 1960. Hindsight will definitively grade the final; but where it sits will depend less on what is past and more on what is to come. The only thing that threatens to diminish it is the evolution of the Barcelona team itself. Real didn't get better after beating Eintracht; Di Stefano and Puskas were gone when the club won another European Cup in the mid-60s. Hampden Park proved to be the culmination of Real's era. Wembley, however, truly established Barcelona's.

Even if, much later on, this final is regarded as a preliminary sketch for some greater art it will still count as a privilege to have been there at the creation. If it isn't, the ticket holder will still be as blessed as my father was at the beginning of a much different decade. It was Masterpiece Theatre, combining education as well as entertainment. I only wish my father could have seen it; and that we could have talked about it afterwards.

Weighty and well-intentioned advice about how United could counter Barcelona's pass-and-move virtuosity, and also contain Lionel Messi, piled up in advance of the final for Sir Alex Ferguson. No permutation was excluded. The virtues of 3-3-3-1 to 4-4-1-1 and all formations in between were stuck to magnetic boards, drawn on to screens in convoluted squiggles and arrows or debated in newspaper columns beneath the bylines of some of the game's foremost professors. As it turned out United, despite holding on at 1–1 at half time, were just briefly in it. The only tactic that might have won them the match was to play the team Ferguson chose and simultaneously field the substitutes' bench as well – and then hope that neither the referee nor Barcelona could count. Eighteen players would probably have been enough to handle Messi; anything less and you were in trouble.

The Thesaurus was long ago picked clean of superlatives to describe him. What remains is the knowledge – profoundly troubling for anyone but Barcelona – that his absolute peak is still some way off. That Messi will get better scarcely seems possible because he frequently looks like perfection – a man in his early to mid-20s with nothing of his trade left to learn. Trying to stop him is like trying to contain the spread of flood water. He spills everywhere – inexorably into and through the narrowest niches, the thinnest gaps. And in dealing with Messi being forewarned is not to be forearmed, for anticipating what he can do is no solution to stopping him. 'Every time I go with the feeling,' he says of the intuition that determines the direction of his attacks and which makes man-marking or second-guessing him hazardous.

Messi pushes off from a standing start. He is usually stationary when he accepts a pass to feet and then his quicksilver speed takes over. He shows the defender the ball before whipping it away from him. This was a recurrent image at Wembley. In the build-up to Barcelona's second goal, he coldly embarrassed Nani close to the touchline. Nani looked horror-struck. In another move an unpredictable change of direction left Vidic as adrift as a shipwrecked sailor. A third found Ferdinand unsure of whether to poke out his leg or use his much longer stride to stay abreast of him; Ferdinand, gingerly at first and then impetuously, decided to attempt the tackle, and Messi hurdled contemptuously over it. His other sideways jinks, which took less than a quarter of a second to execute, demonstrated how difficult it is to wall him in. On another night and in another game, the goal he got – the 53rd of his season – could have been saved. But the manner in which he scored it, capitalising on generous space and shooting powerfully along the floor, also confirmed that skills which others train hard to try to attain, were born into him as a gift. United allowed him space. It was rather like leaving the front door ajar when a sneak thief is lurking.

Like Puskas, his physical presence is not overwhelming until he starts to play. At 5ft 7in, he looks as though he might dissolve at the slightest touch. But he can't be kicked or barged out of a game by rebarbative crudity. He is too strong-muscled and firm-boned for that – a small bull in dancing slippers. In close-up, as he's about to begin a dribble, the eyes are wide and unblinking, as if not a thing (and certainly not another player) could shift his concentration or focus. He looks only at what is ahead of him and beyond the shoulders of the defender; but his peripheral vision is extraordinarily wide, like a landscape painter's canvas, and it absorbs everything in the crowded scene. United's defenders got close enough to put a hand on Messi's back but were, paradoxically, a full light-year from ever restraining him. In his luminous boots, the colour of picked limes, he always found a fresh parcel of energy and just accelerated away from them. I was sitting high behind the goal – the sort of seat my father would have chosen – from where I could admire the architectural splendour of Norman Foster's new Wembley, its turf like ironed baize, and the way in which an unfettered Barcelona dictated their own terms. The surface had been well watered and the ball moved slickly across it, which was perfect for them. As well as Messi's, there was another unquestionably superb performance, from Xavi, whose emphatic passing and vision were faultless, and a roll call of fine ones wherever you looked: Iniesta and Mascherano and Pedro and Villa, the other scorers. But this is emphatically a *team* – not a collection of star-system soloists occasionally interrupting one another's monologues. Looking down from the back row was the optimum vantage point to be constantly astonished by the flow of their build-up play, disciplined and always in sync. No team is more accomplished in retaining possession than Barcelona, who exhausted United. Swarming moves, crammed with short passing, were jigsawed together with hardly a loose or disfiguring joint. What Giggs, Hernandez and Rooney routinely do to others in the Premier League was done to them in the second half when United's suffering was most apparent. For the final 15 minutes Barcelona had the luxury of being able to roll the ball casually between them, as if playing a game within a game from which United were excluded. It was done almost civilly, like a gentle slap with a velvet glove. The flabbergasting thing for me was the lack of height in the side. There wasn't much heavyweight brawn about them either. But, when you pass and dribble like Barcelona, neither is necessary. The very complicated was made to look very simple. The pitch looked bigger whenever one of them had the ball, and the possibilities in using it seemed endless too.

Standing in his technical area, arms folded, Pep Guardiola admired it with an immovably serene expression and appeared as cultured as his team. The managers I first noticed in the 1960s, such as Newcastle's craggy Joe Harvey, looked to have borrowed someone else's clothes. These men wore chequered sports coats, which were too long in the tail for them, and loosely knotted nylon ties. They were dungaree-workers, dressed up for the day and uncomfortable about it. With his suave suit, white shirt, hand-made shoes and dark designer stubble, Guardiola looked as though he could advertise Prada accessories or Breitling watches on the glossy pages of *GQ* or *Esquire.*

Near the end, the Cup out of reach and Barcelona combining poetry and murder within them, I saw the wide screen at the far end of the stadium was showing a close-up of Ferguson, who I suspected looked as Ernst

Berger, the Eintracht Frankfurt coach, must have done at Hampden Park – crestfallen and striving hard not to show the stress of it. Ferguson's fists were firmly clenched, each thumb jabbed into the flesh. Through the oversize black-framed spectacles he always wore, Berger responded to Real's shredding of Eintracht by articulating afterwards the coach's uselessness in such circumstances. 'You are a spectator,' he had said, agonising about it. Ferguson had been a spectator at Hampden Park, too – he and my father were just paying customers – and I wondered whether Barcelona reminded him of that inspired night too. Pride can come from facing facts, and Ferguson earned considerable credit through the rationality of his judgements and the good grace with which he expressed them. Yes, he admitted, United had been given an unprecedented 'hiding'. And yes, he confessed, there was a marked discrepancy between what United had promised and what had been delivered.

Berger baffled himself with questions of how Eintracht might have restrained Real before accepting that the task was always beyond them. Ferguson, though possessing a much clearer sense of where United could have limited the damage, sounded as though he knew Barcelona would give them the slip again if the teams were quickly rematched. To compete with them then must have felt as other playwrights did at the end of the 16th and the beginning of the 17th centuries when only Shakespeare mattered. It was not that United were bad, of course; merely that Barcelona were exceptional, a once-in-a-generation gathering of supreme talent. But that knowledge didn't make defeat at Wembley more digestible for Ferguson any more than being part of a classic compensated Berger for the scale of his loss against Real. The common denominator between 1960 and 2011 is that to scrutinise both matches is to learn something about the game's highest standards. Neither final sustained dramatic intrigue – the result was too obvious too soon. The compulsion to carry on watching came from the sophistication of the winners.

All around me the Barcelona fans were in an acute fever. Among them it was impossible to opt for an observer's detachment. As my father had done in Glasgow, I stayed until the Cup was toted in front of me. Messi wore the huge trophy like a high hat before cradling it against his body, the size and scale of it almost too big for him to carry. Amid the swirl and curl of flags, yet another rendition of the Barça chant and the mirrored glint of phone-camera flashbulbs, I thought of the elderly man, who I'd seen at the beginning of the evening with those Barcelona flags greased on to each cheek. I'd come across him again shortly before kick off. He was on the concourse inside the stadium, sipping pale beer from a half-pint glass and talking animatedly in his native tongue. Now I imagined that voice speaking his fulsome memories and putting the final into perspective for the benefit of his grandsons. There'd be an urge to recall the past simply to put the present into context. I also thought about the final's positive effects – people in the pubs, bars and living rooms across the globe who had seen and savoured it and also coaches who would try to incorporate *something*, however minuscule or rudimentary, from Barcelona's repertoire into their own sides for the coming season. I thought especially about the football-besotted boys who would wake the following morning, grab a ball and turn scruffy parks and small back gardens into Wembley to mimic Messi. I felt a pang of envy about being too old to join in.

In all sport the perpetual question is how one era rates against another. My father drummed it into me that Pele's Brazil of 1970 – Rivelino, Jairzinho, Gerson, Tostao, Carlos Alberto – comfortably outranked Real as the greatest of all time; a side so brilliant it could win the Mexico World Cup without much of a defence and a goalkeeper prone to fumbling. He let me stay up until the bleary, early hours to watch them beamed via satellite from South America, the novelty of football at midnight as captivating as Pele's shot from the half way line or his unforgettable dummying of the Uruguayan goalkeeper. 'It's part of my son's football education,' he'd say to my mother, who was worried I'd sleep at my school desk the following morning. Barcelona aren't Brazil, and perhaps no one ever will be; but the intrepid spirit of their play is the same and the Champions League Final convinced me that football is better now than it has ever been. It isn't just that the game is faster and the players are in far superior physical condition; no half-time smokes for them. It is the variation of tactics and the range of skills – in passing, close control and finishing – that exists in even the most mundane of matches. My father, always attuned to what had gone before, would dispute all this. I know he'd stubbornly find something from the era of Jackie Milburn and Len Shackleton to suggest it wasn't the case. But I'd only have to show him a recording of Messi's Barcelona to come out on top.

Afterwards I thought of my father as I walked alone along Wembley Way, its arch lit up against the night sky. I thought of how often this corner of north-west London had been a junction point in my life – the old Wembley with its Twin Towers and grubby walls and my father's stories of what had happened within them, told and retold. And I also thought of him strolling away, contented and smiling, from Hampden Park in 1960, already reliving what he'd relive repeatedly over the next 30-odd years. I began to eavesdrop on conversations because I felt starved of them; and also because my father wasn't there. The Manchester United supporters I overheard were magnanimous. There was none of the tart disillusion or apportioning of bitter blame that usually follows a Cup Final defeat. 'Better team won – nothing else to say,' I heard one Mancunian confess to another at the conclusion of a long analysis noticeably lacking self-pity. Consoled by it, his friend twisted his expression into one of mournful acceptance and agreed: 'We did all we could,' he said, recognising the feat. 'No one else could have held them as long as we did.' On the tube, a small boy, United's flag furled around a short pole, asked his father why United didn't sign Messi and then whether the addition of George Best would have made a difference to the outcome. His face was speckled with half-dry tears. 'We'd have won then, wouldn't we?' he said, gazing up and seeking reassurance. I supposed only his father could have told him about Best in a way that made him mention his name, as if for comfort. I supposed, too, that the story his father relayed had once come from his own father. And I was sure that this unknown boy, who I had never seen before and will not meet again, would likewise tell his own sons about it.

In this way, football beats on – passed from one generation to the next. My father taught me that much.

Afterword

The Tyne Awaits You
and is Yours

All afternoon I'd tracked the goal updates – from one-nil to three and then the improbable flood. So I knew Newcastle United, previously famished for a result and grubbing around at the bottom of the Premiership, had beaten Sheffield Wednesday 8–0 at St James' Park. After such a dismal start to the season, the result seemed impossibly surreal to me. Which is why it only counted as real, rather than fancifully imagined, when I saw the crowd celebrations. I was home alone, and catching up with the television news. I remember the minute and the hour as well as the day – 19 September 1999 – because of the stamp they left so deeply on me.

On the screen were close-ups of clenched-fist salutes from overjoyed men dressed in black and white, waving scarves and flourishing the occasional banner or flag.

One shaven-headed supporter, arms aloft and eyes closed, wore an expression of absolute contentment. Beside him a fan with the club's badge tattooed on to his right forearm continually punched the air with long, downward thrusts. His action reminded me of a ship-worker I'd once seen hammering metal on a Tyne dock, the sparks flying upwards and all around him. There was a pensioner in an oversized club shirt hugging and kissing his wife, her hair bunched in dyed, gingery curls. At the front, standing where I had once stood, were rows of boys, one of them staring into the camera and holding up eight fingers.

At the end there was the rhythmic chant of a name: Bobby Robson. Alan Shearer had claimed five of Newcastle's goals. For me, however, the match and the moment belonged to Robson – silvery combed hair and a parchment pale face, its inerasable creases like cracks in plaster. He was dressed in a dark suit, the cuffs of his white shirt were visible as he waved gratefully to each corner of the ground.

For a long while my father had wanted Robson to take charge of Newcastle. In the preceding, mostly bitter-sweet, decades managers had come and gone frequently at St James' Park. There were the obscure, such as Gordon Lee and Richard Dinnis. There were the griz-zled, such as Arthur Cox and Jim Smith. There were even two World Cup winners – Jack Charlton and Ossie Ardiles. In between them others had promised fresh starts too, which none had delivered to my father's satisfaction; not even Kevin Keegan. Each year he waited for the major trophy that never came. My father believed the club's old powers would only return under Robson.

Comforting ourselves after another near miss or abject failure, we'd reminisce about the last occasion Newcastle brought back a significant piece of silverware. This was a distant memory. In June 1969, we'd listened to the commentary of the second leg of the Inter-City Fairs Cup Final: Newcastle were in Hungary facing Ujpest Dozsa, a name I could barely pronounce. We strained to hear the feeble radio signal. The broadcast dissolved into spits and long hisses and the commentator's words drifted weakly away from us, as though blown somewhere on a Budapest wind, or were lost completely in a loud crack of static. Often we had to guess the outcome of cliff-hanging attacks and goal-mouth scrambles. At one stage we lay on the floor, each of us with one ear nuzzling the grille of the radio until the volume returned to normal. My father fiddled with the long aerial, picking up the blare of some pop music and then a voice gabbling madly on in Spanish. Newcastle held a 3–0 lead from the first leg. By half time we'd heard enough to know the Hungarians were only one behind and ought to have been in front. We steeled ourselves for a hefty defeat. The weather must have changed – breaking in a clear, wide channel from the Danube to the chimney on our roof. For we heard clearly the description of the corner Newcastle imme-diately got as the second half began. And we heard – as crisply as if the commentator were sitting beside us – an uninterrupted account of the initial, hacked clearance one of the Ujpest defenders made before the ball was pumped back into the box instantly and then slammed into the roof of the net. Newcastle won the game 3–2 and the Cup 6–2 on aggregate. That occasion didn't count as a feast; but what followed it was undeniably a famine. Where Newcastle was concerned, my father decided to choose pessimism as his default setting. It took the sharpest edge off his disappointments, such as Wembley defeats and relegations and the FA Cup catastrophe against non-League Hereford, after which my father's workmates at the pit hung a sign over his locker: NEWCASTLE UNITED: R.I.P. My father stayed loyal nonetheless.

Most children eventually move away from their parents. My parents – at my father's insistence – moved away from me. As soon as it became practicable after his retirement from the mines in the early 1980s, he headed back to the North East coast. He'd spent more than 20 years in Nottingham, always waiting to kiss it goodbye. 'We're just passing through,' he'd say. Home to him was the salt air of Whitley Bay, where St Mary's lighthouse rose from a rocky outcrop like an exclamation mark, the wide-windowed frontage of the Rendezvous Café on its sea front and the smooth, high dome of the Spanish City, which dominated the fading arcades and illuminated signs of the fun-fair below it. Home was also the working-men's club, familiar streets and swapped stories about The Toon. In it he could talk about the minor triumphs and periodic convulsions that shook St James' Park.

Seen in hindsight, a symmetrically bleak pattern emerges – a cycle of raised expectations and false hopes. One manager leaves, another arrives and the best players are sold, subsequently winning medals elsewhere – usually with Spurs, Liverpool or Manchester United. In this way Newcastle fulfilled other clubs' dreams but never their own. In the 1970s Malcolm Macdonald left for Arsenal. In the 1980s Peter Beardsley, Chris Waddle and Paul Gascoigne dazzled before moving elsewhere too. So, in the mid-1990s, did Andy Cole. There was no League Championship, no FA Cup and no hint of success in Europe again. It seemed to my exasperated father that Newcastle's ambition was always too modest for the talent it either found or recruited. He deplored the profligacy of honing skill only to give it to someone else. 'It's as if they're afraid of winning,' he said, thus making the act of selling seem like a form of deliberate self-harm. Even in 1996, with Keegan as boss and Newcastle 12 points ahead in the table, he refused to believe the Premiership was going to be ours. The erosion of that lead, and Keegan's live television 'I'd love it' rant against Alex Ferguson, confirmed he was right. 'Absolutely no chance now,' he predicted gloomily and emphatically to me after watching as Keegan's brain and tongue ran rabidly ahead of his judgement – all passion misplaced. When his forecast of calamity proved accurate, he said exactly what I expected: 'Bobby Robson's the man for us.'

In my father's eyes Robson was 'the man' because he was from the North East and bled black and white. Because he'd grown up watching Jackie Milburn. And because he'd once been a miner. In the month I was born Robson appeared on the cover of *Charles Buchan's Football Monthly*. He was photographed in West Bromwich Albion's stripes and a pair of ankle-high boots, bulky enough to have carried him back down the pit. The once pristine, white laces were long enough to wrap beneath the soles of each boot. A polished brown Slazenger Stadium Super Ball lay at his feet. Buchan wrote on an inside page that: 'What I like best about Robson is his quiet, sportsmanlike behaviour . . . he has no mannerisms, no showmanship.' What impressed my father was Robson's enthusiasm and idealism. He seemed to regard himself as constantly fortunate to be involved in the game. He acted as if he had a blazing faith in those around him; and those around him acted as if it was important to gain his approval and trust and make him proud. My father thought highly of Robson even when, as England boss, he was vilified before the 1990 World Cup in Italy. What happened during it was a vindication for both of them; or at least that's how my father saw it. 'More than a manager,' he said of him, aware of Robson's human qualities as much as his coaching qualifications.

At last Newcastle had him. After seven peripatetic,

but successful years in Europe – in Holland, Portugal and Spain – Robson had returned to the ground which, as a boy, he'd queued outside. It didn't matter that his arrival was long overdue or had come only in response to another crisis. His age – 66 – was immaterial too. Robson was already loved when he finally held up a Newcastle shirt, his name stitched on the back in blue, and posed for one of those clichéd newspaper photographs. Like Bill Shankly, he didn't have to pretend to adore the club he was now working for. Everything was sincere and authentic. Robson also brought a fatherly reassurance that everything would turn out fine. And those eight goals against Sheffield Wednesday, marking his home debut, was a performance so different from what had gone before that only the impact of his personality could have precipitated it. I knew my father would see it as proof of all he'd previously claimed.

Sitting in front of the TV, listening to Robson rationalising the result and striving not to sound over-triumphant, I knew I had to phone my father. To hear him say: 'I told you so.' To listen to him talk about the match. To recognise the pleasure traceable in his voice – all because his wish about Robson had come true. I muted the sound on the next item, which coincidentally was about Brian Clough's return to the City Ground to christen the stand that still bears his name. I walked a step and a half towards the telephone. Only then did I become aware of the one fact my subconscious had briefly suppressed. My father would not be at home. My call to him would go unanswered. He was dead. He had been dead for more than two years.

His funeral had been held during the spring of the Hale-Bopp comet in 1997 – that spit of heat and dust moving imperceptibly across the night sky, the stars around it seeming dimmer beside the fierce brightness of its bulbous head. I remembered the pale oak coffin. I remembered the short, orderly service, exactly as he had demanded – plain and unceremonial, like his life. I remembered the darkness of the small chapel and the message written forebodingly above the altar: 'Ye Know Not When Your Time Will Come'. But the realisation of all this – the unexplainable way my mind had chosen to temporarily block it out and then suddenly bring everything back to me – was like waking from some awful, dense sleep; the sort of sleep that utterly disorients you when it is suddenly broken.

I did something wholly pointless. I went into the hallway anyway, where the telephone sat on the bottom step of the stairs, and I picked up the receiver. I held it uselessly in my hand, shaking slightly as I listened to the soft, constant burr of the connection. The oak-cased clock on the mantelpiece chimed a quarter hour – 7.45 – and then resumed its hard, slow ticking.

I have never forgotten both the absurdity and enormity of the moment when – because of an inconsequential football result – I began to grieve for my father.

* * *

I'd grown up as my mother's child; I was close to her as I was distant from him whenever football wasn't our conversational topic. She was a raven-haired beauty in her Wren uniform during the Second World War. She won her school's English prize. She taught me to read and she read herself. She kept a copy of Palgrave's *The Golden Treasury* in her Sunday handbag. She had a good clerical career ahead of her in the tax office and abandoned it after marrying. I was never sure why she chose my father. Nor could I tell you what sort of glue held them together. I deliberately didn't ask. My mother predeceased my father by four and a half years. I returned from her hospital bed to tell him she had died. I walked up the paved drive, some of the slabs cracked and uneven, the hollows full of old rain, and pushed open the unlocked front door. I found him sitting, as he always did, equidistant between the gas fire and the television, smoking a cigarette. He briefly gripped the hand I offered him and tears wetted his cheeks and fell on to the front of his shirt. It was the only occasion I ever saw him cry – the only occasion, in fact, I saw any release of sorrow from him at all. And it is the only time I remember him holding my hand.

I never fully fathomed my father during his life; and I had not tried to do so since his death. But that night, as the impact of his passing properly struck me and I aimlessly wandered the house in the last of the evening light, I began to think hard about him. Then, and for many months afterwards, I began repeatedly asking myself how someone, ostensibly so uncomplicated, could have been such a maze of a man to me. I'd never really known him; he was all but a stranger. I was sure he didn't understand me; and I certainly didn't understand him. I decided this is why I'd refused to stop for grief and got on instead with the business of living. I shut out his death because I foolishly assumed it would never mark me.

It's said you are your father and he is you. It was certainly true that his face stared back at me whenever I looked into a mirror. We had the same eyes, the same bone structure, the same receding hairline. But – football apart – we were different in every other regard: interests, attitude, outlook and temperament. On the surface, he wanted nothing more than a game on TV, a packet of cigarettes and a glass of whisky, which tasted good on the palate, hot in the stomach and, he insisted, 'killed all known germs'. Of course, there had to have been more to him. What it was had always eluded me. But I knew then – too late – that I should have searched more diligently to find it. From others I learnt of his ambition to have been an RAF navigator rather than a miner. From others I learnt that he'd thought about emigrating to Australia in the mid-1960s because there was no possibility of returning to Newcastle. 'But there's a Newcastle in New South Wales,' he told my mother. And from others I learnt how he'd sit in the pub watching drinkers pass around the *Nottingham Evening Post* and reading what I'd written about Clough. 'He was pleased for you,' said one of his friends. With me, he kept himself to himself. I wasn't able to shake loose any of these confidences from him. We stuck to football. All my sharpest recollections of him – his voice, his expressions, his mannerisms and his manner – were formed purely through the game. I could hear him humming the *De Dum De Dum* of *Sports Report*'s signature tune before the classified football results. I could see him reading a Saturday-night football special, a pink or buff or green, until constant turning made small tears in the pages. I could visualise him dressed for a match as smartly as for a first date.

My mind clicked around to a specific mid-week afternoon when we were the only customers in the Rendezvous Café. Choosing a corner seat, where we were enveloped in a wedge of sunlight, I imagine us resembling escaped figures from an Edward Hopper painting. We drank tea in glass cups and watched winter's foamy waves rising in the distance, the sea slowly reclaiming the beach. The décor of the Café was (and remains) perfectly sealed in the 50s – patterned wallpaper, circular Formica-topped tables, a square-tiled floor. You could be half-fooled into thinking Eden was still Prime Minister. The décor stimulated my father's swell of remembrances about his favourite decade. He reanimated the era, speaking about its footballers, nights out in Newcastle after matches and the weekly jaunts to view a few minutes' highlights of big games shown in art deco news theatres. What I dismissed as another

nostalgic ramble assumed a different meaning in retrospect as I sorted and ordered what we had meant to
one another. I understood that returning to Newcastle
was my father's way of trying to recover what he'd lost:
the sensation of how things felt and looked when life
was most promising for him and he always had money
in his pocket. Everything had gone – the mines, the
miners' houses and many of his former friends. The
landscape was recognisable only through the layout of
the roads rather than the buildings occupying them.
But as a man sees, so a man is – and I was certain my
father always saw himself as he'd been in the 1950s, the
era when Newcastle won FA Cups and Saturdays were
solely about the uphill hike to St James' Park. He was
firmly anchored in that decade – it represented his
happiest days – and he would have rushed back there
if he could have found a way of turning Time's arrow
around. On every occasion, as we arrived back in
Newcastle during my childhood, he'd say to me: 'The
Tyne is waiting for us – and it's ours,' as if he was taking
possession of it.

I repeatedly dwelt on the years we had to ourselves,
thinking of how I had wasted them. With my mother
gone, we were more reliant than ever on football talk
to hold us together. In the early 1990s, however, after
decades of writing about it, I'd grown bored and weary
of the game. I was disillusioned to the degree that I
gave up watching or regularly reading about it. Neither
the matches nor the players held any real interest for

me. I had no choice but to skim off enough information from newspaper back pages to be able to speak knowledgeably to my father about Newcastle. There was no other entry into his world for me. 'That David Ginola's a canny player – even though he looks like a ladies' hairdresser,' he'd say before intricately describing a run or some ball trickery he'd seen Ginola perform on *Match of the Day*. Or he would be rhapsodic about Les Ferdinand – especially his pace and his heading. 'He can float in the air,' he said, as if recalling Wyn Davies. And, after Alan Shearer arrived for £15m in 1996, he conceded: 'Maybe he's *nearly* as good as Jackie Milburn.' On the other end of the line, sometimes only half-listening, I'd murmur my agreement.

I felt remorse – about failing to keep our relationship in constant repair. I felt guilt – about being an absent son. I also felt sad, ashamed, bewildered, brittle and empty. It was much more than the orphaned feeling that comes with the death of a parent. These lines belonging to Norman MacCaig articulated my confusion in poetry.

> How do I meet
> a man who's no longer there?
> How can I lament the loss
> of a man who won't go away?

I didn't visit enough. I didn't talk to him as much as I ought to have done. I allowed distance to estrange us.

Because of it I couldn't explain him to anyone – especially not myself. I experienced the full force of regret, which I had neither anticipated nor thought possible. A period of maudlin introspection led to prolonged mourning, and it wrenched my life out of shape. I can't recall that period now without the acute physical pain of it returning. What comes back is an awful sense of desolation and hopelessness I experienced over my father's absence. F. Scott Fitzgerald once wrote that: 'In the real dark night of the soul, it is always three o'clock in the morning.' It was always three o'clock in the morning for me. I drank myself into stupors. Heavy despair turned into depression. That black dog sank its teeth into me and no doctor's prescription succeeded in ridding me of its bite. This was no mid-life crisis caused by uncertainty about which direction to take next or the realisation of my own mortality. It cut far deeper. The grief was like acid, stripping away the pleasure from almost everything, leaving a dull ache which filled the hollows of my lungs and chest and stomach.

I was sharply aware of the glaring contradiction in my life. Though I empathised entirely with my mother, I had spent my youth and early adulthood seeking my father's approval, constantly trying to please and impress him. My insistent quest for it hadn't worked. I yearned for a closeness to him that I had never attained and which was now unobtainable. I regarded myself as shamefully weak for allowing myself to slide into such a wretched state. At the time I thought I would die purely because I did not care about living. The nadir came in early November 2002. If there'd been enough painkillers in the house, and sufficient Scotch left in the bottle, I know it would have counted as my last day on God's earth. Thank God, there wasn't.

The realisation forced a change in me. Slowly I got myself better. But what didn't go away was the conviction that I'd been a poor child for him; that I'd let my father down and disappointed him. And then, in the winter of 2007, a book I wrote called *Provided You Don't Kiss Me* – about the seasons I spent as Brian Clough's shadow – was short-listed for the William Hill Sports Book of the Year award. Another of the other short-listed authors was Bobby Charlton.

His autobiography, *My Manchester United Years*, began on the snowy runway at Munich, and the question Charlton, at 70 years old, was still asking himself: Why and how did I survive? Charlton explained that Munich lay 'at the heart of my story' and so telling it properly required him to address it in the opening pages. 'Without doing that, I know I couldn't begin to define my life,' he said. The book is powerful and beautifully written. I was convinced it would win. But my overriding thought was how my father would have reacted to the fact that I was competing against Charlton in the first place.

'You . . . on the same pitch . . . as Bobby Charlton?'

I could hear him say it, the triple spaces between the

words served as his astonished punctuation. The amaze-
ment in his voice disguised the pride I hoped – at last
– he would have felt for me and also shared. I thought
of us talking together about the improbability of it –
each as astounded as the other.

Friends wanted me to get Charlton's autograph for
them. I wanted his signature too – the signature I'd
failed to get 35 years earlier outside St James' Park. With
serendipitous timing, I met him on the way into the
ceremony. He was wearing the sort of good suit my
father would have worn. Everything was noisy and
crowded and hot. As he patiently signed away, I watched
the pen gracefully shape his name, which he must have
written on more than a million occasions. I thought
about that shot at Ewood Park and his face dissolving
into tears at the end of extra time in the World Cup
Final, signalling the joy and weariness that follows
glorious exertion, and also the polished European Cup
resting on his right shoulder two years later.

The impossible happened. My book was awarded the
prize. As I came off the stage, the first person waiting
to congratulate me was Charlton, as gracious as ever.
He was standing at the foot of the steps. The handshake,
which he'd given at the end of some of football's most
epic matches to Pele and Beckenbauer and to Eusebio
and Puskas, was offered to me. It seemed scarcely cred-
ible. I wanted to tell him about my father. About the
high esteem in which he'd held him. About the afternoon we'd spent watching his last appearance at St

James' Park. About how he'd never have believed the circumstances of this meeting. But the words would not come, and the chance was lost. All I managed was the feeble: 'My father was a great fan of yours.' I awoke the following morning after a lot of champagne and only a few hours' sleep. I sat on the edge of the bed and picked up Charlton's book. I looked at the 'Good Luck' he'd written for me and then began to randomly turn the pages. At the bottom of page 25 I read:

> *My father's gift . . . was energy and courage and a sense of responsibility to all around him that shaped every day of his life before he died in his early seventies.*

In describing his own father he had described mine too – including the age at which he'd died. I read that sentence half a dozen times before heaving tears made reading it again impossible. I wasn't crying for myself. I was crying for a good man; a man I wished I'd known better. My father had absorbed a series of small defeats and survived them. Like all of us, he could be awkward, irascible, incredibly stubborn and, on occasions, generally impossible. But he was never authoritarian, overbearing or mocking and he seldom interfered. He allowed me to find my own path and he taught me things without making a fuss about them: obligation, patience and self-reliance.

Sometimes it is the things we didn't do that cause us most pain. Whatever my father felt for me went unspoken. He never said he loved me; that wasn't his way. But the bigger tragedy is that I never told him either.

Now I have only you to tell.

He often comes back to me; sometimes when I least expect it.

In mid-summer 2010, I was channel hopping on TV. I came across a group of Newcastle fans inside the club's store, sifting through a rack of shirts for the coming season. One youngster with blonde hair was waiting patiently in a queue with his father. With one hand, the father held the shirt he was about to buy for his son. With the other, he protectively gripped his shoulder. The picture – on the screen for no more than a second or two – sucked me back into 1973. To my own Newcastle shirt. To Frank Brennan's shop. To the quayside, the run of the river, the slow boat, the swoop of a gull and my father's commentary on that 1951 FA Cup Final, a game between Newcastle and Blackpool played before I was thought of, let alone born.

My father left no family archive for me to curate. There were no keepsakes shut away or secretly hidden in a cupboard or the loft. He didn't write letters or send postcards. He eschewed the collection of ephemera or paraphernalia of any kind, as if ownership of trivia was burdensome, like heavy baggage. So there were no cigarette cards or programmes, no ticket stubs and no newspaper cuttings, clipped and folded or glued on to a scrapbook page. I found everything he regarded as important laid into a canary yellow tin box that had contained bars of perfumed soap, which I once gave my mother for Christmas. For a while this box – full of birth certificates and official documents – smelt of his tobacco whenever I opened it. He returned to me whenever I lifted its hinged lid. It was as though he was somewhere in the room, still puffing away like a skittish ghost.

He considered only one souvenir worthwhile or valuable. Most family heirlooms are jewels, a gilt-mounted painting, a collection of silver or a porcelain figurine. Ours is a postcard-sized, black and white photograph of those '51 Cup winners. I was given the photograph as a boy. It was passed on to me by my aunt's employer, a season ticket holder and business associate of some of the club's directors. Arms folded, staring intently into the lens, the players are lined up in two neat rows beside the touchline at St James' Park. Front and centre isn't the captain, Joe Harvey (who stands on the back row) but Jackie Milburn, the ball at his feet. The photograph is signed – slightly faded signatures in fountain pen. I had the photograph silver-framed and my father used to tap the glass with his index finger as he identified each face on it, telling me: 'What you've got here is history.'

He'd then talk about watching them bring the Cup back to Newcastle. About the banner, strung between two pillars inside the railway station, that welcomed the team's chartered train and read: WELCOME HYEM, CANNY LADS. About waiting for the players' and officials' single-decker buses, decorated with rosettes, scarves and bunting as one trailed the other and snaked through the city. About the size of the crowd, 20-deep along the pavements and fanning out into the roads. And about a panoramic photo that captured this street party for football. The camera makes the buses seem miniatures beside tall buildings comprising ornate spindly finials and high, square-headed windows. From these windows torn-up paper was thrown as ticker-tape. My father would point to the vanishing point of the picture, where a street dog-legs to the left. He was 'there somewhere', he'd say, the blur of people making him indistinguishable. My mother was 'there somewhere' too, he added. Long before the two of them became a courting couple, she is in the upper storey of the only stone-bleached façade. 'I saw the Cup as it passed me,' she told me proudly. My father managed to free himself early from the crush and squeeze into St James' Park, where he heard a brass band play 'The Blaydon Races' and Milburn make a speech of tortured gulps. Milburn, witheringly self-conscious, began trying to talk poshly, relying on the polished vowels of the BBC Home Service instead of his own dialect.

'Ha'way man, Jackie, lad,' yelled a voice. '*Taak tiv us in yor own language.*'

When he did, a roaring ovation gusted through the ground. 'You'd think Churchill had announced the end of war,' my father would say. And then he'd describe Milburn's opening goal again – the pass that set him free from his markers, the long clear chase he had into the box and finally the goal itself, precisely taken.

The television clip of the youngster in Newcastle's club shop brought it all back to me again. A stray, separate thought came to me as a consequence and I did some basic sums. The mathematics shocked me. I had reached the age – I was then 51 years old – that my father had been when we stood together beside the serpent bend of the Tyne. The calculation was unsettling because it emphasised how much – and how quickly – Time had passed. I didn't recognise myself as a boy in black and white stripes. In the weeks that followed, the images of that day kept returning to me until retracing our steps and reliving it met a need in me.

I waited until the corresponding week in September before boarding an early morning train. As it slid into Newcastle station, I picked out familiarly reassuring sights: the tower of one church and the spire of another, the hulking shapes of buildings and sloping blue-tiled roofs. I went into the heart of the city, turned right at Grey's Monument and kept walking. As I did so, dodging patches of hoar frost, I realised something else about my father: why he had always wanted to come back here. I now know a little of how he felt; for though several cities have been home to me, I only feel as though I indisputably belong whenever I'm in Newcastle. I can rightfully claim it as my own. Anywhere else and I am an interloper.

He felt so too. My father would be glad to know what Newcastle means to me. He'd be gladder still to find out that I regained my love for football and also unsurprised at what caused it. For someone else's enthusiasm for the game stoked my own. Bobby Robson was such a transparently decent man that I found it impossible not to care about Newcastle again. The adoration Robson felt for Newcastle – the team, the city, the people – made me proud to be a Geordie. I thought of all this as I reached the quay and stood beneath the Tyne Bridge.

The quayside is spruce now; so different from the one my father knew and loved. You can see the red-bricked Baltic, the beautiful curve of The Sage, its glass and silver casing like an armadillo's shell, and the arch of the Millennium Bridge with its harp-string supports. The warehouses are bars, hotels and restaurants now – clean lines and flashes of steel – and joggers and bicycle riders have taken over from workmen in overalls and flat caps. The river rippled placidly and the Tyne Bridge remained exactly as we left it – unchanged and unchangeable, every rivet solid, every cross-girder immovable.

There's a reason why I always see my father standing beside it. It's because I want to remember him as he once was – rather than what he became. I rely on it to blot out a far different and much more disquieting memory.

In a care home, where he stayed for a week under institutional blankets before his final admission to hospital, I found him sitting in an apple-green wing chair. The steep back of the chair propped him upright. He looked careworn and unbelievably tired. Life was leaking away from him. His skin was candle-coloured. His hair had thinned and blue-grey veins were swollen around his temples. His eyes were black stones, almost perfectly still in their sockets, and he lapsed into silences, each thought stillborn. He looked straight through me.

The complicated wiring of his brain had fused. The cerebral cortex had become speckled with plaques, disrupting the mass of neurons and the connections between them. His memory unwound, thread by thread, as incipient Alzheimer's took hold. At first the disease revealed itself in small, mouse-like ways: things 'lost' or misplaced, the insistence that something had been done or not done. After a series of small, intracranial bleeds, his deterioration was rapid. At the end of October 1996 he'd spoken at length about Newcastle's 5–0 thrashing of Manchester United – a team including Schmeichel, Cantona and Beckham. 'Suitable revenge for losing the title,' he gloated. He lamented the death of Tommy Lawton a fortnight later, aware at last that he should have agreed to my invitation to meet him. And at Christmas he was looking forward to the third round of the FA Cup in the early New Year, ardent in his hope that it might be the season Newcastle went back to Wembley. Within another two months he was dying. What my father said – if he said anything at all – was almost always inaudible or incomprehensible.

Shortly after his diagnosis, I spoke to a white-coated doctor, broad and bald with a face as pink as sliced bacon. He produced a blank sheet of A5 and put it down in front of me. He began to draw a series of steps, each steeper than the previous one. He reeled off what I assumed was a practised routine designed for numb-skulls such as me with no grasp of neurology: 'It's like this,' he said, tracing his pen across the marks he'd made. 'Each downward step represents a mini-stroke. Mental capacity diminishes with each one. And then you reach the bottom.' When I'd asked the doctor why no one had found a cure for Alzheimer's, he'd replied: 'We don't know enough about the brain yet. Imagine the cubic space in this room as being the sum total of what we *could* know about how it functions. Now imagine a child's toy brick in the corner. The toy brick represents what we *do* know.' He then added, dejectedly: 'We don't even know whether your father is thinking anything at all really – at least not in the way we define thinking.' I know his words were meant as reassurance. My father was not suffering as his body gently closed down.

I remember leaving the doctor's dowdy, windowless office and breaking into the sunshine. The air was thick with heat. Slow, formless clouds drifted by. There was the drone of traffic and chattering conversations, the regular noise of the turning world simply getting on with its everyday business. I sat on a bench to contemplate what the doctor had told me about the impermanence of memory, the way in which everything my father had seen and heard and accrued was so easily being wiped away. The facts and figures he could recall had always staggered me – goals and goal-scorers, the seasons in which games had been won or lost, the records of individual players. All that knowledge, thirstily consumed, had gone. And the man I'd known was gone too, leaving behind only minor things – spectacles, a watch, his wedding ring and, briefly, the shape of his body in a bed.

All this came back to me again as I stood on the quayside and remembered him and I there together.

I've always comforted myself with this thought: the doctor was wrong.

In his silence and behind that blank expression, my father never stopped thinking. His eyes were still seeing and his brain was still whirring. In spools of bright colour he was replaying something from his past, the pictures travelling by in a timeless parade across his mind.

It's an April afternoon at Wembley in 1951.
Newcastle United versus Blackpool in the FA Cup Final.
Jackie Milburn is collecting a pass and breaking away.
He is running . . . running . . . running.
And then, as he always will, he scores.

Welcome Hyem, my Canny Lad. The Tyne awaits you and is yours.

Notes and Acknowledgements

This book comes out of two obsessions that are both entirely influenced by my father.

Because he saved nothing, I have saved nearly everything to the point of ridiculousness. Only in the past few years – though reluctantly and sometimes painfully – have I begun to discard things. Because he wrote nothing down, I wrote – or more precisely typed out – almost everything that I believed was worth preserving, another habit that I am slowly shedding for the sake of my sanity. In the autumn of 1999, when the need to remember my father truly began, I spent months going over old notes, diary entries, cuttings and reminiscences and putting them in order. To make sense of them was a necessary therapy for me then too.

I am grateful to all those who patiently and speedily

answered what must have seemed to them obscure or odd questions. They are: Chris Styles and Ann Dixon (who was wonderfully efficient) at the Newcastle Chronicle; Andy Smart at the Nottingham Post; Professor Andrew Lees for his insight on Ray Kennedy and the treatment and symptoms of Parkinson's disease; Tom Hall at the Scottish Football Blog; John Lister of the Scottish Football Historian; Richard McBrearty at the Scottish Football Museum; Iain McCartney for his knowledge of all things Manchester United; Jill Tingey; Louis Massarella of *FourFourTwo* magazine; Matt Eastley and Mike Berry of Backpass magazine; Roy Adlard and Brian Tansley for taking me back to my days at Nottingham Sport; David Instone (helpful as ever); Robert Weir; Mike Kirkup; Rev Judith Oliver and the churchwardens of St Francis', Dudley; John Barrett, who was Duncan Edwards' boyhood team mate, and the gentleman who tends Edwards' grave. (To see it was so poignant that I stupidly forgot to ask his name.)

Staff at the following libraries were a credit to their profession and underlined the importance of a flourishing library service, which, sadly, successive Governments seem not to care about: Nottingham Central, Newcastle Central, Stirling Central, Glasgow Central, Seaton Delaval, the British Newspaper Library. The staff of Woodhorn Museum at Ashington were similarly supportive.

A special salute to Wyn Davies, who adorns the cover of this book. Another to Brian Glanville for educating me about the playing style of Tommy Lawton. And third to Paul Joannou, whose knowledge of Newcastle United is limitless, for talking to me about the St James' Park boardroom of the 1950s.

I also thank Lee Hall for permission to quote from *The Pitmen Painters* and Norman MacCaig's son Ewen for allowing me to use lines from the poem *Dead Friend*.

At Century, I wouldn't have survived without my editor Ben Dunn or the indispensable Briony Gowlett, and I can't say thank you enough to Natascha Spargo for her superb cover design.

My agent, Grainne Fox, deserves (as ever) a special mention for putting up with me.

Finally, a new definition of love.

On the morning of the Champions League Final – with noon fast approaching – I found myself sitting on a train that was stuck in Leeds station. The apologetic guard spoke of problems with power lines between Grantham and Stevenage. I rang home in utter panic. My wife, Mandy, had her own weekend planned. She sacrificed it – unhesitatingly and uncomplainingly – to drive me to Wembley. I was due to spend the night in a central London hotel. But traffic, time and parking restrictions made the booking redundant. We made another close to Wembley. We found the hotel was in need of 'some refurbishment', a handy euphemism for its dilapidated, shabby state. The television set was the most modern thing in it by at least three decades. The cobwebs were spun by spiders alive when Ted Heath formed a Government. This is where Mandy watched the game, and I returned from Wembley amazed to find:

- She hadn't driven home and left me to it
- My marriage was still intact.

Anyway, my heartfelt message to Mandy is very simple. I have no idea how I'd cope without you.

Picture
Acknowledgements

The author and publishers would like to thank the following copyright-holders for permission to reproduce images in this book:

© Press Association; © Getty Images; © Action Images; © Mirrorpix; © Newcastle Evening Chronicle / Newcastle Photos; © Colorsport

All other images are care of the author.

The author and publishers have made all reasonable efforts to contact copyright-holders for permission, and apologise for any omissions or errors in the form of credits given. Corrections may be made to future printings.

Index

(the initials DH and JH in subentries refer to Duncan Hamilton and Jim Hamilton)

DUNCAN HAMILTON

The Unreliable Life of Harry the Valet

The Great Victorian Jewel Thief

17 October 1898.

An impossibly daring jewellery heist aboard a train at Paris's Gare du Nord station captures the attention of the world.

Who would have dared to pull off such a feat?

Award-winning writer Duncan Hamilton reveals the true story of Harry the Valet, the notorious crook who was the scourge of Victorian London.

Harry conned and stole his way into high society, living a life of excess in London's best hotels and hang-outs. Dressed in bespoke suits and handmade shoes, Harry outwitted Scotland ard with his trademark guile and panache.

With dozens of pseudonyms, no fixed address and a knowledge of his city that allowed him to hide in its shadows, Harry seemed almost invisible. Until, blinded by love, he carried out the robbery that would prove his downfall.

'A tale that rattles along like a hansom cab across the cobbles.'
THE TIMES

'Duncan Hamilton tells a lovely tale with verve and panache.'
COUNTRY LIFE